Management of Tourism in India

Management of Tourism in India

Awadhesh Kr. Singh
Abdul Majeed Mulla

MADHAV BOOKS
GURGAON (HARYANA)

First Published – 2011

ISBN: 978-93-80615-01-1

Published by

MADHAV BOOKS
F-2562, Palam Vihar
Gurgaon-122 017 (Haryana)
Phone : 0124-2365193, 9810373248

Contents

Preface and Acknowledgement

Tourism has emerged as the biggest industry of future. The importance of tourism has been well recognized worldwide. Now tourism has ushered into a new area of expansion and importance however, it faces numerous emerging challenges and competition both from within and outside the country. In fact, tourism has enormous potential of employment generation and poverty alleviation. India has shown potential to emerge as a leading player in the global tourism. The recent policy changes also envisage strategic planning, management and development of tourism in India.The present book has been arranged into nine chapters, which focus on emerging perspectives, issues, trends and strategic implications. Chapter Ist is introductory one, which dealt with conceptualization of tourism resources, and tourist destination development. Chapter IInd is concerned with development of tourism in India. Emerging trends, paradigm shifting and economic significance of tourism have been discussed in the chapter. Chapter IIIrd deals with tourism planning and policies in India. Tourism development during plan periods, national tourism policy and action plan etc. have been critically reviewed in the chapter. Chapter IVth focuses on tourism resources. Evolution of eco tourism concept, prospects for nature based tourism, evolution of eco-tourism, tourism prospects in mountain eco-systems, tourism in protected areas, wild life tourism and heritage tourism as well as analysis of carrying capacities have been dealt in the chapter. Chapter Vth is concerned with assessment of tourism impacts which mainly focuses on social, cultural, natural and environmental impacts of tourism. Chapter VIth deals with tourism profile of Karnataka. The chapter highlights on cultural and natural heritage resources of Karnataka. Chapter VIIth deals with management of tourism in Karnataka. It also provides detailed analysis of data pertaining to service providers and tourists. Chapter VIIIth focuses on strategic planning, environmental analysis, setting goals and objectives, man power planning, marketing segmentation, marketing communication, and marketing of tourism resources. Chapter IXth is concluding one which highlights the analysis of emerging trends, constrains and also policy recommendations.

A.K. Singh
Abdul Majeed Mulla

1

Introduction

As we have already entered in the new millenium, tourism has emerged as the biggest industry of the future. Often ranked as the world's largest industry, tourism plays a major role in the economies of 125 of the 170 nations in the world. For many countries, it is their biggest economic activity. Over 70 per cent of the Island country Maldieve's foreign exchange earning comes from tourism, for instance. World Tourism Organization (WTO) has estimated that there were more than 693 million international travelers in 2001. Spending by these tourists was estimated at more than $ 462 billion. Tourist arrivals are predicted to grow by an average of 4.1 per cent a year over the next two decades, surprisingly a total of over billion international travelers by the year 2019 and reaching 1.6 billion by the year 2020. Importantly, tourism is the world's largest employer, generating, directly and indirectly, nearly 200 million jobs or some 10 per cent of the jobs globally. However, in 2001 the industry has suffered because of the September 11 terrorist attacks in USA. For the first time since 1982, the worldwide number of international tourist arrivals showed a slight decrease (-0.6 per cent or 4 billion down from 2000). The impact of the events of 11th September, 2001 has been very severe on travel and trade. Thus, tourism crises posed a services challenge to the tour and travel management.

The fastest growing segment in tourism is eco-tourism. WTO has estimated that eco-tourism generated 7 per cent of all international travel expenditure and 20 per cent of all international travel. Today, nature tourism is the largest foreign exchange earner for South Africa, Kenya, Ecuador and Costa Rica. Moreover, tourism industry has an estimated annual growth rate of 4 per cent, nature tourism boasts of a growth rate between 10 per cent and 30 per cent. Even a fraction of these revenues can go a long way to help the local economy and ecology (Vania, 2002). However, India's position globally both in terms of tourist inflow and tourism earnings have almost constant primarily because other countries have moved even faster. Average annual growth rate of tourism has been reported 4.13 per cent in India against the average growth of 4.56 per cent at global level during 1980-1997. The future growth rates of tourism in India are projected to be 6.5 per cent during 2000-2010 and 5.8 per cent during 2010-2020. India will remain the pre-dominant position within South Asia with 8.9 million tourist arrivals out of a total 18.75 million (47.47 per cent) by 2010.

Concept of Tourism

The concept of tourism as a phenomenon involves the movement of people within their own country or accesses the national borders. Tourism involves basically three elements (Wahab, 1975), namely man (human element as the creator of the act of tourism), space (the physical element to be necessarily covered by the act itself), and time (the temporal element which is compared by the trip itself and the stay at the destination). Conceptually, tourism is defined as the sum of the phenomenon and relationships arising from the travel and stay of non-residents in so far as they do not lead to permanent residents and are not connected with an earning activity (Burkart & Medlik, 1984). The concept of tourism is characterised by:

- Movement of people and their stay at various destinations;
- Giving rise to activities at the destinations;
- Developing social and physical infrastructure and amenities to facilitate visitors;

- Giving rise to recreational and other cultural events to attract tourists;
- Developing pleasure activities and professional service providers and
- Giving rise to various service demands which are provided by commercial sense of two tourist industry.

Tourism has to be regarded as an industry although, strictly in accordance with the classical definition of the term, it is not industry, however, tourism would be regarded as an industry which contributes to its economic and social development and activates many productive sectors. In economic terms, tourism creates a demand or provides a market for a number of quite separate and varied industries (Robinson, 1976). The appellation of the term industry to tourism has been also justified because of the modern approach to the definition of industry as a group of firms producing identical goods, which the consumer regards as being substitutes for one another although they may be physically different (Wahab, 1975). Tourism is one of the new industries that are capable of providing rapid economic growth in income and standards of living. It includes as a complex sector industries in the classical sense of the terms like lodging, transport and handicrafts industries (Tewari, 1994). Lundberg has described tourism as business. He is of the opinion that tourism is the business of the transport, care, feeding and entertainment of the tourists (Lundberg, 1972). Mill and Morison have treated it as system consisting of inter-related parts and expressed the view that tourism is not an industry (Mill Morison, 1985).

A conceptual framework has been given by After Vandermay (1984) in the context of regional tourism resources (Chart 1). It focuses on two primary dimensions. The first represents the various sectors of tourism industry on a regional level, while the second dimension recognizes both public and private tourism coordinating organizations that function in the region.

Normally, the conceptual framework of tourism has three dimensions: one, the input, and the impacts of local people and area; local input provided on voluntary basis is a limited

Source: After Vandermey (1984), Tourism Management, Vol. 5 (2)

RDACs = Regional Development Advisory Committees
RDAs = Regional Development Associations

Chart 1: A Conceptual Framework of Regional Tourism Resources

but valuable resources, three, in terms of content community wishes to support in tourism development (Chart 2).

Tourism Demand

Tourism demand has increased significantly in the recent past. There has been a dramatic expansion of domestic tourism also in many developed countries (Christopher & Holloway, 1998). There are many factors which have contributed to the increase in the demand for tourism. Population growth, rising standards of living, more leisure time and greater discretionary spending have boosted the numbers of travelers. Both the public and private sectors of economy have fosters this demand and encouraged the expansion of the tourist industry. The technological development in transport, telecommunication, and media have brought down the relative cost of travel and encouraged travel. However, tourism demand is characterised

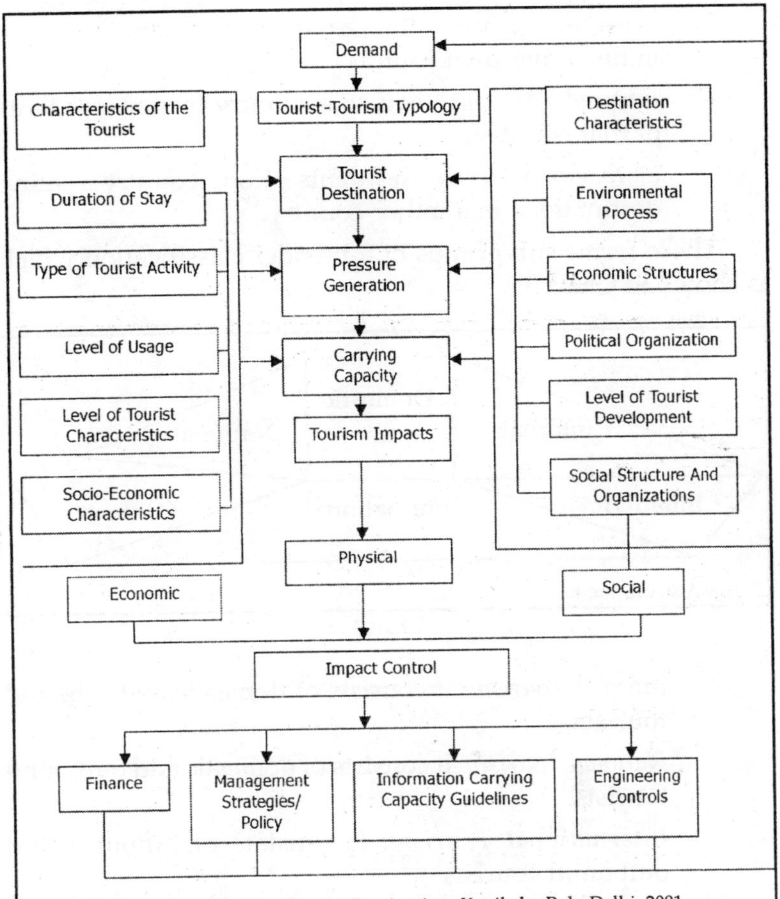

Source: Kamra, K.K. Managing Tourist Destination, Kaniksha Pub. Delhi, 2001.

Chart 2: Tourism: A Conceptual Framework

by three important factors viz. (i) elasticity; (ii) sensitivity and (iii) seasonality. Tourism is also affected by internal and external environment. Terrorism, violence, political instability, insecurity, poor health and physical infrastructure, etc. severely affects the tourism growth. However, tourism demand is highly dynamic in nature.

Classification of Tourism

Tourism can be classified by resident origin :

- *Domestic Tourism:* When a persons visits another place in his or her own country.
- *Inbound Tourism:* Visits to a country by non-residents of that country.
- *Outbound Tourism:* Residents of one country visiting destinations in another country.

These forms sub-groups of a broader classification which is shown in Chart 3.

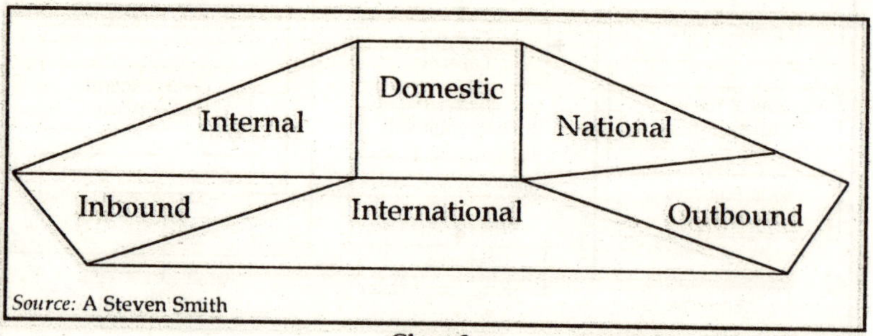

Chart 3

- *Internal Tourism:* It consists of domestic and inbound tourists.
- *National Tourism:* It consists of domestic and outbound tourists.
- *International Tourism:* It consists of inbound and outbound tourists.

Importantly, travel industry identifies the following motivations :

- Relaxation and physical recreation.
- Touring, sightseeing and culture.
- Visiting friends and relatives.
- Business trips and conferences, meetings and seminars.
- Specialist trips for health, study, sporting etc.
- Visitation to eco-tourist sites viz. protected areas; man groves, mountain, deserts, oceans, forests, flora and fauna, etc.

Tourism Resources

A destination's tourism resource base is the essence of that location's tourism appeal (Godfrey and Clark, 2000). Tourism resources are all of those features, which draw people into a destination. They form the core of visitor attractions, but also include other services and facilities, which center to accommodate and entertain tourists while in the destination area. The tourism resources can be classified in the main points:

- *Natural Resource:* Flora, landscape, fauna climate, water etc.
- *Cultural Resource:* Religious places/sites heritage, dance, dress, songs, language/dialect, music, art crafts, local traditions, rituals etc.
- *Event Resources:* Festivals, tournaments, business, exhibition, carnivals, parades, fairs, haats, contests auctions, pilgrimage etc.
- *Activity Resources:* Recreational (water sports, boating, windsurfing, driving, hunting and shooting, fashion shows); services, (theatre, cinema, health, resorts, conference centre, crafts, gallaries etc.); facilities (wildlife centres, aquarium, gardens, production centres etc.)
- *Service Resources:* Transport, accommodation, reception, catering services etc.

Tourism Organizations

Successful tourism development will depend on effective functioning of tourism organization. Therefore a number of core operators and activities, which should be considered by all tourism groups, including coordination and leadership, policy, marketing and communications, hospitality, training and customer care and monitoring and reach etc. are crucial for sustainable development of tourism. In brief tourism organizations are classified as :

- Travel agency
- Tour operators

- Hotels and other accommodations
- Road & Railways, Transport agencies
- Air and Sea transport agencies
- Information centres
- Tourism development Corporations
- Tourism and Travel Organizations
- Travel Associations (TATA), UFTAA, ICAO, IATA, TAAI, FHRAI, IATO etc.)

Tourist Destination Development

The concept of tourist product is focal to understanding the innovation and practice of management in all sectors of the travel and tourism industry as tourism has generated analytical exploration of the various dimensions and details perceived as an economic activity having a consumption, or demand, aspect and a production or supply, aspect. The tourist products from the industry perspective can be apprehended at two levels (Kamra, 2001):

- The total tourist product, consisting of a combination of all the service elements consumed by the tourist from the time tourist sets off home, to the time of return.
- The explicit product such as attractions, accommodations, transport and other facilities are elements of the local tourist products.

The main components of the total product are as follows :

- Attractions (landscape, seascape, beaches, climate and ecology, built attractions (historic and new townscape as in newly built resorts and purpose built attractions), cultural attraction (festivals, folk songs, dances, theatre, traditions) and social attraction (life styles, experience, interaction etc);
- Accessibility which can be specified in terms of the extent of comfort or hassle with which visitors can reach the destinations of their liking;

- Destination facilities which imply the elements within the destination or linked to it, and facilitate the tourists stay at the destinations and their participation in the tourist activities.

Facilities are purpose built around the wants and needs of the potential visitors from the targeted segments in quantities identified by the market feasibility studies. These facilities subsume accommodation, restaurants, cafes and bars, transport at the destination and other ancillary services such as retailing visitor information etc.;

- Images, which typically reflect the intrinsic qualities of the tourist product, its design, quality, style of attractions, and its built and social environment. Images are characteristics of all forms of tourist product meaning the perceptions i.e. ideas and beliefs tourists hold about the products they invest in. Images are, in fact, significant in the sense that they affect the buyer's behaviour;
- Price which is the sum, total of the costs on product elements such a travel, accommodation and involvement in a range of selected services at the destination.

A destination comprises a core of facilities, amenities and services fashioned to cater the needs of the tourists, generally represented as 4A's. Nevertheless, all the elements (i) attractions; (ii) access; (iii) amenities; (iv) ancillary services has to be in order in the form of a complete mix before tourism experience is delivered and tourism in general is patronized and a mix of these elements is perceived as an amalgam. Proper planning of the strategy for destination development as also for any other product, tourism or general, would therefore, seem to be of paramount importance. A well thought out and formulated plans or strategy would go a long way towards ensuring a successful take off and sustenance of the destination project. The dynamics of destination development can be seen in Chart 4.

There is, in fact, a complex interplay of inference on decision takers between development advocates and control lobbyists. In the process, a dialogue develops between the

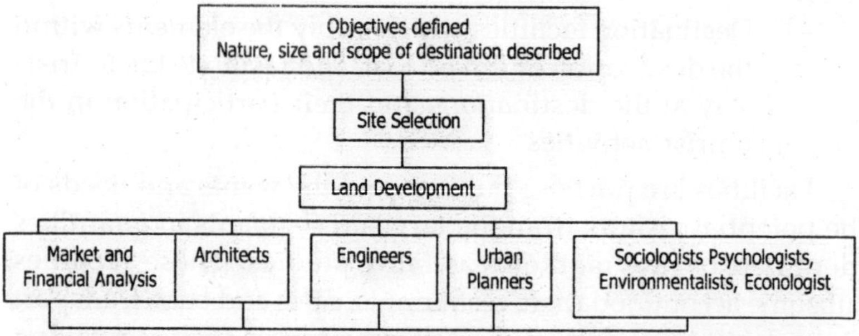

Programme Development	Research Regional Concept & Theme	Analysis of impact of destination development on social and environmental patterns
Analysis of competitive destinations, total visitor market, market share, preliminary economic and financial analysis	Protect Technical Description Critical Mass-Services and facilities requirements sizing and costs	Analysis of site potential
Market analysis of trends timing and size of increments, financial analysis of earnings cash flow and return on investment	Polish of offsite/onside Services and facilities requirements Schematics and Design developments. Detailed project cost estimates	Complete Master Plan for Region
Working drawings and specifications	Manpower requirements, Government's role in destination area development	
Development Allies ——	Funding ——	Construction

Source: Kamra, K.K. Managing Tourist Destination, Kanishka Pub. Delhi, 2001.

Chart 4: Destination Development

consultants and the advisors representing the developers and planning agencies. The leverage of different factors and interest groups on decision taking and the development policy is illustrated in Chart 5. Importantly, tourism destination development highly depends on the government support for tourism investment, planning and marketing approach. However, private participation in terms of investment in tourism, infrastructure and services is most crucial. Again, community participation in tourism promotion is also needed.

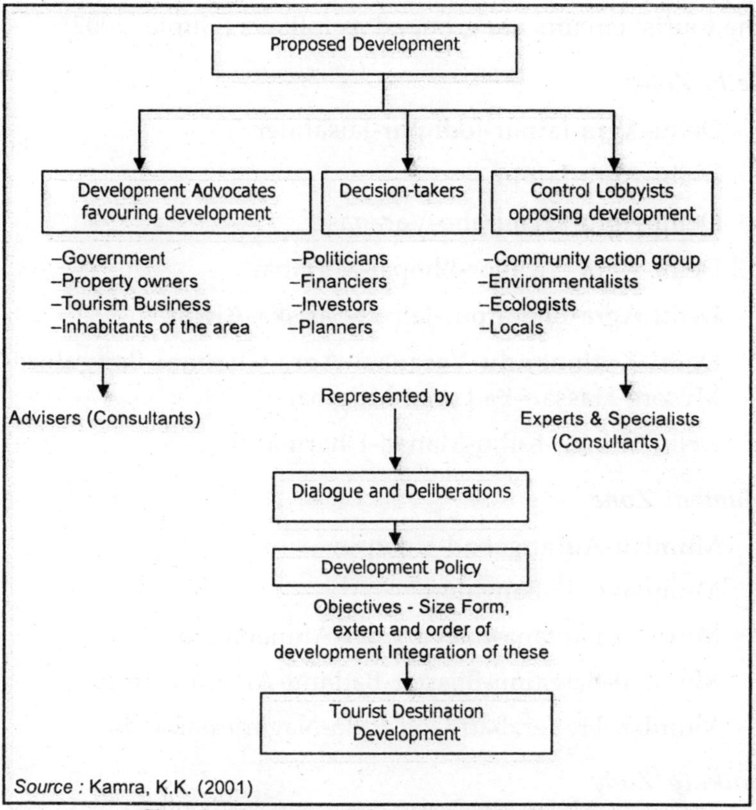

Chart 5: Dynamics of Destination Development

Tourist Circuits In India

India, a multi-faceted country, offering varied tourist attractions, has been segmented into a different travel circuits. The travel circuits are aimed at spreading tourism geographically so that every state in India is enabled to offer its attractions to the visitors. These circuits are also identified as the 'Golden Triangles' of Indian tourism offering the most coveted heritage sites as well as other tourism varieties around its location. To be accessible to the domestic as well as the foreign visitors, these spots are connected with their nearest metropolitan cities of Delhi, Mumbai, Kolkata and Chennai.

The tourist circuits are grouped as follows (Gupta, 2002):

Delhi Zone

- Delhi-Agra-Jaipur-Jodhpur-Jaisalmer
- Delhi-Agra-Jaipur
- Delhi-Agra-Khajuraho-Varanasi
- Delhi-Agra-Gwalior-Bhopal-Mumbai
- Delhi-Agra-Bharatpur-Jaipur-Sariska-Alwar
- Delhi-Kathmandu-Varanasi-Agra,Chennai-Bangalore-Mysore-Hassan-Badamai-Mumbai
- Delhi-Shimla-Kullu-Manali-Dharmasala

Mumbai Zone

- Mumbai-Aurangabad-Udaipur
- Mumbai-Goa-Bangalore
- Mumbai-Palitana-Bhavanagar-Ahmedabad
- Mumbai-Belgaum-Bijapur-Badami-Aivalli-Hampi
- Mumbai-Hyderabad-Golconda-Nagarjunakonda

Kolkata Zone

- Kolkata-Bhubanesvar-Konarka-Puri-Chilka Lake
- Kolkata-Gaya-Kathmandu
- Kolkata-Guwahati-Shillong-Kaziranga
- Kolkata-Darjeeling-Gangtok

Chennai Zone

- Chennai-Tiruchchirappali-Thanjavur
- Chennai-Bangalore-Mysore-Bandipur
- Chennai-Madurai-Kodaikanal-Thekkadi-Koch
- Chennai-Coimbatore-Udagamandalam (Ooty)-Madurai-Mystore-Bangalore
- Chennai-Kanchipuram-Mamallapuram-Pondicherry

The above analysis and description demonstrate that India has large potential of tourism and the phenomenon growth in this sector also indicates that India may be emerged as one of the largest tourism markets of Asia, however, strategic planning and management of tourism resources may provide avenues to avail the benefits of tourism industry in future.

References

Burkart & Medlik, S. (1974), Tourism Past, Present And Future, Heinemann, London.

Christopher, J. & Holloway (1998), The Business Of Tourism, Longman, London.

Godfrey, K. & Jackie Clarke (2000), Tourism Development Casell, London.

Gupta, S.P., et.al. (2002), Cultural Tourism In India, D.K. Printwell (P) Ltd., Delhi.

Kamra, K.K. (2001), Managing Tourist Destiantion, Kanishka Pub. Delhi.

Lundberg, D.E. (1972), The Tourist Business, Kahner, Pub. Com. Chichago.

Mill, R.C. and Morrison, A.M. (1985), The Tourism Ssytem, PHI, New Jersy.

Robinson, H.A. (1976), A Geography of Tourism, Macdonald and Evans, London.

Tewari, S.P. (1994), Tourism Dimensions, Atma Ram & Sons, Delhi.

Vania, Rustam (2002), Eco-Tourism, *Down To Earth*, July 31.

Wahab, S. (1975), Tourism Management, Tourism International Press, London.

2

Development of Tourism in India

Tourism as an industry has ushered into a new area of expansion and importance. The significance of tourism has been well recognized in both the developed and developing countries. In fact, tourism has enormous potential of employment generation and poverty alleviation. Tourism has also changed the landscape and nature based tourist destinations have emerged as most potential alternative forms of tourism. The recent policy changes will help in realizing the full potential of India in tourism growth, however, it faces numerous new challenges and a lot of competition both from within and outside of the country.

Tourism has emerged as one of the most important area in the planning process of different countries. For a number of countries, it is one of the major source of foreign exchange earnings. However, India's entry to this sector has been quite late. Its share is less than 0.4 per cent in world tourists traffic, though India has large potential of tourism (cultural, heritage, ecological and other form of tourism). Tourism has also emerged as one of the lucrative business in India. Globalization has shown the path of tourism development and promotion in the new millennium. Importantly, new tourism policy of India has envisages strategic planning, management and development of the tourism sector in India.

Emerging Trends in Tourism Growth

The growth of international tourism was slow in the first part of the Century, rapid in the later part and phenomenal since 1980. In 1950, the total arrival was only 25 million generating receipts of $2.1 billion. The absolute number of arrivals multiplied two and a half times between 1960 and 1970 and thereafter, it has almost doubled every decade. The receipts from tourism have grown even faster. $18 billion in 1970 increased to $105 billion in 1980. It is well known now that as a contributor to the global economy, tourism has no equal. In 2000, the arrivals reached 698 million with a total international tourism receipt of $476 billion. Over the past 15 years, international tourism receipts have grown 1.5 per cent faster than world GDP. John Naisbitt, in his book "Global Paradox", had estimated in 1994 that with about $3.4 trillion of output, it was the largest industry in the world. According to the World Tourism Organization (WTO), "In 1998 international tourism accounted for an estimated 8 per cent of the world's total export earnings and 37 per cent of exports in the services sector. International tourism receipts and passenger transport amounted to more than $504 billion, putting it ahead of all other categories of international trade as shown in Table 1.

Table 1
International Trade

Category of Trade	*$ Billion*
International Tourism	504
Automotive products	496
Chemicals	490
Food	458
Petroleum and other fuels	435
Computers and office equipment	394
Textiles and clothing	332
Telecommunications equipment	279
Mining products	163
Iron and steel	141

The estimates of WTO project astounding growth of travel and tourism during the coming decades. It is estimated that (Bejbaruah, 2002) :

- by 2020 there will be 1.6 billion international tourist arrivals world-wide;
- they will be spending about $2,000 billion;
- the sustained annual average growth rate in tourism will be 4.3 per cent in arrivals and 6.7 per cent in receipts—which is far above the probable expansion of the world's wealth, which will be growing only at about 3 per cent per annum;
- between 1995 and 2005, 144 million new jobs would have been created in this sector—112 million of them being in the Asia-Pacific region alone.

Today, international tourism has emerged as a huge economic giant, accounting for 11.6 per cent of the world's GDP generating over US $4.1 trillion (2000) output and employing 10.4 per cent of worldwide employment. The tremendous pace of development in this industry in further evident from the fact that the industry will generates 12.5 per cent of GDP employ 13.9 per cent of employment and the receipts will touch US $ 1500 billion by 2010.

Fortunately, after a period of sustained world wide growth rate, international tourism has entered into an unsettled era. There were 25 million arrivals (1950). But fifty years later, the number reached 664 million (2000) arrivals. As per the forecasts made by WTO, the growth rate (1990-2010) of world tourism arrivals should increase of about half the rate of that achieved in 1950-90. This indicated an average annual growth rate in between 3.5 per cent to 3.8 per cent. However, the WTO and WTTC have demonstrated that the growth rate in Asia Pacific Region (2000-2010) would be double the world average, where India will occupy the top position (Chand & Chauhan, 2002).

Incidentally, the volume of international tourism arrivals in India is very low. It accounts for only 0.39 per cent (1000) of the world's total tourist (664 million) traffic (2000). Whereas the share of India in terms of tourism receipts have been varying in between 0.6 per cent to 0.7 per cent over the last five years. Table 2 depicts the time path of foreign tourist arrivals and tourist receipts in India during the period 1951-2000. It is evident from the table that tourist arrivals as well as foreign receipts have increased over the period under consideration but at a decreasing rate. The foreign tourist arrivals have increased from 16825 in 1951 to 5081504 in 2007. The growth during 1950-60 was around 25 per cent, which declined to 8.6 per cent during the period 1960-70 and a sharp increase has been noted during 1970-80. However, during 1991-2000 there has been a tremendous rise in the growth rate i.e. 56 per cent. The annual growth of foreign tourists arrival in India is above 14 per cent. India's share in worldwide tourist arrivals was reported 0.56 per cent only in 2007.

Table 2
Tourist Arrivals in India and World

Year	*India (number)*	*World (million)*	*Per cent Share of India*
1951	16,829	–	–
1960	1,23,095	69.3	0.18
1970	2,80,828	159.7	0.18
1980	8,00,150	284.8	0.28
1985	8,36,908	332.9	0.25
1990	17,07,258	443.8	0.38
1991	16,77,258	466.0	0.36
1992	18,67,657	503.6	0.37
1993	17,64,830	518.3	0.34
1994	18,86,433	546.3	0.35
1995	21,23,683	567.4	0.37
1996	22,83,579	595.0	0.40
1997	23,74,094	610.8	0.39
1998	23,58,629	625.2	0.38
1999	24,71,848	650.0	0.38
2000	26,41,157	664.0	0.39
2001	25,37,282	684.4	0.37
2002	23,84,364	704.7	0.34
2003	27,26,214	692.2	0.39
2004	34,57,477	761.4	0.45
2005	39,18,612	803.0	0.49
2006	44,47,167	807.0	0.53
2007	50,81,504	903.0	0.56

Source: India Tourist Statistics, 2007.

Further table revealed that during the year 2000 tourist traffic has increased a marginal rate i.e. 5.7 per cent over 1999. The past some decades of tourism, have been marked foremost by its tremendous expansion. Between 1950 and 1999 the number of international arrivals has shown an evolution from a mere 25 million international arrivals to the current 664 million, corresponding to an average annual growth rate of 7 per cent.

In 2007 tourism arrivals maintained the growth of 6.6 per cent of 903 million and tourism receipts (excluding international transport) growing to US $ 857 billion. These trends were mainly determined by the set back of international tourism in East Asia and the Pacific in 1998. The average annual growth in receipts declined from 10 per cent between 1989 and 1993 to 5.9 per cent from 1994 to 1998. However, due to the sharply fluctuating value of the US dollar over the past ten years—the base currency used from global comparisons—this slowdown and the annual fluctuations in international tourism receipt need to be interpreted with caution. In 1998, for example, the 2 per cent rise in receipts over 1997 is mere reflection of the strong appreciation of the dollar against the currencies of major tourism source markets, than a real decrease in tourism spending. In the case of important destinations, such as France, Italy and Spain, the total receipts from international tourism in US dollars shows an increase of 6.3 per cent in 1998 over 1997, reflecting a booming tourism activity. The contribution of regions in international tourist arrivals was reported highest 53.6 per cent for Europe followed by Asia and the Pacific (20.4 per cent), America's (15.8 per cent), Middle East (5.3 per cent) and Africa (4.9 per cent) in 2007. The highest contribution of tourist receipts worldwide was reported by European region (50.6 per cent).

The annual trends in arrivals represent a reliable indicator of industry growth. The 5 per cent annual increase in international tourist arrivals worldwide between 1989 and 1993 demonstrates that the industry is remarkably resistant to economic fluctuations and other problems. In the second half of the decade between 1994 and 1998 the average annual increase in arrivals did slow economic recovery, sustained high unemployment in major industrialized countries and the Asian financial crisis.

The strong recovery of tourism travel worldwide was further confirmed by the growth rate for air traffic world wide in 1996. Nevertheless, preliminary traffic figures for 1998, released by the International Civil Aviation Organization (ICAO), point to a 1 per cent increase over 1997 both for total and for international scheduled traffic of the world airlines.

This substantial slowdown from an average increase of 7 per cent in the previous five years and 8 per cent in 1997 reflects, in particular, a small decline in traffic of the airlines of the Asia/Pacific region which contributes more than a third to world traffic and until recently achieved high rate of growth. With the reception of airlines of the Middle East and Africa, which showed little change in traffic, airlines of other regions continued to achieve traffic growth, but at levels below recent annual trends (Table 3).

The present scenario of tourism in India can be summed up in three broad parameters. First, that India has tremendous potential, which are not yet fully achieved. Second, that the future of tourism in India looks extremely optimistic but realization of that optimism will depend on removal of a large number of small impediments. The future action plan should be based on realistic assessment of these impediments. Third, in a competitive global environment, we also need to adopt new strategies to be able to meet the future challenges (Bezbaruah, 2002).

India's position in tourism industry is shown in Table 4. It is expected that India's growth will be much higher than the world average.

The growth pattern of regionwise world tourism in India is reflected in Table 5.

About 50 per cent of the total people were only from Europe who visited India during the period under study. 5.84 lacs tourists visit from South Asia in 1997 followed by 3.58 lacs tourist from East Asia and the pacific and 3.40 lacs from America in the same year. In 1999, the maximum growth of

Table 3
International Tourist and Receipts Worldwide

	1989	*1990*	*1991*	*1992*	*1993*	*1994*	*1995*	*1996*	*1997*	*2007*
Arrivals (millions)	426	458	464	503	519	550	565	597	611	903
% annual change	8.02	7.45	1.25	8.49	3.12	6.05	2.73	5.49	2.39	6.6
Receipts (US $ billion)	221	269	278	315	324	354	405	436	436	856
% annual change	8.31	21.54	3.21	13.52	2.85	9.23	14.44	7.52	0.09	15.4

Source: World Tourism Organization (WTO).

Table 4
Comparative Tourism Growth

	India	*China*	*Thailand*	*Malaysia*	*Singapore*	*World*
Travel and tourism industry GDP (US $M) Real growth between 2001-2011 (percent annualized)	10.0 (1)	9.0 (3)	7.5 (9)	6.1 (20)	6.7 (14)	3.3
Travel and tourism economy GDP (US $m) Real growth between 2001-2011 (percent annualized)	9.1′ (3)	8.8 (4)	7.2 (10)	5.9 (25)	6.8 (13)	3.6
Travel and tourism employment GDP (US $m) Real growth between 2001-2011 (percent annualized)	3.6 (41)	2.0 (101)	3.0 (62)	3.5 (47)	3.2 (55)	2.4
Travel and tourism economy employment Real growth between 2001-2011 (percent annualized)	2.8 (73)	1.8 (113)	2.8 (70)	3.3 (50)	3.3 (49)	2.3

Source: WTO : Tourism 2020 Vision, 1998.

Table 5
Arrivals by Region in India

('000')

Countries	1993	1994	1995	1996	1997
Africa	60	61 (1.67)	84 (37.70)	86 (2.38)	99 (15.12)
America	220	245 (11.36)	284 (13.73)	322 (13.38)	340 (5.59)
Europe	693	745(7.50)	825(10.74)	897 (8.73)	899 (0.22)
East Asia and the Pacific	215	251(16.74)	289(15.14)	335(15.92)	358(6.87)
South Asia	466	480(3.00)	540(12.5)	544(0.74)	584(7.35)
Middle East	109	103(-5.50)	101(-1.94)	97(-3.96)	94(-3.09)

Source: WTO.
Note: Figures in bracket are in percentages.

tourist arrivals in India was found from Africa i.e. 15.12 per cent over the previous year while from middle east, the number of tourist go down from 97 to 94.

There has been significant increase in the tourist arrivals from Australia (274.29 per cent) followed by Central & South America (243.51 per cent) and North America (165.62 per cent) during 1991-2000. Again, during the year 2000 Western Europe constituted 30.7 per cent while South Asia accounted for 25.1 per cent in the total tourist arrivals in India. It shows that there is significant increase in the tourist arrivals in the region of North America, Australia, and South East area while the share of region in the total tourist arrivals in India declined sharply in case of South Asia and West Asia (Table 6).

The forecasts for the period of 2010 & 2020 are shown in Table 7.

Europe will remain the largest receiving region. East Asia and the pacific, increasing at 7.0 per cent p.a. will pass the Americas (Up 3.8 per cent) as the record largest receiving region, holding a 27 per cent market share in 2020 as against 18 per cent by Americas. The respective share of Africa, the middle East and South Asia will all record some increase to 5 per cent, 4 per cent and 1 per cent by 2020.

When India got Independence, the total international tourist arrivals were at the very low ebb, i.e. only 17000. But with the allow of policy of industrialization, the number of international tourist arrivals has got slight momentum. However, since the beginning of the decade of eighties there

Table 6
Region-wise Tourists Arrival in India

Region	2000	(%)	1999	1998	1997	1996	1995	1994	1991	(%)	Percentage Change 1991-2000
North America	4077	15.4	334859	324820	322864	302894	267188	232938	153502	9.2	165.62
Central & South America	40600	1.5	37988	23701	17011	19346	16072	11805	11819	0.7	243.51
Africa	1437711	5.4	136595	110708	102361	89148	87238	64134	62127	3.7	131.41
Australia	114291	4.3	101237	80212	65387	63063	49941	43865	30535	1.8	274.29
Western Europe	810139	30.7	807885	853411	831329	821222	754182	664820	514541	30.7	57.44
Eastern Europe	57048	2.2	59893	48443	45097	55673	53276	66080	46073	2.7	23.82
West Asia	128995	4.9	110806	95589	112607	114262	114748	114096	118530	7.1	8.82
South Asia	663581	25.1	624945	558772	583706	543967	540209	480142	590621	35.2	12.35
South East Asia	147166	5.5	142358	133524	146205	132808	129491	1135535	78966	4.7	86.36
East Asia	127825	4.8	125108	129366	146880	144266	109916	93844	67793	4.0	88.55
Grand Total	2641157	100.00	2481928	2358629	2374094	2287860	2123683	1886433	1677508	100.00	57.44

Source: Statistical Abstract of India, 2001.

had appreciable increase in the volume of international tourists. But still the share of India in global tourist arrivals has been insignificant i.e. only 0.38 per cent. Tourism in India has registered a record increase of more than 67 per cent during the decade of eighties. But the trends have been highly fluctuating and erratic nature. Interestingly, in the year 1990, there ha been a negative growth rate, i.e. 0.5 per cent and thereafter there had been a tremendous increase in volume of foreign tourist arrivals in India and the rise as high as more than 26 per cent. Again, it went down to 11.3 per cent in 1992. But the most alarming decline has been witnessed in the year 1993 i.e. a decline of nearly 6 per cent. The highest growth of tourist arrivals was reported in 1986 (15.2 per cent) followed by 1995 (12.6 per cent) and 1992 (11.3 per cent) while it showed negative trend during 1984, 1990, 1991, and 1993.

Table 7
Forecast of International Tourist Arrivals by Region (2000-2020)

	Tourist Arrivals (Million)			
Regions	*1995*	*2000*	*2010*	*2020*
Europe	335	390	527	717
East Asia/Pacific	80	116	231	438
Americas	111	134	195	284
Africa	20	27	46	75
Middle East	14	19	37	69
South Asia	4	6	11	19

Source: World Tourism Organization (WTO).

Importantly, at the end of the 20th century India is experiencing a negative growth in tourism, particularly in terms of foreign exchange earnings. The statistics of the Ministry of Tourism show that India earned US $ 2820 million from tourism industry in 1998. This represents a decline of 3 per cent as compared to the foreign exchange earnings in 1997 though the country received almost the same number of foreign visitors. The earnings in the first 9 month of 1999 in US dollar terms were particularly at the same level as they were in 1997 despite having a higher volume of arrivals. Significantly, India's share of global foreign exchange earnings also declined to 0.62 per cent in 1998 as compared to 0.67 per cent in 1997. This decline was registered at a time where there was an increase in foreign exchange earnings across the world (Dixit, 2001).

Over a period of 44 years (1951-1995), the arrivals of tourists increase to 2.12 million and half of which is accounted by ethnic Indians from the United Kingdom and the neighbouring countries. Tourism is presently, India's third largest export industry - after readymade garments and gems and jewellery. The foreign exchange earnings from tourism during 1995-96 was of the order of Rs. 10,000 crores. Moreover, the direct employment in this sector during 1994-95 was about 7.8 million persons accounting for about 2.4 per cent of the total labour force. The multiplier effect of tourism in employment generation is farily high and as such the total employment including indirect employment is 18.4 million. It would be possible to generate additional direct employment for 4.73 million persons within the next five years if the international tourist arrivals could be increased to at least five million. Interestingly, labour capital rate is much higher than industries.

During 1997 foreign earnings from tourism of world were reported to be $ 433.8 billion while in the corresponding year foreign earnings in India were reported to be $3151.7 million constituting 0.71 per cent share in world tourism earnings. Interestingly, India's share in world tourism earnings was reported highest in 1997 as compared to previous years. It was least reported in 1999. Interestingly, receipts from international tourism show variance over the years. The highest growth rate was reported in 1973, 1977, 1988, 1978, 1980, 1990, 1979, 1975, accounting more than 20 per cent growth as compared to previous year while it was found lowest in 1.9 per cent in 1981 and even negative growth in 1982. In India, estimated income from tourists also shows variance. The highest growth was reported in 1975-76 (107.1 per cent) followed by 1991-92 (87.3 per cent) and 1986-87 (35.1 per cent) while it was reported negative in 1981-82 and 1985-86. Importantly, foreign exchange earnings were reported lowest in India as compared to other selected countries. In India 2.12 million tourist arrivals were reported as compared to USA where 44.73 million tourist arrivals were found. Similarly, $ 2.76 billion foreign exchange earnings from tourist arrivals were reported as against $ 58.37 billion in USA.

Tourists from all over the world are coming to our country. There is a steady increase in the number of foreign tourists visiting India. Inspite of crossing two million marks; India accounts for only 0.4 per cent of world's total tourist traffic. Interestingly, during 1997, 1.97 million tourists (excluding Pakistan and Bangladesh nationals) visited India and out of total tourists 42.12 per cent tourists were from Western Europe while 16.36 per cent tourists were from North America. Again, there has been significant change in percentage share of North American tourists during 1993 to 1997. Similar is the case of Western European tourists. Interestingly, share of Asian countries tourists was also reported to be significant. Importantly, during 1970 to 1987 there has been phenomenon growth of tourist arrivals in India. Out of total tourist arrivals in India United Kingdom (14.3 per cent) and West Europe (13.3 per cent) accounted for largest share while USA accounted for 11.6 per cent in total tourist arrivals in India in 1987. Significantly, share of tourists from West Asia, West Europe and East Europe has risen significantly while it declined in case of USA, Australia and South East Asia. Again, during 1997, UK constituted 18.7 per cent share in total tourist arrivals in India while USA accounted for 12.4 per cent share in tourist arrivals in India. Interestingly, there has been sharp rise in the share of tourist arrivals in India in case of USA, Japan, Canada, Malaysia and significant decline in case of UK, Sri Lanka, France, Italy and Singapore (Dixit, 2001).

Importantly, an estimated 41 per cent of the foreign tourists visiting India have a per cent capita income of over Rs. 4 lakh per annum, while about 19 per cent between Rs. 50,000 and Rs. 2 lakh and 26 per cent less than Rs. 60,000 per annum. Going by the findings of the latest survey conducted by Ministry of Tourism (1998-99), the category of tourists with highest income (over Rs. 4 lakh per capita per annum) constitutes only 41 per cent of the total traffic to India.

During 1991-2000 there has been a tremendous rise in the growth rate i.e. 56 per cent. The growth of tourism during 1950-60 was around 25 per cent which declined to 8.6 per cent during the 1960-70 and a sharp increase has been noted during 1970-80. Thus, it is clear that tourism growth during the post-reform period has been tremendous. During the year 2000 tourist traffic has increased a marginal rate i.e. 5.7 per cent over 1999. It has been estimated that tourism in India will grow higher than China, Thailand, Malaysia, Singapore etc. during 2001-2011. Importantly, tourist receipts in India are gradually increasing since 1981. During 1999-2000 tourism industry achieved 6.4 per cent growth rate which was below 6 per cent of the forecasted rate. A comparative analysis of tourist arrivals in India from different regions and important countries depicts that foreign tourist arrivals in India from various nations have increased from 1987 to 2000. UK and USA both have continued to occupy the top two positions since 1981. The inbound tourist traffic from UK has increased by 6.2 per cent during 1981 to 2000, while tourists from USA have increased by 6.4 per cent during the last two decades. Srilanka occupied third position in inbound tourist traffic to India. France, Germany, Canada and Japan occupied important place in India's international tourist arrivals.

Rajasthan, Maharashtra, Karnataka, Uttar Pradesh, Tamil Nadu, Andhra Pradesh, Bihar, Gujarat, Kerala, Orissa, are some of the states, which attract larger number of tourists in India. Foreign tourist preferred to visit Maharashtra, Tamil Nadu, Uttar Pradesh, Rajasthan, Bihar, Himachal Pradesh, Andhra Pradesh and Kerala (Table 2.8). The ranking of states in domestic tourism simply demonstrates that Andhra Pradesh, Uttar Pradesh, Tamil Nadu, Karnataka, Rajasthan, Uttarakhand, Maharashtra, West Bengal and Madhya Pradesh account larger share in tourist arrivals. Delhi, Maharashtra, Tamil Nadu, Uttar Pradesh, Rajasthan, West Bengal, Andhra Pradesh, Karnataka and Kerala recorded important position in the foreign tourist arrivals during 2007.

Table 8
State-wise Tourist Arrivals in India

	2001		2002		2007	
State/Union Territory	*Domestic*	*Foreigner*	*Domestic*	*Foreigner*	*Domestic*	*Foreigner*
Andhra Pradesh	52533647	67147	60487370	210310	127933333	769724
ArunachalPradesh (A)	6349	323	4372	187	91100	2212
Assam	1010651	6171	1953915	6409	3436833	12899
Bihar	6061168	85673	8660207	112873	10352887	177362
Goa	1047342	260071	1325296	271645	2208986	388457
Gujrat	8272969	30930	5735286	34187	13477316	104158
Haryana	276287	898	6426763	85281	6252945	64711
Himachal Pradesh	5211772	135760	4958917	144383	8481988	339409
J & K	5246948	21298	4570583	7821	7915271	52754
Karnataka	14117464	140703	8678670	59545	37825953	534563
Kerala	5240009	208830	5568256	232564	6642941	515808
Madhya Pradesh	5048851	107824	4903242	67319	13894500	234204
Mahara-rashtra	8479695	9153399	9802527	768935	19226716	1928052
Manipur	76527	183	89633	221	101484	396
Meghalaya	178697	2390	268609	3146	457685	5267
Mizoram	28771	152	29417	259	43161	669
Nagaland (A)	9948	920	14263	657	22085	936
Orissa	3109976	22854	3289205	23279	5944890	41880
Punjab	474305	3258	317904	7558	368593	5470
Rajasthan	7757217	608283	8300190	428437	25920529	1401042
Sikkim	203306	31028	159342	8566	329075	17498
Tamil Nadu	23812043	773073	39873160	804041	70254972	1753103
Tripura	254912	1512	260586	2602	244795	3181
Uttar Pradesh	68790000	795000	71490000	710000	116244008	1493157
West Bengal	4943097	284092	8844232	529366	18580669	1154770
Andman & Nicobar	84064	5539	90629	5101	136015	10975
Chandi-garh	482133	15203	554948	13706	928159	26567
Daman & Diu	580322	10290	595449	6569	446490	5315
Delhi (A)	1324636	830092	1228059	543036	2388330	2018848
Dadra & Nagar Haveli	452000	400	452100	202	473489	5625
Laksh-deep	3501	650	9173	912	16642	2933
Pondi-cherry	476804	22115	480522	20094	798528	57682
Uttaran-chal	9551669	44429	10606504	45070	19803280	95976
Chhatis-garh	969342	792	1058565	993	414322	1232
Jhar-khand	353177	2979	313134	2244	4906394	4004
Total (A)	236469599	5436261	269598028	5157518	526564364	13230839

Source: Tourist Statistical Book, 2007

Tourism Infrastructure and Services

Tourism infrastructure is the backbone of the tourism industry. It facilitates the tourists in terms of easy movement of tourists in a comfortable manner; offer them a variety of accommodation to suit them, efficient coordination of the movement and stay of tourists. Therefore, travel agencies, tour operators, tour promoters, transport operators and other service providers have come up to operate their business and facilitate tourists.

Travel Agency

The travel agency business in India is a lucrative business and is growing steadily with the increasing pace of life and the acute necessity of a swift and more frequent travel. The main functions of a travel agency are to ensure a smooth, comfortable and definite travel by taking all responsibilities of making reservations and assisting the passengers in completing all the formalities involved in the travel. In order to get the benefits of commissions and credit facilities from its principles, the airlines, hotels and transporters, a travel agency has to be approved by IATA (International Air Transport Association) and the respective departments of the government. In the state of Uttar Pradesh (including Uttaranchal), there were 5 travel agencies in 1997.

A full fledged travel agency mainly consists of three departments: (i) international passage booking, (ii) domestic passage booking, (iii) tour operation. Importantly, international passage booking facilitates only those passengers who intend travelling abroad. It has four small units : (i) documentation unit, (ii) reservation unit, (iii) visa unit, (iv) sales unit. Interestingly, domestic passage booking unit facilitates domestic air travel and deals only with Indian airlines. This unit takes the requirements of the passengers on telephone and gets the tickets delivered to the clients.

Tour Operation

This department of a recognized travel agency has a very vital role to play in promoting the tourist traffic to India and thus earning a considerable amount of foreign exchange for the country. The basic function of this unit is to get tourists from abroad and make arrangements for their hotel accommodation, sight-seeing and ground transportations all over the country according to their individual requirements. In the state of Uttar Pradesh, there were 7 tour operators in 1997.

Tour Promotion

Tour promoters are mainly agents and are called (i) retailer, (ii) whole seller. Retailer is the agent who normally operators individually, who are called FITS, and small groups depending solely on his own contact and business potential. Importantly, whole seller is the one who plans a tour and prints detailed pamphlets with detailed itinerary of the tour its price and circulates the same among all the travel agents in an around his area. The retailers feed the whole seller with passengers taking the tour and get a certain amount of commission on whatever sales they make. The whole seller thus forms a group of requisite number of passengers and sends the itinerary and details concerned with India to the agent in India who in turn obtains all the hotel and air confirmations and quotes his price for the tour to the operators abroad.

Package Tours

Most of the agencies in India and abroad, are devising means and ways to cut the volume of correspondence short and acquire facilities of instant reservations with the hotels and the airlines. 'Package Tours' is a developing vital attempt in this direction. Now the agents divides the whole country in various small units and plans package tours, covering fully at least one unit and offers fixed services and uses fixed hotels at a fixed price. A detailed pamphlet of these package tours containing 7 to 10 different package tours with detailed itinerary and price of each tour, is then printed and circulated among the agents and airlines abroad.

Transportation

The tourist industry of a country depends on two major factors conveyance and accommodation. The greater the facilities available in these fields, more brisk the trade turnout will be. Tourists have the choice of three types of travel: by air, by surface, and by sea. While international tourism depends primarily on air travel, the domestic tourism depends mainly on surface transport. Importantly, numerous incentives are being regularly offered by the air companies to make the air journey substantially cheaper. Interestingly, growth of motor-car industry, particularly in the developed countries, road transport by bus and by private or hired cars both have become the demand of the day.

Air Services

There is government run and privately run air services in India. Air India is a international air service while Indian Airlines is a domestic air service. Sahara and Jet Air, Deccan Air services, the two main private operating companies, have good domestic network. Apart from this, a number of Air Taxi operators are providing non-scheduled air services. A helicopter service is provided by Pawan Hans Helicopters with flight to ONGC offshore operations as well as to Vaishno Devi Shrine. However, in the state of Uttar Pradesh, such services are lacking. Moreover, there are no international airports, which may facilitate international fights operations. Importantly, direct flights are not available to network major cities and tourist destinations. However, government has approved the services of charter flights from abroad to Goa, Agra, Varanasi, Jaipur and Bangalore.

Rail Services

The second largest railways system in the world under a single management, the Indian Railways provides the principal mode of transportation for freight and passengers. Indian railways have bound the economic, cultural and social life of the country, helping in development of industry, agriculture, and of course tourism which is the greatest revenue earner in the Indian economy.

The Indian Railways presently has 84,370 kms. running of tracks laid between 7,068 stations with a fleet of over 11,000 locomotives (Table 9). The Indian Railways has nine administrative zones. They are:

- Central Railway (Bombay)
- Eastern Railway (Kolkata)
- Northern Railway (New Delhi)
- North Eastern Railway (Gorakhpur)
- North Eastern Fronteir (Guwahati)
- Southern Railway (Chennai)

- South Central Railway (Secundrabad)
- South Eastern Railway (Kolkata)
- Western Railway (Mumbai)

Indian Railways has bifurcated the existing nine zones into seven more administrative zones for smooth functioning of service. They are:

- West-Central Railway (Jabalpur)
- East-Central Railway (Bhubaneshwar)
- South-Western Railway (Bangalore)
- South East- Central Railway (Bilaspur)
- North-Western Railway (Jaipur)
- North-Central Railway (Allahabad).

Table 9
State-wise Rail Route Length

State	*1990-91*	*1991-92*	*1992-93*	*1993-94*	*1994-95*	*1995-96*	*1998-99*
Andhra Pradesh	5023	5086	5055	5063	5073	5057	5057
Arunachal Pradesh	1	1	1	1	1	1	1
Assam	2467	2467	2467	3728	3734	2441	2392
Bihar	5309	5315	5316	5288	5291	5283	5178
Delhi	168	168	168	168	214	214	200
Goa	79	79	79	79	79	79	69
Haryana	1500	1499	1499	1499	1452	1452	5312
Himachal Praddesh	267	266	266	266	266	266	269
Jammu & Kashmir	77	77	88	88	88	88	84
Karnataka	3065	3065	3089	3078	3124	3124	2974
Kerala	984	984	1028	1053	1053	1053	1050
Madhya Pradesh	5869	5904	5987	5987	5987	6000	5922
Maharashtra	5435	5440	5455	5459	5462	5462	5447
Manipur	1	1	1	1	1	1	1
Mizoram	1	2	2	2	2	2	2
Nagaland	9	9	9	9	9	13	13
Orissa	2002	2002	2002	2002	2009	2191	2340
Punjab	2160	2160	2121	2121	2121	2121	2102
Rajasthan	5827	5826	5740	5808	5935	5924	5917
Tamil Nadu	4012	4010	4023	4021	4005	4005	4188
Tripura	45	45	45	45	45	45	45
U.P.	8926	8917	8901	8947	8929	8934	8893
West Bengal	3816	3816	3825	3825	3815	3817	3786
Chandigarh	11	11	11	11	11	11	8
Pondicherry	27	27	27	27	11	11	11

Source : Annual Report, 2000, Indian Railways.

A number of high speed trains are operated with comfort and in time saving journeys. These are the Rajdhani Express, Shatabdi Express, Jan Shatabdi Express, Palace on Wheels, Shivalik Express, Shivalik Palace, Fairy Queen, 'Royal Orient' etc. Metro rail services in several cities have provided cost effective public mode of transport.

The railways offers hill stations concessions. It also has launched several trains, which take religious tourists throughout India in package tours of three to four months. For students and other groups of people, the railways provide tourist coaches. Bonafide students and their groups also get concessions for their tour. There is another aspect of railway concessions. It concerns package tour for sight-seeing which are becoming more popular with people all over the world.

Communication Services

In India VSNL and several other private agencies are providing communication services. Important private operators are Airtel, Vodafone, Tata, Reliance and Idea, while digital communication has changed the way of life. Most tour operators, travel agents, transporters etc. are depending on e-marketing of their services. Mobile communication has broken the geographical boundaries and such services are available even during bad weather, natural disasters etc. Importantly, expansion of telephone exchanges have enhanced telephone connectivity and network. There were 24869 telephone exchanges in India during 1997-98. In eastern U.P., there were 1438 telephone exchanges while in western U.P., there were 840 telephone exchange. During 1994-95, 1603 telephone exchanges were reported in east and western U.P. (Table 10).

Table 10
State-wise No. of Telephone Exchanges

State	*1990-91*	*1991-92*	*1992-93*	*1993-94*	*1994-95*	*1995-96*	*1997-98*
A. P.	2010	2010	2008	2029	2038	2058	2171
Assam	218	225	240	269	286	284	366
Bihar	461	515	636	743	776	790	892
Gujarat	1027	1070	1161	1262	1338	1387	1553
Haryana	411	483	548	605	681	750	856

Contd.

State	1990-91	1991-92	1992-93	1993-94	1994-95	1995-96	1997-98
H. P.	311	345	369	410	461	539	646
J & K	138	155	175	197	202	220	264
Karnataka	1631	1707	1799	1866	1927	2021	2239
Kerala	649	675	688	715	727	765	850
M. P.	1261	1566	1953	2337	2630	2667	2790
Maharashtra	1674	1779	1927	2073	2268	2467	2905
North East	168	172	176	200	216	231	306
Orissa	472	338	596	655	674	695	794
Punjab	550	583	632	691	784	836	1100
Rajasthan	882	923	1045	1240	1380	1441	1777
Tamil Nadu	1244	1252	1262	1276	1313	1353	1523
U.P.(E & W)	1237	1309	1431	1502	1603	–	–
U.P. (E)	–	–	–	–	–	963	1438
U.P. (W)	–	–	–	–	–	760	940
W. B.	473	485	504	511	511	556	828
Delhi	70	76	84	111	123	127	165
All India	15091	16091	17455	18956	20169	21160	24869

Source: Annual Report, 2000, Dept. of Tele Communication.

Accommodation

In India, hotels, rest-houses, dharmashalas, guest-houses, retiring rooms, etc. are providing facilities to tourists for their stay. Accommodation and its tariff may be of several types, depending on the nature of its establishment and the facilities offered to the guests by them. Some of the different kinds of establishments available in India are : (i) hotels; (ii) motels; (iii) travelers' lodges; (iv) youth hostels; (v) cottages; (vi) dak bungalows; (vii) circuit houses; (viii) camping sites and holiday camps; (ix) guest houses; (x) railway retiring rooms; (xi) dormitories; (xii) dharmashalas. However, hotels are being preferred due to availability of services and facilities. Hotels are of different categories, ranging from one star to five star hotel and crowned by super deluxe hotel, while government (central and state government) run rest houses, guest-houses, dak bungalow, circuit houses are available to government officers only on subsidized rate, though concerned departments may book such accommodation for a short period on approval by higher authorities for eligible persons. Similarly, dormitories and railway retiring rooms are available only who have already traveled by train and have valid railway tickets. Such accommodations are available only for a short period of 3 days maximum.

Category-wise details regarding number of hotels and rooms available are presented in Table 11.

Table 11
Number of Approved Hotels and Availability of Rooms

	No. of Hotels		*No. of Rooms*	
Category	*2006*	*2007*	*2006*	*2007*
One Star	46	53	1435	1774
Two Star	217	231	582	6637
Three Star	477	587	20342	24496
Four Star	111	116	7354	7584
Five Star	71	81	8470	9792
5* Deluxe	86	93	20943	20110
Apartment Hotel	5	5	334	461
Time Share Resort	-	1	-	62
Heritage Hotel	67	83	2211	2450
Unclassified	133	175	8924	10415
Total	1213	1425	75836	83781

Source: India Tourism Statistics, 2007.

State-wise number of hotels and rooms are shown in Table 12.

Table 12
State-wise Number of Hotels & Rooms During 2007

State	*Hotel*	*Rooms*
Andhra Pradesh	87	5976
Assam	11	491
Bihar	06	294
Chhatisgarh	05	160
Delhi	48	8855
Goa	47	4241
Gujarat	54	3097
Haryana	28	1520
Himachal Pradesh	23	852
Jharkhand	07	249
Jammu & Kashmir	04	286
Karnataka	43	4007
Kerala	313	8487

Contd.

State	Hotel	Rooms
Madhya Pradesh	37	1848
Maharashtra	190	16318
Meghalaya	04	119
Orissa	13	768
Punjab	88	2281
Rajasthan	112	5454
Sikkim	01	28
Tamil Nadu	162	9976
Uttar Pradesh	53	3866
Uttarakhand	17	697
West Bengal	34	2756
Total	1425	83781

Source: India Tourism Statistics, 2007.

During 2007, 438 tour operators, 337 travel agencies and 160 tourist transport operators in India were found engaged in facilitating tourist. The number of tour operators was reported high in Delhi, Maharashtra, Tamil Nadu and Kerala. Most of the tour operators were found active in Delhi only. The numbers of travel agencies were reported high in Delhi, Maharashtra, Tamil Nadu and Karnataka (Table 13).

Emerging Trends and Paradigm Shifts

The following trends have emerged in the recent past, which have implications on government policies and planning. The analysis of these trends and paradigms shifts is quite relevant for policy imperatives:

- Eco-tourism has emerged as one of the most lucrative, fast growing and sustainable tourism development form in the worldwide tourism industry. India has also paid attention towards development and promotion of eco-tourism, however, regulation of tourism in protected areas and other nature based tourist destinations has to be ensured through enforcement of laws relating to environment protection and sustainable development of the resources.
- Rural tourism has shown tremendous scope for development and promotion since cultural tourism

Table 13
State-wise Number of Tour Operators & Travel Agencies (During 2007)

State/UT	*Tour Operators*	*Travel Agencies*	*Tourist Transport Operators*	*Adventure Tour Operators*	*Domestic Tour Operators*
Andhra Pradesh	6	11	4	-	-
Arunachal Pradesh	1	-	-	-	-
Assam	4	-	-	-	-
Bihar	2	3	-	-	-
Goa	13	4	-	-	-
Gujarat	5	8	2	-	-
Haryana	5	4	-	-	-
Jammu & Kashmir	5	1	-	-	2
Karnataka	9	22	13	-	2
Kerala	17	5	22	-	-
Madhya Pradesh	1	2	2	-	-
Maharashtra	40	77	12	1	3
Orissa	5	-	-	-	-
Punjab	-	3	2	-	-
Rajasthan	5	2	-	-	-
Tamil Nadu	22	47	24	-	5
Uttar Pradesh	9	5	3	-	-
Uttarakhand	-	1	-	1	-
West Bengal	3	15	1	-	-
Delhi	285	121	73	22	7
Total	438	337	160	24	19

Source: India Tourism Statistics, 2007.

particularly folk dances, folk songs, rituals, theatre groups, ethnic traditions etc. have promoted the cultural heritage of India with intrinsic value as a tourism asset. Thus, government has to diversify the tourism products and promotion of our cultural heritage in a proper manner.

- Sustainable development of tourism has demanded the enhanced role of community based organizations in development of tourism, management and preservation of natural resources and protection of environment and ecology. Globalization has shown tremendous scope for tourism development and its promotion. However, strategic planning and management of tourism resources and destinations have to be ensured so that in the changing business environment and governance sustainable tourism development may be ensured.
- A newly emerging trend in tourism is that senior citizens who live in isolation because of the daily busy schedules of their children and their attitudes are now focused for enabling them to pass their time in a lively manner. However, more incentives and facilities have to be provided them for their comfort and safe travel and stay at destinations.
- Heritage tourism has emerged one of the potential tourism alternative form. It entails the following parameters of management viz. conservation and mass tourism, uniqueness of the site, strategic planning and community participation in conservation and preservation of historical sites, natural and built up environment etc. (Kamara, 2001).

References

Bezbaruah, M.P. (1999), Tourism-Current Scenario and Future Prospects, Yojana, August.

Bezbaruha, M.P. (2002), Fronteirs of New Tourism, Gyan Pub. Delhi.

Chand, M. and V. Chauhan (2002), Indian Tourism : A Retrospective and Prospective Appraisal In Tourism In The New Millenium, By S.P. Bansal, et al (Ed.), Abhishek Pub. Delhi.

Dixit, M. (2001) , Dimensions of India Tourism, Bharat Book Centre, Lucknow.

Kamra, K.K. (2001), Managing Tourist Destinations, Kasnishka Pub. Delhi.

3

Tourism Planning and Policies

Tourism Planning is an essential activity for every destination and a must for the tourism development and promotion. However, tourism planning in India is a recent initiative in the international tourism market. Tourism planning has following main attributes and advantages (Tewari, 1994) :

- Planning is paramount to avoid situation caused by haphazard development. It is required to ensure that the natural and created assets are concerned and protected to maintain their tourist appeal;
- There are numerous examples which show the consequences of the unplanned development of destination areas. These related to negative impacts of the lack of planning particularly on the physical environment leading to the permanent damage, alteration or degradation;
- Tourism development involves heavy outlays and investments. The resources, of the state are in most cases, limited and also required for several other development activities. Thus, state needs to undertake tourism planning in order to ensure the proper utilization of the finances so that the maximum economic and other benefits may be desired;
- Both the public and private sectors have important roles in the development of tourism which is not always clearly demarcated. The success of the tourism

development to a large extent depends on the availability of the appropriate facilities at the right time and in the right place. Thus, tourism planning ensure balanced growth of demand and supply.

- Tourism development can be most effective if it is undertaken within the context of a plan and form a part and parcel of the national economic development programme design to lead to the optimum growth of the economy of the country as a whole.

A process for tourism planning involves several steps, which may be broadly, grouped under five essential phases. Each of the five phases involves many participants and activities and its outcome leads to the development of subsequent steps. The five phases of tourism planning are (Mill and Morison, 1985) :

- Background analysis phase;
- Detailed research and analysis phase;
- Synthesis phase;
- Goal and objective setting phase; and
- Plan development phase.

The key phases in tourism planning can be (Gupta et al, 2002) :

- Tourist Demand and Supply
- Create Objectivities
- Environmental Planning
- Basic Tourism Infrastructure
- Monitory or Financial Planning
- Man Power Planning
- Administrative Planning
- Tourism Marketing and Promotion
- Monitoring, Evaluation and Performance Appraisal.

The first step in development of tourism in India was the setting up of the Sargent Committee in 1945. The Committee recommended a separate department of tourism at the Centre level with regional offices. In 1948, an ad hoc committee was constituted under the Transport Ministry. However, in 1949 Government of India set up a tourist traffic branch under the Ministry of Shipping and Transport with a view to increase tourist traffic in India. In 1958, a separate Department of Tourism was established under the Ministry of Transport and Communication. Jha Committee in 1963 was constituted with a view to examine the prevailing conditions for promoting tourist traffic; to access the basic requirements for tourists in respect to hotel accommodation, transportation etc. and to recommend necessary measures for the expansion of tourist traffic and to protect the breakage of foes. The committee pointed out that the downward trend in tourism was due to two reasons: (a) Chinese aggression, (b) declaration of emergency. The committee suggested 15 points plan for certain organizational changes and other measures to improve the existing tourist trend. The committee also recommended that public sector in tourism should play a vital role (Dixit, 2001). During 1965-66 three public sector corporations were established while the corporations were merged into one corporation called Indian Tourism Development Corporation Ltd. In March, 1967, Department of Tourism and Civil Aviation was separated and converted into Ministry of Tourism.

The Government of India has formulated several plans, which have been already successfully implemented. Along with the government, various associations are involved in activities relating to planning and development of travel and tourism. In India the National Tourism Administration is the Department of Tourism and Culture. The Department of Tourism and Culture coordinates with various departments of the government in tourism-related activities (Chart 1).

The functions of the Ministry covers both promotional and organizational activities under the following divisions :

- Planning and programming.
- Publicity and conference.
- Travel trade.
- Hospitality and accommodation.

- Supplementary accommodation and wildlife.
- Market Research.
- Administration.

The activities of the Ministry cover a wide range of subjects:

- Collection, compilation and dissemination of tourist information in India and abroad, attending to enquiries from international tourists, tour operators and travel industry such as airlines, steamship companies and hotels.
- Co-operation with international travel and tourist organizations at government and non-government levels.
- Development of tourist facilities of interest to international tourists.
- Publicity at home and abroad with the object of creating an overall awareness of the importance of tourism.
- Simplification of frontier formalities in respect of international tourists.
- Regulation of activities of the various segments of the travel trade such as hotels, youth hostels, travel agents, wildlife outfitters, guides, tourist car operators and shopkeepers catering to tourist needs.
- Compilation of statistics and market research on international tourist traffic to India and their utilization for more effective tourist promotion.

In 1950, India established Planning Commission and adopted planned model for the overall development of the country. During the First Five Year Plan (1951-56), total outlay was Rs. 1960 crores. However, no amount was allocated for the development of tourism, as tourism was not a separate sector of Indian economy (Chand and Chauhan, 2002). Although , tourism cell was formed in 1949 and was looked after by Ministry of Transport. In spite of no plan allocation, Govt. adopted some measures to increase/attract foreign

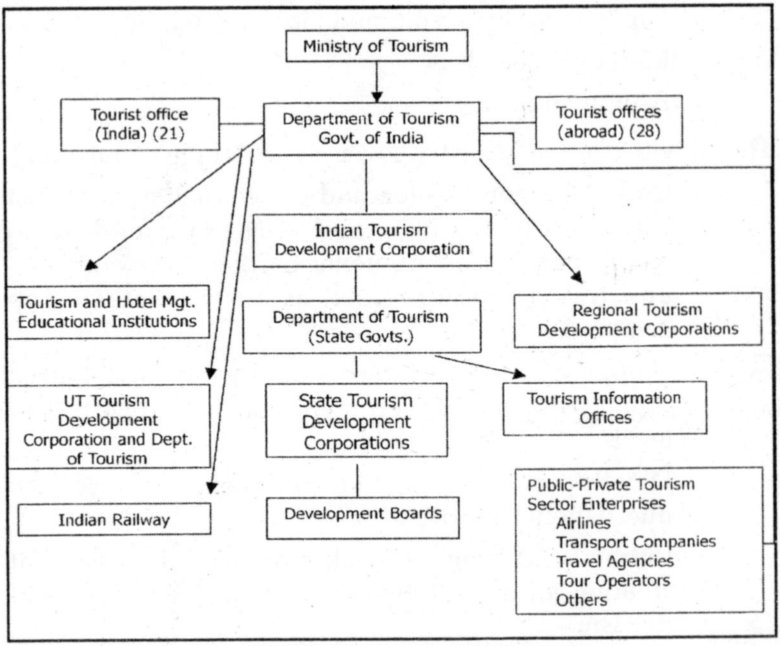

Chart 1: Ministry of Tourism

tourists such as opening of tourist offices in India and abroad, production of tourist literature and publicity material and involving travel agents and tour operators to organize tourism promotional activities etc. In fact, the first planned effort towards the development of tourism was taken by the Govt. during Second Five Year Plan (1956-61). A separate fund of Rs. 3.36 crores, which was just 0.7 per cent was set aside for the development of tourism. Table 1 shows the share of the tourism to total plan allocation during the different five-year plans. The main thrust during this plan was to develop tourism infrastructure especially accommodation and transport facilities at the destination which could be the first choice for both foreign and domestic tourists. During 10th Five Year Plan, 1160 projects were sanctioned in tourism sector while Rs. 2011.67 crores were spent on tourism development. The outlay for 11th Five Year Plan was reported to be Rs. 5156 crores.

Moreover, this approach mainly concentrated on developing random and isolated facilities in important tourist destinations.

Table 1
Tourism and Plan Allocation

Plan	*Tourism Outlay (in Crores)*	*Total Plan Outlay (in Crores)*	*Per cent of Tourism*
1st Five Year	Nil	1,960	–
2nd Five Year Plan (1956-60)	3.36	4,600	0.07
3rd Five Year Plan (1961-66)	8.00	4,600	0.11
Annual Plans (1966-74)	7.00	6,757	0.10
4th Five Year Plan (1969-74)	36.00	15,902	0.23
5th Five Year Plan (1974-79)	73.95	39,304	0.19
6th Five Year Plan (1980-90)	187.46	97,500	0.19
7th Five Year Plan (1985-90)	326.16	1,80,000	0.18
8th Five Year Plan (1992-97)	773.62	4,34,100	0.17
9th Five Year Plan (1997-2000)	485.75	8,59,200	0.056
10th Five Year Plan (2000-2007) (Expenditure)	2011.67	–	–
11th Five Year Plan(2007-2011)	5156.00	–	-

Source: Compiled From Plan Documents, Various Issue.

Practically, tourism promotional activities were divided into three part schemes. The first part scheme were intended to create tourist facilities like accommodation.

The first two development plans mainly concentrated on developing random and isolated facilities in important tourist centres. Third Five Year Plan observed the setting about of an era for the development of tourism activities, particularly adventure tourism through the installation of winter sports complex at Gulmarg in Jammu and Kashmir but with only a marginal increase in allocation of funds for the sector. The Indian Tourism Development Corporation (ITDC) was also set up in 1966 to develop tourism infrastructure and promote India as a tourist destination. During the Fourth and Fifth Plans, tourism development approach was focused augmentation and betterment of tourist facilities so as to promote destination traffic. The Sixth Plan can be considered as a critical turning point in the history of Indian tourism when the first ever tourism policy of the country specifying the tourism development objectives and furnishing an action plan based on travel circuit concept to maximise the benefits of tourism was announced in 1982 (Bezbaruah, 1999). The development of tourism got priority and was specified as a plan objective in the Seventh Plan (1985-90). The sector was accorded the states of an industry and the plan turned out to be a landmark for Indian Tourism. For the first time a National Action Plan for Tourism worked out and presented in the Parliament on 5th May, 1992 made up the principal element of the development plan for tourism during Eighth Plan (1992-97). It recommended to realise diversification of tourism product, accelerated growth of tourism infrastructure, effective marketing and promotion efforts in the overseas markets and removal of all impediments to tourism (Kamra, 2001).

National Action Plan for Tourism, 1992

A National Action Plan includes a set of strategies for achieving a phenomenal growth in tourist arrivals, foreign exchange earnings and employment generation through:

- Improvement of tourism infrastructure.
- Developing areas on a selective basis for integrated growth and development.
- Restructuring and strengthening of the institutions for development of human resources.
- Creation of special category of heritage hotels, resorts and providing them financial assistance.
- Introduction of tourist trains and river cruises.
- Revamp of foreign offices and tracking output.
- Usage of IT in promotion of India in all leading markets.
- Formulation of special airline hotel packages.
- Open sky policy.

National Strategy for Development of Tourism, 1996

In October 1996 the government evolved a national strategy for the development of tourism. Proposals were discussed with the Planning Commission and state governments to be worked on. The proposals covered along with a setting up of the Board of Tourism Industry and Trade were as follows (Gupta, et. al. 2002):

Transport

- Modernization and upgradation of airports.
- Sanctioning of charter flights.
- Permission to private airlines to operate international flights.
- Private airlines to be allowed to fly to remote tourist centres with small aircrafts.
- Improvement of railway network to important tourist centres.
- Comfort in travelling to important tourist and pilgrimage centres.
- Road signs along tourist routes.
- Modernization of road infrastructure.
- Construction of high speed tracks.
- Development of water transport.

Infrastructure Development

- Environmental planning.
- Development of telecommunications.
- Development of cultural tourism, eco-tourism, and water cruise and adventure tourism.
- Short-term visa for charter tourists.
- Smooth immigration and custom clearance.
- Market research.
- Focussed marketing strategy.
- Introduction of information technology.
- Publicity and promotion.
- Environmental protection and cultural preservation.

National Tourism Policy, 1997

The main feature of the policy are :

- Identification of domestic tourism, inbound tourism and outbound tourism.

- Focus on the significance of tourism in poverty alleviation and employment generation.
- Diversification of tourism product in the form of going for new destinations to reinforce the mainstream of cultural tourism.
- Preservation and protection of natural resources, environment and ecology for tourism development.
- Sustainable development of tourism within the carrying capacity of the area.
- Foreign collaborations and investment in tourism industry in view of liberalization and its application in the tourism sector.
- Enhancing the role of people's associations, NGOs, and other community based organizations to promote tourism.

National Tourism Policy-2002

The policy has taken into consideration seven key words to promote tourism in India viz. *Swagat* (welcome), *Suchana* (information), *Suvidha* (Facilities), *Suraksha* (safety), *Sahyoga* (co-operation), *Sanrachana* (infrastructure) and *Safai* (Cleaniness).

The National Tourism Policy-2002 has laid significant importance upon the following basic principles (Govt. of India, 2002):

- Positioning of India as a global brand to take advantage of the burgeoning global travel trade.
- Providing a legislative framework to regulate tourism trade and industry, ensure safety and security and create basic infrastructure and healthcare facilities.
- Encouraging private sector to co-operate with government sector for safeguarding the stability and also the social and economic advancement of the local communities.
- Improvement and environmental upgradation of the protected monuments and the areas around them.

- Effective linkage of departments as Civil Aviation, Environment, Forest, Railways, Home, etc.
- Emphasis on Eco-tourism.
- Over-exploitation of natural resources to be prevented.
- Encouragement to tribal and local crafts leading to enhancing the status of women and eliminating poverty.
- Special thrust to rural tourism and tourism in small settlements.
- Importance to domestic tourism, particularly pilgrimage tourism.
- Development of infrastructure for encouragement to adventure tourism.
- Effective use of yoga, nature therapy, siddha, Indian cuisine for attracting tourists.
- Adoption of a Code of Ethics by the tourist industry and the travel agents.
- Creation of tourism circuits based on India's unique civilization, heritage and culture in partnership with states, private sector and other agencies.
- Section of the State police to be earmarked and trained as tourist police.
- Highlighting India's cultural and spiritual heritage at the international meetings of World Tourism Organization, World Tourism and Travel Council, Earth Council, etc.
- Improvement of civic administration.

The Policy Framework

The national policies with regard to tourism for achieving the objectives enumerated in this statement have to be consistent with the existing global scenario as well as national priorities and ethos. Taking into account these considerations, the following policy guidelines have seen formulated:

- The economic and social benefits of tourism and its importance as an instrument of economic growth have to be fully recognized.
- Tourists desire for peace, stability, safety, security, friendly host society, effective and efficient facilities and services.
- Tourism consists of several goods and services consumed by the tourists at their places of visit. Therefore, tourism development can not be the responsibility of any single agency.
- The infrastructure for tourism consists of not only the one site facilities like hotels, restaurants, entertainment facilities etc. but also includes all forms of transport and communications infrastructure and basic amenities. Therefore, an integrated approach for tourism development is the need of hour.
- Policy envisaged a selective approach based on travel circuit concept in the provision of tourism infrastructure to achieve intensive development of selected centres.
- The main strength of Indian tourism at present is its cultural and heritage attractions. The country is also endowed with nature based tourism resources such as wildlife, forests, mountain peaks, rivers and adventure sites etc. Therefore, diversification of tourism products is called for.
- The prnciple of sustainable development stipulates that the level of development does not exceed the carrying capacity of the area.
- Tourism is a multi-sectoral activity and the industry is affected by many others sectors of the national economy. Therefore, inter-governmental linkages and coordination have to be ensured. Both the public sector and private sector participation in tourism development is required.

- The potential tourism destinations have to be identified and developed through proper marketing and strategic management.
- Tourism development needs to be properly guided and regulated to avoid adverse impact on the natural environment and cultural heritage.

An analysis indicates that the Department of Tourism, Ministry of Tourism, Govt. of India has taken several concerted steps in the promotion and development of tourism industry at national, regional and state level such as identification of travel circuits, liberalized charter policy and air taxi scheme, open policy, assistance for the development of specified area, provision of various financial and non-financial incentives, tax concessions, publicise the traditions, fair and festivals, discovering roots for ethnic tourism, conducting surveys, setting tourism committees, developing human resources, introduction of innovative marketing strategies, strengthening tourism product, correlating information technology with development process, development of infrastructure and superstructure, formulated tourism policies, plans strategies and so forth. Importantly, National Tourism Organization by WTO on Tourism 2020 Vision has highlighted that the following areas are to prioritized to focus tourism development:

- More focussed and more aggressive marketing.
- Constraint striving for a competitive edge through a combination of product differentiation, quality and price.
- Growing recognition of the need for sustainable tourism development to ensure long term prosperity.
- More privatization of tourism related services and infrastructure.
- Active participation of community in tourism activities and services.
- New marketing approach for targeting market segments and developing destinations.

- Strategic management of infrastructure, services, and destinations for catering the emerging tourism needs.

References

Bezbaruah, M.P. (1999), Tourism Current Scenario and Future Prospects, Yojana, August.

Chand, M. and Vinay Chauhan (2002), Indian Tourism. A Retrospective and Prospective Appraisal in Tourism inthe New Millenium by S.P. Bansal et. al. (Ed.), Abhishek Pub. Delhi.

Dixit, Manoj (2001), Dimensions of Indian Tourism, Bharat Book Centre, Lucknow.

Govt. of India (2002), New Tourism Policy, Ministry of Tourism and Culture, Govt. of India.

Gupta, S.P. et.al. (2002), Cultural Tourism In India, D.K. Print Well, Delhi.

Kamra, K.K. (2002), Managing Tourists Desination, Kanishka Pub. Delhi.

Mill, R.C. and Morison, A.M. (1985), The Tourism System, Prentic Hall, New Jersey.

Tiwari, S.P. (1994), Tourism Dimensions, Atma Ram and Sons, Delhi.

4

Tourism Resources

Tourism as a multifaceted activity has been focus of planners, managers and researchers since it tends to generate substantial resources and employment. The recent paradigm shifts in tourism sector demands proper planning regulations and strategic approach to ensure sustainable tourism development. Moreover, nature based tourism has become an effective way to raise the living standards of rural communities and conservation of nature. Against this backdrop, present paper purports to review the perspective of eco-tourism alongwith the analysis of the carrying capacity and environmental impact of tourism on nature.

World Tourism organization has estimated that international travelers will account 1.6 billion by the year 2020. The tourism industry accounts for 200 million jobs or 10 per cent of the jobs globally. Average annual growth of tourism in India has been reported 4.13 per cent against the average growth of 4.56 per cent at global level during 1980-97. The future growth rates of tourism in India are projected to be 6.15 per cent during 2000-2010 and 5.8 per cent during 2010-2020. The state of Uttar Pradesh (including Uttaranchal) accounts for 13 per cent of the total foreign tourist arrivals in India. Even state attracts a number of domestic tourists.

Today, tourism is the second largest net foreign exchange earner in the country. Some other benefits of tourism apart from employment generation can easily be counted:

- Tourism is a multidimensional activity and it covers a large number of economic activities. The spread effect of tourism, therefore, is much wider than any other economic activity.
- The return on investment in tourism from the point of view of employment generation is much higher compared to agriculture and manufacturing sector.
- Tourism helps development of backward regions because they are not only area specific but can be promoted wherever tourism attractions exist.
- Tourism also helps promotion of handicrafts and handlooms as well as arrival of traditional culture and preservation of heritage if properly managed and controlled.

Eco-Tourism

Eco tourism is one of the fastest growing trends in the worldwide tourism industry. Environment has an intrinsic value which out weighs its value as a tourism asset. It is also agreed upon by environmental experts that the three elements, viz, political acceptability, social responsibility and sound environment with a perfect balance between quality and quantity, in tourism development/promotion, can ensure quality tourism. Whilst there is a general support for a symbiotic relationship between the two, i.e., tourism and environment; the dilemma is that the residents lay greater stress on tourism development whereas the tourists focus on environmental protection. In this context, 'eco tourism' is being promoted as a means of 'giving nature value' and hence of achieving sustainable tourism. The term 'eco tourism' has been defined in many ways and is usually used to describe tourism activities which are conducted in harmony with nature. It is a form of tourism which fosters environmental principles with an emphasis on visiting and observing natural areas, the emphasis on tourism as much as this can be separated from recreation is deliberate. Eco tourism relates to the quality of the environment and to ensure that the impacts from the activity are controlled comprehensively. Eco tourism can be defined as "purposeful travel to natural areas to understand the cultural and natural history of the environment, taking care not to alter the integrity of the eco system, while producing economic opportunities that make the conservation of natural resources financially beneficial to local citizens".

Eco tourism is one of the most popular alternative tourism forms. Its advocates believe that it engenders a sense of need for environmental protection among local population once the latter realize conservation does not mean loss of economic opportunity. Hopefully, eco tourism can provide the local community with jobs, enabling a shift away from unsustainable practices such as over grazing, mining or logging in environmentally sensitive eco-systems.

Eco-tourism is responsible travel to natural areas which conserves the environment and improves the welfare of local people. In some countries eco-tourism has got important place in the economy and practices of sustainable development. Kenya earns some $500 million a year in tourism revenues. Coasta Rica generated $336 million in tourists revenues in 1991 and registered 25 per cent growth in income over the previous three years. Nature based tourism is the engine of many tropical island economies in the Caribean Pacific and Indian Oceans. It is to be noted that eco-tourism generated about 7 per cent of all international travel expenditure in 1989.

Eco-tourism requires a multidisciplinary approach, careful planning and strict guidelines and regulations that will guarantee sustainable operation. Governments, the private enterprises, local communities and non-governmental organizations all have an important role to play. Eco-tourism is a complex and multidisciplinary phenomenon. There are many facets that must be addressed. In the changed context parks are becoming more and more interested in eco-tourism. Not only are they receiving greater numbers of visitors but park managers are starting to see tourism as a new source of funding and employment. Eco-tourism is already producing concrete benefits in the fields of conservation and sustainable development. In many countries eco-tourism has become an effective way to raise standards of living of rural communities and conservation of nature. Fillion (1992) estimated that nature tourism is contributing more than $223 billion to the national income of various countries.

Concept of Eco-Tourism

Mexican architect and eco-tourism consultant Hector Ceballos-Lascurain, who is given the credit for introducing the term eco-tourism, defined it as travelling to relatively undisturbed it as travelling to relatively undisturbed or uncontaminated natural areas with the specific objective of studying, admiring and enjoying the scenery and its wild animals and plants, as well as any existing cultural manifestations found in these areas. The International Eco-Tourism Society (TIES) includes in its definition the improvement of the environment and the well being of local people; it considers eco-tourism to be 'responsible travel to natural areas which conserves the environment and improves the well being of local people'.

The term eco-tourism as mentioned above was coined by Hector Ceballos-Lascurain in 1983, and was initially used to describe nature based travel to relatively undisturbed areas with an emphasis on education. The concept has, however, developed to a scientifically based approach to the planning, management and development of sustainable tourism products and activities. It is an enlightening, particularly travel experience to environments, both natural and cultural, that ensures the sustainable use, at an appropriate level, of environmental resources and, while producing viable economic opportunities for the tourism and host communities, makes the use of these through conservation beneficial to all tourism role players. Eco-tourism focuses on local cultures, wilderness adventures, volunteering, personal growth and learning new ways to live on our vulnerable planet. It is typically defined as travel to destinations where the flora, fauna, and cultural heritage are the primary attraction. Responsible eco-tourism includes programmes that minimize the adverse affects of traditional tourism on the natural environment, and enhance the cultural integrity of local people. Therefore, in addition to evaluating environmental and cultural factors, initiatives by hospitability provides to promote recycling, energy efficiency, water re-use, and the creation of economic opportunities for local communities are an integral part of eco-tourism. Historical and cultural conservation, preservation, sustainable development etc. are some of the fields closely related to eco-tourism. Many professionals have been involved in formulating and developing eco-tourism policies. They come from the fields of Geographic Information Systems, Wildlife Management, Wildlife Photography, Marine Biology and Oceanography, National and State Park Management, Environment Sciences, Women in Development, Historians and Archaeologists etc.

Nature-based Tourism and Eco-Tourism

Nature Tourism denotes all tourism directly dependent on the use of natural resources in a relatively undeveloped state, including scenery , topography, water features, vegetation and wildlife. Thus, it includes hunting, countryside motor-biking and white water rafting, even if the use of the natural resources by the tourists is neither wiser nor sustainable. Nevertheless, nature based tourism is a rapidly growing sector of the tourism economy. Its global value for 1988 has been estimated to have been as high as US $ 1 trillion (Filion, et al, 1992). Nature tourism generates 7 per cent of all international travel expenditure (Lindberg, etal 1997). The World Resources Institute (1990) found that while tourism overall has been growing at an annual rate of 4 per cent, nature travel is increasing at an annual rate between 10 per cent to 30 per cent (Reingold, 1993). Data which supports this growth rate is found in Lew's (1997) survey of tour operators in the Asia Pacific region who have experienced annual growth rates of 10 per cent to 25 per cent in recent years (Lindberg, 1997). Fillion (1994) outlines the magnitude of the eco-tourism market through the use of general tourism statistics. Fillion identified, through an analysis of in bound tourist motivations to different worldwide destination, that 40 - 60 per cent of all intervention tourists are nature tourists and that 20 - 40 per cent are wildlife related tourists.

Uncontrolled mass tourism this time and again contributes to the degradation of many areas of natural and cultural significance, enabling the loss of biological and cultural diversity, as well as of important sources of income. Therefore, sustainable tourism approach is needed to be adopted. In recent years a specific category of nature based tourism is developed along these lines. 'Ecological Tourism' is environmentally responsible travel and visit to relatively undisturbed natural areas, in order to enjoy and appreciate nature that promotes conservation, has low visitor impact, and provides for beneficially active socio-economic involvement of local population'.

Evolution of Eco-Tourism

The origins of nature travel are remote. Herodotus was one of the first nature tourists. His extensive travels included visits to the Black Sea, Egypt, Southern Italy, Athens and Aegean Sea. He was deeply interested in geography, the natural environment and ancient monuments. Aristotle also practiced nature tourism. Other notable precursors of eco-tourism include Pytheas, Strabo and Pliny the Elder, all of whom travelled, moved by a desire to see the natural and cultural environments of the world in which they lived. Later on, Marco Polo, Ibn Batuta, Bernerdino de Sahagun, Joseph de Acosta and Eusebio Kimo have left vivid accounts of the new lands they discovered. Recently, Charles de la Condamine, James Cook, Alexander Von Humboldt, Louis-Antonine de Bougainville, Charles Darwin, John, L. Stephens, Henry Bales, Alfred Rusell Wallace, David Livingstone, Sven Hedin and Carl Lumholtz dedicated themselves to travel to remote areas with the fundamental purpose of discovering, studying and describing landscapes, life forms and different cultures. However, nature travel as a popular programme of tourism could not considered until late 19th century. Nature travel during the 19th century was essentially a quest for spectacular and unique scenery. During this time, the national park concept was created and while the founders of national parks wanted to protect the environment rather than provide resorts, it was the tourist who provided the economic and political rationale needed to translate philosophy into accomplishment. With the expansion of communication and transport facilities, tourism developed in 20th century. After World War II, the tourism industry exploded worldwide. But as the numbers increased, the image of tourism deteriorated with the emphasis on sustainable development in 1992, at Rio Conference on 'Environment and Development', focus of tourism shifted to sustainable tourism i.e. nature tourism. Furthermore, protected areas such as National Parks, Sanctuaries and Biosphere Reserved Areas provided base for eco-tourism.

Despite India's varied and spectacular wildlife and cultural heritage its share in the world tourist arrivals is a dismal 0.31 per cent. Wildlife areas attract only a fraction of the tourists coming to India. Moreover, tourism revenue generated by these areas is meagre. Promotion of eco-tourism in these areas can generate revenue exceeding the expenditure incurred in their management. Such revenue generation is an urgent and dire need, as in face the increasing biotic threats the wildlife areas have to economically justify its existence. Significantly, eco-tourism has become popular and has been implemented successfully in many countries. However, India despite its stunning array by natural, culture and anthropological attractions has been unable to attract eco-tourists due to a variety of reasons, including lack of facilities, poor marketing efforts, and a poor carrying capacity. Considering the large number of Indian and a smaller segment of foreign tourists visiting protected areas, the staff and infrastructure of management of tourism is inadequate. Infrastructure, staff and facility to address the major objectives of creating nature conservation have been reported to be inadequate. Only a few partks (Kanha, Corbett, Gir, Bandipur etc.) have developed interpretive programmes for park visitors and have organized training courses for park guides. Even, in most of the protected areas very little has been done to streamline tourism management. Most of them, either do not encourage tourism or allow unmanaged tourism to continue. A study of about 200 protected areas of India, by Indian Institute of Public Administration, New Delhi, 1989, reveals that 37 per cent national parks and 83 per cent sanctuaries are officially opened to tourism but over 70 per cent of them do not have visitors orientation centres management infrastructure. The report also revealed that most of the Indian Protected Areas are suffering from high level of disturbance in them, 56 per cent of the sanctuaries allow collection of a variety of non-food forest produce and 67 per cent of national parks and 83 per cent of the sanctuaries are subjected to livestock grazing pressures (Kumar, S.).

Since long, tourism development was taken in isolation with little regard to ecological and social character of the area. But now in the changed scenario, the close relationship between tourism and the environment and the importance of environmental and sustainable tourism development planning are becoming increasingly recognized. In the arena of tourism and culture, India has been a sleeping giant. Now, it is rediscovering its vast bounties of nature and also great treasures of art, architecture and improving their approaches and elevating their surroundings. It is also tapping all opportunities for hill, adventure, rural and wildlife tourism and placing before the world, through tourist sports, its unique techniques of Yoga, Sidha, Ayurveda and Unani system of medicines dealing with physical and mental illness. It is lying down an enchanting network of 572 nature endowed areas (89 national parks and 483 wildlife sanctuaries) and 3606 protected monuments under the Ancient Monuments and Archaeological Sites and Remains Act.

Nature tourism is largest industrial activity in South Africa, Kenya, Ecuador and Costa Rica. The combined viewing value of marine creatures of the exquisite coral alloys of Maldives one in excess of US $ 19 million. The viewing value of the reef shark alone may be 10 times the entire export value of all sharks presents. In addition, Scuba diving alone generated in excess of US $ 41 million in 1996. This represents average net earning for each resort of approximately US $ 0.56 million per year. The country has a clear interest in maintaining its fragile ecology. Maldives is learning fast that environment is the basis of their business (Vania, 2002). It is estimated that 30 - 35 per cent of all tourists to the Maldives go for diving. There were a total of about 77,000 shark watcing dives (at seven most important sharks watching sites of Maldives) compared to the total 500,000 dives made annually in the Maldives. Thus, Maldives has $ 2.3 million direct revenue from shark watching dives. Anderson and Ahmad pointed out that each living elephant in Kenya may be worth US $ 900,000 over its lifetime in terms of tourism revenue (Agarwal, 2002).

Tourism Prospects in Mountain Eco-systems

The mountain eco-systems are the unique creation having altogether distinct characteristics. They have been regarded as an abode of gods, symbols of peace, tranquility and austerity and credibility of civilizations. Mountains are fragile eco-systems and are globally important as water towers of the earth, repositories of rich biological diversity, minerals and forests, target areas for recreation, and as a hub of cultural integrity and heritage (Yadav, 2002). The mountains provide a direct life support base for one-fifth of humankind as well as goods and services to more than half of the world's population. India has seven principal mountain ranges and the most important amongst them are the Himalayas. The Himalayas run across the top of the Indian sub-continent stretching over some 2,500 kilo metres. These mountains were formed in between 50 to 60 million years ago. The most recently formed are the lower foothills known as the Shivaliks. Beyond the Shivaliks are the lower Himalayas which have the most popular hill resorts of India like Shimla, Dalhousie, Musoorie, Nainital and Darjeeling at the height of four to eight thousand feet above sea level. Beyond the lower Himalayas are the great Himalayas or the Himadaris. In the Himadaris are Everest and Annapurna peaks which lie in the boundaries of Nepal and within Indian and Kanchanjanga, Nanya Parbat and Nanda Devi. The Aravallis, one of the oldest ranges in the world, run between Delhi and Gujarat to the South West. A number of hill resorts are located in this range. Again, the Vindhyas divide the wide gangetic plains of northern India from the Southern parts of the country. They are stretched over a length of 1000 kilometres with an average altitude of 874 feet. The Satpuras which are south of the Vindhyas, run parallel to them. It has one hill resort, Pachmarli which is located near the highest point in the range, Dhupgarh at a height of 4429 feet. The Sahyadris run for 1600 kms. down the western edge to the southern most point of India. The hill resort in this area is Ootacamund or Ooty, known as Udhagamandalam which stands at the foot of the 8615 feet height Doda Betta Peak. This peak is located in the Nilgiris. Beyond the Nilgiris are the Anamalai or Elephant Hills. The famous hill resort of Kodaikkanal is located in Palani Hills. The Eastern ghats which run on the opposite side of the Sahyadaris have summits over 3200 feet. To their south east are the Shivroy hills and the hill station of Yercand. Pauvanchal or eastern mountain ranges are the last great mountain ranges of India running along the Indo-Myanmar border in North East India (Table 1).

Table 1
Famous Hill Stations in India

State	*Name of Hill Stations*
Himachal Pradesh	Chail, Chamba, Dalhousie, Dharmshala, Kasauli, Kangra, Kullu, Manali, Naldehra, Parwanoo, Shimla
Jammu & Kashmir	Gulmarg, Jammu, Patnitop, Sanamarg, Srinagar
Jharkhand	Ranchi
Kerala	Munnar, Nelliyampathy, Wayanad, Devikulam, Peermade, Ponmudi, Thiruvananthapuram, Idukki, Palakkad, Kannur.
Uttaranchal	Almora, Dehradoon, Kasauni, Mussoorie, Nainital, Lansdown, Rishikesh, Gomukh, Joshi Math, Ookhirmath, Gopeshwar, Bageshwar, Ranikhet, Pithoragarh
Madhya Pradesh	Bhedaghat
Rajasthan	Mount Abu
Maharashtra	Mahabaleshwar, Panchagani, Lonavala, Khandala, Kerala, Matheran, Amboli Jawahar, Panhala, Chickalava
Sikkim	Gangtok
Tamil Nadu	Kederi Kanal, Yercaud, Courtalam,Ooty
West Bengal	Darjeeling

Tourist Trends in Eco-tourist Destinations

Since the essence of eco-tourism lies in admiration of nature and out door recreation, it encompasses a wide range of activities such as trekking, hiking, mountaineering, bird watching, boating, rafting, biological explorations and visiting wildlife sanctuaries. The shrines, temples, archaeological sites, historical monuments etc. attract a number of tourists. The shrine of Mata Vaishno Devi is one of the most venerated shrines of India. It is connected with the cult of Shakti which is connected pre-Aryan cult of the Mother Goddess. The shrine, which is really a natural cave temple, is located in the Trikuta hills, about 45 km. from Jammu. The Management of Shrine is under the control of a Board, known as Mata Vaishno Devi Shrine Board. With the rapid improvement on built environment, particularly the entire route of 14 km., lighting, water supply, sanitation, shelter houses etc., the shrine attract more than 50 lakh visitors per annum (Table 2).

Table 2
Tourist Arrivals in Vaishno Devi Shrine

Year	*No. of Visitors*
1960	2,00,000
1986	13,95,000
1987	18,57,000
1988	19,92,000
1989	23,12,000
1990	21,69,000
1991	31,15,000
1992	35,16,000
1993	33,68,000
1994	37,04,000
1995	40,11,000
1996	43,35,000
1997	44,34,000
1998	46,22,000
1999	46,70,000
2000	52,17,000
2001	50,57,000

Source: Deptt. of Tourism, MVDSB, Katra, Jammu.

Similarly, shrines of Vindhya in U.P. attract about one million of visitors annually. Similarly, Kumbh fair at Haridwar where millions of people congregate at one place and take a holy dip. The influx of tourists in Kullu valley in Himachal Pradesh has increased in multiple phases increasing from 13,310 in 1979-80 to 67,132 in 1991-92, this figure further raised upto 1,20,867 in 1996. Earlier the majority of tourists were domestic but the pattern of foreign tourists is gradually improving in the Upper Kullu Valley (Table 3).

Table 3
Tourist Influx in Manali (Himachal Pradesh)

Year	*Tourists*	*Percentage of Domestic Tourists*	*Percentage of Foreign Tourists*
1975	11062	94.9	5.1
1976	14477	95.0	5.0
1977	15792	93.2	6.8
1978	11003	93.0	7.0
1979	13310	94.0	6.0
1980	15306	93.0	7.0
1985	22595	87.0	13.0
1987	48744	84.9	15.1
1988	52745	83.9	16.1
1989	57116	82.9	17.1
1990	61596	80.3	17.2
1991	67132	80.8	18.2
1996	120867	73.36	26.64

Source: Tourist Information Centre, Manali, 1999.

The total number of foreign tourists increased from 9757 in 1989 to 12,910 in 1991-92. This figure further increased upto 32,204 by 1996 (Pandey, 2002). The growth of tourism and the process of urbanization goes hand in hand. The infrastructure required to provide basic amenities to the tourists lead to acceleration in the process of urbanization (Pandey etal, 1998). Growth in urban population has increased from 15.89 per cent in 1961 to 40 per cent in 1991. There has been a surpassing increase in the number of hotels and guest houses since last decade, more precisely between 1975-1996. The number of hotels has gone up from 2 to 640 in an around Manali (Table 4).

Table 4
Growth of Hotels & Guest Houses in Upper Kullu Valley

Year	*No. of Hotels & Guest Houses*
1975	2
1980	5
1985	10
1988	100
1990	200
1996	640

The increasing tourist activity in Mussoorie attracted as many as 14.47 lakh visitors in the year 1993 whereas 1994 and 1995 saw 12.21 and 13.15 lakh respectively. During 1988 to 1995 there has been significant growth of tourists in Mussoorie. In 1988 there were 12.26 lakh visitors which reached to 13.51 lakh in 1995 (10-19 per cent). Similarly, in Nainital, there has been phenomenon growth of tourists from 4.91 lakh in 1986 to 16.00 lakh in 1996 (225.86 per cent). The visitors to Badrinath were reported to be 4,61,465 in 1995. There has been significant growth of visitors to the shrine during 1985 to 1995. Even Corbett Park attracted 42,230 tourists in 1995-96. There were 7799 visitors to the valley of flowers in 1994-95. In 1999, the visitors to Hemkund and Valley of Flowers accounted 1,09,298. However, the visitors at Valley of Flowers are showing declining trend since 1997. Importantly, tourists in Corbett Park were reported to be 69,231 in 1998-99. There has been significant growth of visitors to Park since 1990-91, in the year 1990-91, there were 39,078 visitors, which reached to 69,231 in 1998-99 (77.16 per cent). There has been increase of 80.87 per cent of tourist flow in hill regions of Uttaranchal during 1989 to 1999. While tourist increase in Garhwal region was reported to be 55.47 per cent during the corresponding period.

The share of tourist arrivals in Garhwal region was reported 72.84 per cent in 1989 which declined to 68.61 per cent in 1999. This shows that major tourist destinations are located in Garhwal region. There has been significant growth of tourist flow to Badrinath (88.94 per cent), Gangotri (116.0 per cent) and Yamunotri (254.17 per cent) during 1975 to 1999.

There has been phenomenon growth of tourist flow in lesser known areas of Garhwal such as Gaumukh, Dodital, Harkidoon, Auli Chopla, and Deoriatal. The increase in tourist traffic has been reported high during 1991 to 1998 in Mussoori (22.8 per cent).

Tourism in Protected Areas

The long term conservation status of an area is almost certainly linked to the legal category of protection given to it. The Wild Life Protection Act (1972) and Indian Forest Act (1988) allow several levels of protection. There are (rodgers and Panwar, 2000): (i) National Park, (ii) Wild Life Sanctuary, (iii) Game Reserve, (iv) Closed Area, (v) Reserved Forest, (vi) Protected Forest. Importantly, the terms like 'Biosphere Reserve',. 'Nature Reserve', 'Sacred Forest' etc. have no legal status under Indian Law. These land use categories have implications for long term conservation of biological values. Significantly, rapid growth of human and livestock population since the turn of the century and consequent pressures of land hunger and development have taken an increasingly heavy toll of the country's wilderness. The conservation measures have been largely slow and inadequate. The growing concern at the scale of environmental degradation has emphasized the development of protected areas in many parts of the country. This network has grown and India today has a total of 426 wild life protected areas covering 109,652 sq. km. or 3.3 per cent of the country's land surface. As per information available from Wild Life Institute of India, Dehradoon, there were 54 national parks covering 21003 km2 and 372 sanctuaries covering 88649 km^2 giving a combined coverage of 109652 km^2 or 3.334 per cent of the country's geographical area in 1988. This network has grown steadily and in 2000 India had a total of 566 wild life protected areas covering 153,000.34 km^2 or 4.66 per cent of the country's geographical area (Table 5).

This review contains recommendations to bring the total protected area network to 858 totalling 187191.89 Km^2 or 5.69 per cent of the country's geographical area respectively. This network contains areas designated as national parks and as

Table 5
Distribution of Biogeographic Zones

Particulars	*Total (All India)*	*Trans-Himalaya*	*Himalaya*	*Desert*	*Semi Arid*
Zone area (Km^2)	13287263	5.62%	6.41%	6.56%	16.60%
No. of NP's	86	3	12	1	8
Area (Km^2)	37648.57	3.55%	3.57%	1.47%	0.24%
No. of WLS	480	4	55	5	83
Area (Km^2)	115351.77	5.65%	6.35%	5.99%	2.56%
No. of NP's + WLS	56	7	67	6	91
Area (Km^2)	153000.34	9.20%	9.92%	7.45%	2.80%

Contd.

Western Ghats	*Decan Peninsula*	*Gangestic Plain*	*Coasts*	*North-east*	*Island*
41.03%	41.99%	10.79%	2.52%	5.21%	0.25%
12	21	6	5	9	8
2.51%	0.62%	0.67%	2.09%	1.13%	14.03%
44	116	30	21	28	94
7.6%	3.08%	1.49%	4.70%	1.41%	4.51%
56	137	36	26	103	566
10.12%	3.71%	2.16%	6.79%	2.54%	18.84%

Source: Wild Life Protected Area Network In India: A Review, WII, Dehradoon, 2000.

wild life sanctuaries. Thus, the cumulative growth has been computed 854 in case of protected areas, 694 in wild life sanctuaries and 160 in case of national parks.

In India the Protected Areas (PA's) began to be recognized as a category of landuse by the third decade of this 19th century's gained momentum after the year 1970 and have assumed special significance following the Rio-conference. Of the ten categories of Protected Areas designated by the IUCN, India has four viz. national parks, wild life sanctuaries, biosphere reserves and world heritage sites (Sawarkar, 1999). Notwithstanding the ecological basis of government directions, the main operating interpretations have came to be (i) PA's have and will significantly reduce economic opportunities and there by adversely affect social and economic interests in a variety of ways at national, regional state, local and specific community levels, and therefore PA's are anti-development; (ii) since PA's are specific landuse categories set aside for conservation of wild life, the areas outside including the managed forests have no such management responsibilities except providing protection to wild life as mandatory under the law; (iii) conservation of wild life is incompatible with other landuse; (iv) by virtue of protection afforded by PA's to wild animals of various kinds, their population have grown to great proportions and are causing economic loss in agricultural production, livestock depredation in the surrounding areas besides certain species being responsible for injuries to human and occasionally for loss of human life (Sawarkar, 1999). However, Protected Areas serve the interest of a variety values, principally natural. Natural values come in different categories-the biological e.g., interest endangered, threatened, rare, endemic species, communities of plants and animals, ecological processes and functions etc. Moreovr, animals and plants exhibit a specific pattern of distribution following major events in the history of the land, the environmental gradients, and the interactions between living beings and abiotic factors called the bio-geographic pattern of distribution. The PA's need to represent such bio-geographic patterns to secure the national interest in biological diversity and they need to be networked through ecological connectivity.

Principles for Tourism In Protected Areas

The principles such as conservation, enjoyment, development of infrastructure and facilities, designing and management of sites and marketing tourism sites etc. should be adhered. The tourism industry should help to protect the distinctive landscape and wildlife of national parks by supportive practical conservation measures. Similarly, the activities and interests promoted by tourism should draw on the special character of national parks, with their many opportunities for quite open air recreation and their distinctive beauty, culture, history and wildlife. Significantly, the social and economic well being of the residents of the national parks is an essential consideration if the statutory objectives of national parks are to be met. Thus employment in the tourist and related service industries is an important element of the economy of national parks. The tourism industry should support the economy of local communities by employing local people, and local products and services, and by supporting the skills and economic activities which are traditional in national parks areas. Importantly, appropriate facilities must be available to enable tourists to enjoy the national parks. But tourism development must respect the quality of the landscape and environment. Moreover, the scale, setting, planning, design and management of new tourism developments should be in keeping with the character of the landscape, and seek to enhance it. In last, tourism industry should be publicity, information and marketing to deepen people's enjoyment appreciation and understanding of the concern for national parks (Lascurian, 1996).

Eco-tourism is different from other kind of tourism as it involves travel to wilderness areas for enjoying and understanding the bio-diversity and cultural heritage of the area (Negi). The term eco-tourism in the present day context is used for travel to protected areas or wilderness areas. Interestingly, our country is endowed with unique and rich animal and plant life which is mainly attributable to a vast range of habitats from high mountain to the coasts. India considered 6th among the 12 mega bio-diversity countries of the world. The country supports some 15000 species of plants, 1693 of fish, 181 amphibians, 395 reptiles, 1175 birds and 372 mammals, 60,000 of insects and 5000 of molluse. This is known bio-diversity and there may be several thousand more which are yet to be discovered. Significantly, scientists estimate that there are 10 to 30 million species on the earth, of these, only about 1.4 million have been either named or at least briefly described (Kumar). Significantly, nature tourism or eco-tourism denotes all tourism directly dependent on the ue of the natural resources in the relatively undeveloped state, including scenery, topography, water features, vegetation and wildlife. Thus, it includes hunting, countryside motobiking, and white water rafting. The nature based tourism is a rapidly growing sector of the tourism economy. Its global value for 1988 has been estimated to have been as high as US $1 trillion

Despite India's varied and spectacular wildlife and cultural heritage its share in the world tourist arrivals is dismal 0.31 per cent. Wild life areas attract only a fraction of the tourists coming to India. Moreover, tourism revenue generated by these areas is meagre. Promotion of eco-tourism in these areas can generate revenue exceeding the expenditure incurred in their management. Such revenue generation is an urgent and dire need, as in face the increasing biotic threats the wild life areas have to economically justify is existence. Significantly, eco-tourism has become popular and has been implemented successfully in many countries. However, India despite its stunning array by natural, cultural and anthropological attractions has been unable to attract eco-tourists due to a variety of reasons, including lack of facilities, poor marketing efforts, and a poor carrying capacity. Considering the large number of Indian and a smaller segment of foreign tourists visiting protected areas, the staff and infrastructure for management of tourism is inadequate. Infrastructure, staff and facility to address the major objective of creating nature conservation have been reported to be inadequate. Only a few parks (Kanha, Corbett, Gir, Bandipur etc.) have developed interpretive programmes for park visitors and have organized training courses for park guides. Even, in most of the protected areas very little has been done to streamline tourism management. Most of them, either do not encourage tourism or allow unmanaged tourism to continue. A study of about 200 protected areas of India, by Indian Institute of Public Administration, New Delhi, 1989, reveals that 37 per cent national parks and 83 per cent sanctuaries are officially opened to tourism but over 70 per cent of them do not have visitor orientation centres and tourism management infrastructure. The report also revealed that most of the Indian Protected Areas are suffering from high level of disturbance in them, 56 per cent of the sanctuaries allow collection of a variety of non-food forest produce and 67 per cent of national parks and 83 per cent of the sanctuaries are subjected to livestock grazing pressures (Kumar).

Tourists Arrival in Protected Areas

Data for tourists visiting wildlife parks and sanctuaries are available since 1962. However, figures on wildlife tourism are not available in the published or documented form since the system of data collection and maintaining records is not being followed in most of protected areas of country. There has been a phenomenon increase in the number of visitors arrival in the national (Shullai, 1980) parks like Corbett, Kanha, Shivpuri, Kazirunga, Bandipur etc. during 1962-63 to 1966-67. Importantly, during 1970-71 to 1978-79 visitors arrival in Gir sanctuaries recorded the increase of 158.29 per cent and 5.07 per cent, Indian and foreign tourists arrival, respectively (Johnsingh, 1993). The estimates of eco-tourism are shown in Table 6.

During 1987-92, average annual revenue from visitors was computed in tune of Rs. 12,50,000 in case of Corbett National Park and Rs. 12,40,000 in case of Pariyar. Moreover, during 1997-98, Gir, Pariyar, and Corbett attracted al large number of Indian visitors while Ranthambhor, Pariyar and Bharatpur attracted a large number of foreign tourists (Bharti). Importantly, potential of eco-tourism revenue estimates is given in Table 7.

It was reported much higher in case of Gir followed by Kabini Lodge and Parambikulam. Average number of visitors in a year has been reported highest in case of Periyar, Corbett

Table 6
Visitors Arrival in Indian Protected Areas

Particulars	*Corbett*	*Kanha*	*Ranthambhor*	*Periyar*	*Bharatpur*	*Gir*
Visitors Arrival during 1987-92						
Indian	34,040	40,000	–	2,25,600	22,560	40,022
Foreign	2,960	1,384	–	14,400	940	940
Average Annual Revenue	2,50,000	–	–	12,40,000	5,40,000	–
Visitors Arrival in 1997-98						
Indian	46,999	42,569	19,394	4,27,000	32,943	89,173
Foreign	4,937	2,408	20,603	23,000	22,043	2,424
Student	–	–	1,111	–	16,030	–
Total	51,936	44,977	41,966	4,50,000	70,915	91,597
Revenue (in US$)	2,03,488	52,047	88,395	1,39,535	87,488	52,429

Source: Wildlife Institute of India, Dehradoon, Uttaranchal.

Table 7
Potential Eco-Tourism Revenue Estimates

Particulars	*Bandipur*	*Kabini Lodge*	*Parambikulam*
Average No. of visitors/year	23,500 (4%)(987-92)	6,680 (33%)(1988-93)	20,640(1987-91)
Average Annual Revenue @	5,400,000	5,900,000	39,400
Average Annual Expenditure (Rs.)	–	4,200,000	–
Potential Revenue (Rs.)	16,000,000	24,000,000	20,000,000

Contd.

	Periyar	*Gir*	*Corbett*
	2,40,000 (6%)(1997-92)	32,878(1987-92)	37,000 (8%)(1987-91)
	1,240,000	4,92,400	12,50,000
	–	20,000,000	24,300,000
	16,000,000	24,300,000	16,000,000

Note:
1. Data on visitors for Kabini Lodge refers to number of bednights and in all other cases to actual number of visitors.
2. @ All revenue stated in Indian Rupees; convert conversion rate is approximately Rs. 30 to 1 US $.
3. Percentage in parenthesis refers to percentage foreign visitors.
4. Years in parenthesis refers to the period for which data is given.

Source: Wild Life Institute of India, Dehradoon, Uttaranchal, 1993.

Table 8
Visitors Arrival in Dudhwa National Park (UP)

Year	Indian		Foreigners		Total Visitors	Revenue (Rs.)	Per Visitors (Rs.)
	Day	Nighthalt	Day	Nighthalt			
1991-92	1245	2881	91	157	4374	90732	20.74
1992-93	785	1831	23	70	2709	65281	24.09
1993-94	1850	9025	65	74	11014	203040	18.43
1994-95	3693	2054	72	30	5849	241359	41.26
1995-96	5529	2156	106	24	7815	245713	31.44
1996-97	3584	2513	77	37	6211	441635	71.10
1997-98	2260	2016	16	46	4338	387700	89.37
Total	18946	22476	450	438	42310	1675460	39.60
Growth 1991-92 to 1997-98	81.53	-3	-82.42	-70.70	-0.82	327.30	330.91

Source: A. Shankaran, Management Plan of Dhudhwa Tiger Reserve, Lakhimpur Kheri (U.P.), 1997-98.

and Gir. However, proportion of foreign tourists against total visitors was computed high in case of Kabini Lodge (33 per cent). Interestingly, visitors arrival in Dudhwa National Park has shown marginal decline due to decline in number of foreigner visitors. However, during 1991-92 to 1997-98, increase in Indian visitors has been computed 81,53 per cent. But this increase has been found in case of day visitors while number of night halt visitors has significantly declined over the period.

During 2001-2002 to 2004-2005, tourist arrivals have declined sharply. Moreover, night halt of the tourists has also declined sharply. However, per visitor revenue received has increased slightly (Table 9).

It is to be noted that economic success of eco-tourism depends on the beauty of the natural area and the charisma of its wildlife and the ease with which wildlife is seen, accessibility of the area and the comfort of accommodation and the quality of nature interpretation and other guided services.

Analysis of Carrying Capacity

Carrying capacity is a complex term which can be defined as the 'maximum use of natural and cultural resources by the community and tourism of a given geographical area for Mountain Community Development and Mountain Tourism Development without adverse impact on the socio-cultural, economic or biophysical environment'. In other words, carrying capacity can be simplified to consist of three interrelated dimensions; the environment, the economy, and the social and institutional aspects (See Chart 1).

Thus, critical factors are those which need to be changed from their current stage, or alternatively, conserved for protected on their current state, in order to increase the carrying capacity of environment on the basis of pre-determined standard. Critical factors can have negative or positive effects on both community and tourism and hence on natural resources. Negative factors result in overall deterioration in the state of mountain community and tourism development and natural resources, whereas positive factors improve their current state (Nigam, Devesh, 2002).

Table 9

Visitors Arrival in Dudhwa National Park (U.P.)

Year	Indian			Foreigners			Grand Total	Revenue (Rs.)	Per Visitor Revenue (Rs.)
	Day	Night Halt	Total	Day	Night Halt	Total			
2001-2002	3329	2226	5555	46	19	65	5620	651372	115.90
2002-2003	2870	1880	4750	31	21	52	4802	567868	118.26
2003-2004	2438	1938	4376	42	47	89	4465	736560	164.96
2004-2005	2381	1287	3668	22	44	66	4634	762825	164.61
Total	11018	7331	18349	141	131	272	18621	2718625	146.00

Source: Field Survey.

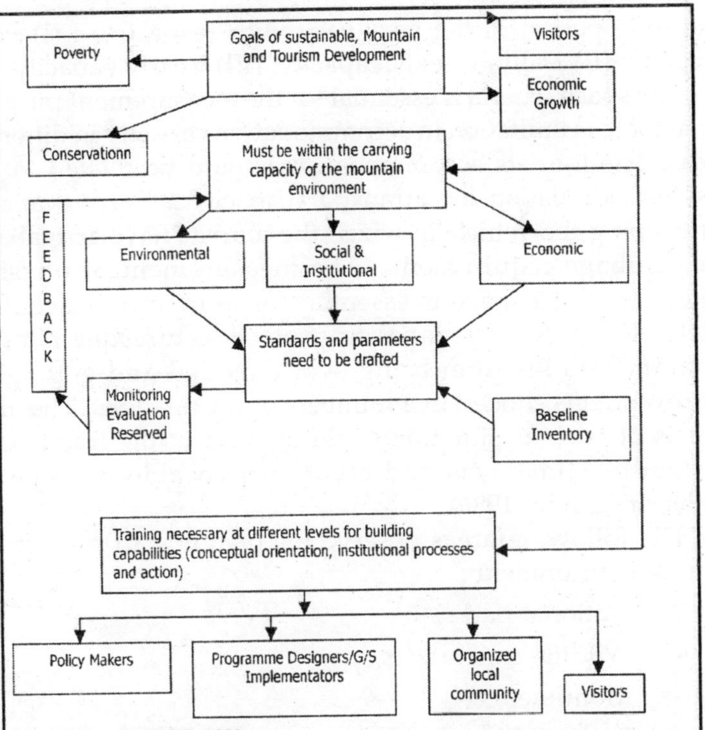

*Source:*After, ICIMOD, 1998.

Chart 1: Essentials of the Carrying Capacity

The measurement of the carrying capacity of a tourist destination is effectively considered as a point from where the negative factors start to operate (O'Reilly, 1986). The hills of Uttaranchal, where the place is limited for the stay of tourists may not be able to cope with such a big number of visitors, have great bearing on carrying capacity. The concept of carrying capacity is created as a management tool to limit and control tourism which may threaten the sustained use of its limited resources such as places for comfortable stay, the places where the load of their vehicle could be parked without pollution in the vicinity of the tourists area, and to the discomfort of the local people, the availability of duly needs to be visitors such as the food products, and the availability of hospitals and medical needs (Martin and Usyal, 1960). Again, physical criteria could be broadly divided into time and space.

The time period in the year vary with respect to : (I) Peak capacity; (II) Daily/weekly capacity; (III) Yearly capacity.

The space criteria is essential for the measurement purpose since there is limitation in accommodation capacity in different areas. The tourists accommodation should be related to the resident population, local transport capacity, the area available for keeping the vehicle in which the tourists have arrival and the drainage requirements. The measurement of physical criteria such as space is essential for tourism management (Getz, 1983). It is essential to protect picturesque sites of Uttaranchal hills from being over-crowded and getting its narrow streets choked in a numbers of destinations. The after effects of such as situation could also affect the fragile eco-system of Himalayas and create irrevocable damage by pollution (Singh, 1986).

The following areas deserve for planning to protect the natural environment :

- National parks,
- Wildlife sanctuaries,
- Monuments,
- Protected landscapes,
- Anthropological reserves,
- Biosphere reserves,
- Resource reserves.

In order to develop the physical aspect of the carrying capacity of the tourist in hills, a number of projects are being approved by the Directorate of Tourism.

The tourism carrying capacity though depends largely upon the physical factors but there are too many aspects, which could limit and hamper the development of tourism. These are associated with the economic factor, which could not be ignored and should be incorporated into broader planning process of the carrying capacity (Cleaverdon, 1979). These are:

- Saturation problem which disturb the economic level of the place of tourism when there is a figure to stagger departures due to large concentration of tourists during school holidays, better climatic condition and fairs and festivals;

- Bottle neck in the transit zone due to non-availability of transport to carry the tourists upto destination zone, since these effect the economy of the place directly;
- Damages in the overall environment in the destination zone that becomes a problem to the local inhabitants and a cause for dissatisfaction to the visitors, and hence requires large expenditures that effect the economy of the place.

The carrying capacity with the respect to the infrastructure has been measured with respect to access, utility services and support population (Bhatia, 1982). The roads, telecommunication, transports, electricity, basic civic amenities etc. at the destinations are required to facilitate tourists. Therefore, a development plan, specific for a particular areas be drawn at the regional levels, keeping in view of infrastructural requirements (Bryden, 1973) One popular approach to visitor management in protected areas in carrying capacity borrowed from the range and wildlife management professions, it was hoped that a maximum number of visitors could be specified. Carrying capacity is viewed as a means of guarding protected area resources. The resurgent interest in carrying capacity as a management framework has its roots in several factors (Borrie, etal, 1999) : (1) the increasing complexity of management; (2) accelerating demands on natural resources to provide a wider diversity of goods and services; and (3) the search for a defensible answer that can be implemented in a wide variety of setting. Butler (1996) argues 'to avoid at least some of the negative impacts associated with visitation, it must be ensured that capacity limits are identified and not exceeded' (Chart 2).

There are nine necessary conditions for the application of carrying capacities and subsequent use limits in recreational settings (Borrie, etal, 1999). These conditions are as follows :

- There must be agreement on the type of desired social and resource conditions, including the type of recreation opportunity;

- The recreation activities and or experiences to be provided must be density dependent;
- There must be agreement on the acceptable level of impact;
- A clear, specific known relationship must exist between use levels and social and resource conditions;
- Use level must be more important then visitor behaviour in determining the amount of impact;
- The protected area management authority must control access in the area;
- The protected area management authority must have the resources (personnel, financial, information etc.) to administer the carrying capacity limit;
- There must be agreement on the objectives of a rationing system in implementation carrying capacity;
- There must be agreement that the carrying capacity limit represents either the maximum or the optimum number of people visiting an area.

Chart 2
Visitor Capacity for Selected Sites

Site/Activity	*Visitors Per day/hectare*
Forest Park	15
Sub-urban nature park	15 - 70
High density picnicking	300 - 600
Low density picnicking	60 - 200
Golf	10 - 1'5
Fishing/soiling	5 - 30
Speed boating	5 - 10
Water skiing	5 - 15
Skiing	100 (per hectare of trails)
Nature trail hiking	40 (per km.)
Nature trail horse riding	25 - 80 (per km.)

Source: E. Inskeep (1991). Tourism Planning : An Integrated and Sustainable Development Approach, Van Nostrand. Reinhold, New York.

Environmental Impact of Tourism

Environmental protection has become a major issue in the recent years. In general, most people realize that the planet has quite limited resources and therefore attempt to identify various methods which will enable its preservation. Tourism is an economic activity has an inevitable effect on the environment, especially at the destination level. Environment is a core feature of the tourist product. Tourists are therefore, consumers of environment 'travelling to producers' locations, the tourist destination, in order to consume the product (Goodall, 1992). Again, tourism has been responsible for a great number of environmental problems. The major problems arise because the environment is a zero priced public good, and as with any zero priced good, is subject to excess demand and over utilization. This over utilization of the natural resources, especially during the peak periods of tourist activity as well as often ill planned tourism development, have provided a number of examples where tourism is in conflict with the environment (Mathieson, and Wall, 1982). Consequently, the natural of the tourism-environment relationship is quite difficult to analyse and the estimation of environmental impacts associated with tourism development is an extremely complex issue. Apart from the positive and negative environmental impacts, which are caused directly by the tourism industry, there are several impacts which can be indirectly attributed to tourism activity within a destination. These impacts result from the tourism supporting industries, which supply the destination with essential products to meet the tourist demand (Buhalis and Fletcher, 1995). Thus, tourism development is dependent on environment and therefore essential measures should be taken in order to maintain and even improve the quality of the natural resources. The General Secretary of the WTO suggests that there is a peaceful co-existence of tourism and the environment, which is illustrated by the following propositions (Savignac, 1992) : (i) travel promotes environmental awareness; (ii) well managed tourism is a good friend of the environment; (iii) a successful tourism industry needs a high quality environment. Consequently, conservation and preservation of natural areas, archaeological sites and historic monuments have emerged as important spill over benefits of tourism. In turn, the promotion of these prime tourist resources enhances and perpetuates tourism by maintaining its very foundation (Mathieson and Wall, 1982). Tourism often stimulates the creation of natural parks, sanctuaries, eco development, man-made attractions and marine conservation units. However, visual pollution may result from several sources (Inskeep, 1991) :

- Poorly designed hotels and other tourist facility buildings that are not compatible with the local architectural style and scale or well integrated into the natural environment;
- Use of unsuitable building materials on external surfaces;
- Badly planned layout of tourist facilities;
- Inadequate or in appropriate landscaping;
- Overhead utility lines and poles;
- Obstruction of scenic view by development and;
- Poor maintenance of buildings and landscaping.

Increased danger of fire is another environmental impact emerging from tourism activity. As more people are gathered in a destination the fire risks are greatly increased. Careless actions have ruined the vegetation and wildlife of particular areas. In addition, fire can arise from the variety of indirect tourist activities in a destination.

The key elements of environmental change connected with tourism development primarily focus on aspect of land and landscape in the built and natural environment. These physical impacts tend to be the most visually apparent, because the development of tourism, like any other development activity, will change the physical location to some extent, wherever it exists. Tourist has in many places provided both means and justification for the conservation of built environment or man-made heritage.

The positive aspects of tourism in connection with environment are (Godfrey & Clarke, 2000) :

- Stimulation of funds for conservation and rehabilitation of historic buildings;

- Building image of former significance by re-establishing individual buildings and places;
- Renovation of many redundant industrial and commercial sites into new shops and services, visitor attractions, hotels, apartments and exhibitions space which could not likely exist;
- Development and promotion of civic amenities, infrastructure and facilities in eco-sites for conservation and preservation of fauna and flora.
- Creation of park areas and renewed attention on the importance of wildlife and biological preservation;
- Increased awareness on environmental issues and concerns.

Certain, negative change in ecological and environmental systems due to tourism activities may result in form of (Godfrey and Clarke, 2000) :

- Problems of architectural pollution, where new buildings are somewhat at odds with the original character of an area;
- Creation of strip or ribbon development and urban sprawl particularly on the approach or access to destination areas;
- The straining of local service infrastructure, causing break down in the supply of fresh water, sewage systems and electricity;
- Traffic congestion and parking problems leading to local aggravation, noise and environmental damage;
- Fullness from tourist vehicles and its effect on building facades;
- Compaction of roadways and implications for underground sewers;
- Structural damage caused by traffic vibration;
- Graffiti and vandalism;
- The loss of vegetation for the car parks and other visitor facilities;

- Trampling of plants and reduction in local bio-diversity;
- The compaction and erosion of the soil;
- The general spread of garbage and litter;
- Poor quality of water supply, ground water pollution, reduction in water tables etc.
- Disruption of predator pee relationships and breeding patterns in wildlife parks and sanctuaries;
- Loss of natural habitat to development;
- Direct loss of wildlife population through trophy and souvenier hunting and the trade in exotic species.

The present developments and prospects of eco-tourism across the country no doubt will promote and conserve nature however; it is difficult to imagine that the eco-tourism parameters will be met by the managers of protected areas and policymakers. The limits of acceptable change planning process demand to evolve the sound mechanism of assessing recreational carrying capacity of the eco-tourism destinations and minimizing the negative impacts of tourism on local built up environment, eco-system and nature. Moreover, effective visitor impact management programmes must be pragmatic, making the most efficient use of available resources and emphasizing flexibility and innovation. Again, users of environmental resources should pay for the social cost of their activities. In this task, closer cooperation between the private and the public sectors is essential. The environmental impacts of tourism can be assessed with an input-output model which could demonstrate the environmental requirements associated with the tourism.

Wild Life Tourism

Wild life tourism is increasingly becoming a popular recreational pursuit and major concern for government. Though, wildlife tourism is a controversial issue and many environmentalists believe that wildlife tourism may jeopardise the integrity of eco-system, wildlife behaviour, and forest resources. However, wildlife tourism has been promoted in many countries and the development of eco-tourism in protected areas has boosted the economies of many African countries.

Wild life refers to some fame species (exclusively birds, mammals, fish etc.) that people hunt. In a broader terms, wildlife is related to bio-diversity i.e. flora and fauna. The Cooperative Research Centre for Sustainable Tourism (2001) has defined wildlife tourism as "tourism that involves encounters with non-domesticated animals either in their natural environment or in captivity. It includes a wide range of activities, such as bird watching, whale-watching, general wildlife viewing, visiting zoos and acquired, sharkelling to view underwater life, hunting and recreational fishing".

Many tourists prefer to see and interact with wild species in their habitats and experience a much more intimate closeness to authentic habitats. The wildlife tourism developed rapidly after Second World War, viewing wild life is being promoted in much government controlled protected areas in Australia and overseas. In view South Wales, tourism has been promoted in protected areas, and to a lesser extent in wildness areas. Recently, in India too, wildlife tourism has been promoted in protected areas.

Wildlife tourism can be classified according to the motivation of tourists and their level of interactions with wildlife. Non-consumptive tourism and consumptive tourism are two broad categories of wildlife tourism. The first category involves recreational activities that neither catch nor kill wild animals. Wildlife watching, view recording and photography are the most common forms of non-consumptive recreational activities. However, a study of impacts of tourism at a wildlife refuge in Florida showed that wildlife photographers are the most disruptive among the different recreational users in the area. It can be in the form of (a) recreational hunting of waterfowl and big game; (b) recreational fishing; (c) trophy hunting and fishing (Freese, 1998). Recreational hunting in Australia includes game bird hunting, Kangaroo and wallaby hunting, feral animal hunting, game rench hunting of exotic species, and safari hunting (Common Wealth Australia, 1998). While there is demand for trophy hunting, the opportunity to hunt to diminished because of tough government regulations and declining number of wildlife. The current hunting regulation is based on the theoretical concept of ecological carrying capacity. It involves regulated removal of excess populations that would otherwise be lost to natural predation, diseases and overcrowding.

The wildlife tourism promotion requires a perspective plan and strategic management of visitor's impacts on eco-system and wildlife. Knowledge of the ecology, habitat preference and distribution of wildlife within its range also involves the identification of wildlife resources, recreation facilities and basic amenities to visitors. Thus, management of wildlife tourism should consider developing a zoning plan to define and delineate site within the protected areas as well as in common or private property that should be allocated for wildlife tourism (Chawla, 2003). Spatial zoning is the most common technique to reduce the negative impact of tourists on wild life. The special l structures provide tourists a sense of security in an unknown place and enhance their appreciation of nature. These structural elements also serve as a protective barrier between tourists and wildlife (Dredge, 1999). Wildlife tourism management also involves full supervision, monitoring and control so as not to disrupt the breeding behaviour and reduce the breeding success of the animals (Sinha, 2001).

The impact of tourism on wildlife resources is mostly negative. However, it varies according to number of tourists and their behaviour towards wildlife, nature and magnitude of tourist activity has stated that captive characteristics of wildlife, the recreationist's behaviour and the context of the disturbance all seem to be important in understanding tourism impacts on wildlife. The ecological sensitivity of wildlife habitats, seasonal vulnerability of wildlife, the animals individual characteristics, population attributions of species, inter and intra specific interactions and animals adaptability to human induced disturbances are among the many factors that may affect wildlife's recreation to tourism (Green & Higginbottom, 2000). Thus, due to promotion of tourism in National Parks and Sanctuaries, man-animal conflict has been documented (Edinglon, 1986). There is high probability of population imbalance of birds in natural habitats due to forceful displacement of other species by those that are more habituated to human.

Benefits and Values of Wildlife Tourism: The benefits of wildlife tourism are related to economic, social, environmental and recreational. The economic benefits from wildlife tourism are in form of employment, supporting commercial enterprises, and income generation. Wildlife hunting, in form of recreational hunting, generates income from visitors per visitor and hunting/fishing fees, from sales of hunting/fishing gears and from hiring fees of boats, and land vehicles. Non-consumptive wild life tourism also generates income from park fees, admission fes, leases, services, sale of materials, and other tourism related entrepreneurs (Freese, 1996). The values of wildlife resources include ethical, cultural, commercial, recreational and environmental uses. There exist intimate relationships between wild animals and our society, tradition, culture, education, economy, recreation and ecology. They have a major role to play in making our planet a place of joy, enjoyment, peace and prosperity (Negi, 1991). The positive values of wildlife have been:

Positive Value: Ethical value, cultural value, ecological value, scientific value, aesthetic and recreational value, commercial and economic value, game value etc.

Negative Value: Damage to agriculture, competion, disease, conflicting landuse priorities.

Wildlife in India: India has rich bio-diversity in form of flora and fauna. India is abode of thousands of species of wild animals viz. mammals, birds, reptiles, fishes, amphibians and invertebrates. They live in and around the country's diverse vegetation that varies from the open throng desert forests of Rajasthan in the west to the evergreen forests of Kerala in Suth, the rain forests of north east India and the alpine pastures of Kashmir in the north and also in the inland and marine waters, swamps and marshes. The ecology is the basis for all animal life and their habitat to live and flourish. The country has diverse ecological conditions. On the basis of flora, fauna, climate and edaphic conditions, India can be divided into the following ecological zones :

- *Western Himalaya:* Jammu and Kashmir, Himachal Pradesh and Uttaranchal.
- *Eastern Himalaya:* Darjeeling Hills of North Bengal, Sikkim, and Arunachal Pradesh.
- *North-eastern Hills:* Assam, Mizoram, Manipur, Tripura, Meghalaya and Nagaland.
- *Indo Ganga Plains:* Plains of river Ganga and its tributaries and the tributaries of river Indus, viz. Ravi, Beas and Sutlaj.
- *Desert Zone:* Arid and semi-arid tracts of Rajasthan, Punjab, Haryana, Gujarat and U.P.
- *Central India:* Madhya Pradesh, Orissa, Gujarat and Maharashtra.
- ***Decan Plateau:*** Parts of Maharashtra, Karnataka, Tamil Nadu, Andhra Pradesh and Kerala.
- ***Western Coast:*** Western Coast of coutnry extending from Gujarat coast in the north to Kenya Kumari in the south.
- *Bay Islands:* Andman andNicobar Islands in the Bay of Bengal.

Wild Animals: Thousand of species of mammals, birds, reptiles, fishes and amphiboles are found in the different ecological zones of the country. The important species of Indian animals have been listed and may be categorized into :

Mammals: India is the home of more than 300 species of mammals which include ape, cat family, elephants, and marine mammals. Many of these like 'Kashmir stag and Asiatic Lion are threatened with extinction.

Birds: India is abode of thousands of species of both resident and migratory birds. Among them are terrestrial, aquatic and littoral species.

Reptiles: Important reptiles are crocodiles, lizards, tortoises, snakes, etc.

Fishes: In India, fishes are found in rivers, streams, swamps, marshes, lakes and marine habitats, from the cold waters of Kashmir to the Indian Ocean.

Indian sub-continent is rict vits variety of wildlife. India's diverse wildlife base is the second largest in the world and there are 85 National Parks and 480 Wildlife Sanctuaries established here (Table 10).

Table 10
National Parks and Sanctuaries in India

Region	*Wildlife Sanctuaries*	*National Parks*	*Total*
Trans-Himalaya	4 (0.83)	3 (3.53)	7 (1.29)
Himalaya	55 (11.46)	12 (14.12)	67 (11.86)
Desert	5 (1.04)	1 (1.18)	6 (1.06)
Semi Arid	83 (17.29)	8(9.41)	91 (16.10)
Western Ghats	44 (9.17)	12 (14.12)	56 (9.91)
Decan Peninsula	116 (24.17)	21 (24.71)	137 (24.26)
Gangetic Plain	30 (6.25)	6 (7.06)	36 (6.37)
Coasts	21 (4.37)	5 (5.88)	26 (4.60)
North-East	28 (5.83)	9 (10.59)	37 (6.55)
Island	94 (19.58)	8 (9.41)	102 (18.05)
All India	480 (100.00)	85 (100.00)	565 (100.00)

Source: Wild Life Institute of India, Dehradoon, 2000.

Most of the National Parks are located in Decan Peninsula (24.71 per cent) followed by Western Ghats (14.12 per cent) and Himalaya (14.12 per cent). Similarly, most of the wildlife sanctuaries are situated in Decan Peninsula (24.17 per cent) and Islands (19.58 per cent). Wildlife and National Parks provide shelter to largest number of tigers, one horned rhinoceros in the world. India's protected reserve is about 153000 sq. km. and constituting more than 3.3 per cent of surface land and 12 per cent of forest area of India. India's wildlife sanctuaries houses more than 500 species of mammals, over 2000 species of birds, over 500 species of reptiles and amphibians and around 30000 species of insects (Chawla, 2003).

Among the important wildlife sanctuaries and parks include Corbett National Park, Ranthambore Tiger Reserve, Kanha National Park, Periyar National Park, Bandipur National Park, Bharatpur Bird Sanctuary, Sunderban National Park, Kaziranga National Park, Sariska National Park, Bandhavgarh National Park, Dudhwa Tiger Reserve, Simpipal National Park, etc. The exotic wild life in India include Asiatic Lion, Indian Elephant, King Cobra, one horned Rhino, Royal Bengal Tiger, etc. Bird watching is popular in Sariska Wild Life Sanctuary, Bharatpur Bird Sanctuary and Corbett National Park.

Tourism Scenario: Traditionally, Corbett is one of the most important destinations for wild life tourism in India. Tourism in Corbett remained more or less static till the eighties. A limited number of visitors came and stayed inside the National Park in accommodation maintained by the Forest Department. Corbett National Park has accommodation at twelve different places, there being only one tourist complex at Dhikala with 92 bed accommodation. Accommodation in other places consists of Forest Rest Houses, most of them having been constructed during the British period, and more than a century old. The visitors would come in their own vehicles, bring their own provisions as food is available at Dhikala only, and enjoy wildlife by driving around, sitting in the watchtowers or going on elephant rides. Interpretive facilities consisted of a good library at Dhikala, audio-visual shows at Bijrani and Dhikala, and museum at Dhangari. Ramnagar township located on the boundary of park, where the headquarters of park is located, remained unaffected by tourism.

During the nineties, there was a sea change in both the numbers and pattern of visitation. The number of tourist increased dramatically. Today, Corbett annually receives around 50,000 visitors out of which nearly fifteen per cent visitors are foreigners. This is almost equal to visitor arrival at Kanha Tiger Reserve in Central India and Ranthambore Tiger Reserve in Western India but is much lower than in Periyar Tiger Reserve in South India and Gir Lion Reserve in West India. However, owing to differences in rates for visitor facilities in different States, Corbett has one of the highest revenue from tourism in any protected area in India.

Private sector began to dominate the development and marketing of tourism in the region. Major investments were made by private entrepreneurs in accommodation, transport, and other facilities for tourists. Earlier, tourism was markedly seasonal as remains closed from 16th June to 14th November every year. In order to increase the occupancy, the private resorts have made enormous effort to attract visitors during the monsoon period when park remains closed by encouraging conferences, bird-watching activity and offering attractive packages for groups for wildlife viewing outside park. These efforts have converted tourism into an activity which goes on round the year.

Tourism developments had a tremendous, impact on both the biological resources and socio-economy of the park's landscape. Owing to the major changes in the land use pattern in the park's landscape, there has been a marked increase in man-animal conflict, particularly cases involving elephants and incidents of road kills of wild animals along the State highways forming. The local residents raised an agitation resorted to demonstrations at the park's HQ and blockade.

Due to increasing pressure of human and cattle population most of our protected areas have become islands of vast resources surrounded by needy population. Legal regulations deny access of local population to these areas who have been traditionally using these areas for various day-to-day needs. It is almost impossible to bring home the idea of bio-diversity conservation in the minds of people particularly when they find free access being allowed to outsiders. This causes conflict between managers of these areas and the local population. In order to protect these vast wilderness areas rich in their bio-diversity, it will be necessary to frame the tourism policy of the protected areas in such a way that the areas of conflicts are minimized and local people get their fair share out of the eco-tourism plan of the area. The hostality of the surrounding population may cause much more damage to these areas than an unregulated tourism policy. It is, therefore, most important to harmonise the tourism plan of the area to accommodate the local needs in such a way that the conservation of the area gets top most priority. The objective has to be to create public awareness for conservation in general and to build up a sizeable public support for the protected area in particular.

With increasing frequency, managers of national parks and sanctuaries are substituting decision-making frameworks like limits of acceptable change or visitor experience and reduce protection for more traditional methods. These frameworks, which are similar to each other, often more guidance and promote greater flexibility in addressing management problems. Importantly, monitoring programmes provide the mechanism to periodically evaluate resource conditions, management standards on the effectiveness of implemented action. Resource monitoring may be defined as the systematic collection and analysis of data at regular intervals to predict natural and human induced changes and to provide the basis for appropriate management response. Thus, a principal benefit of visitor impact monitoring programmes is that they provide an objective permanent record of resource conditions. Managers may find valuable information for preparing visitor management actions. Managers are supposed to evaluate the potential effectiveness of alternative strategies compared to their management costs and visitor's costs. park related attributes such as level of development, accessibility and type and level of visitation also influence strategy selection. Park managers need to focus on the prevention of future impacts by planning and development of traits and facilities in the resistance locations. They also need to provide training facilities for local guides and service providers for low impact tourism activities on eco-system, environment and wild life behaviour.

In sum, some of the key points are (Jefray, at. al. 1999):

- Visitor use can negatively affect vegetation, soil, water and wildlife resources, as well as the quality of visitor experience;
- Visitor crowding and conflict can reduce the quality of visitor experiences;

- Environmental attributes such as vegetation and soil resistance and resiliency, influence the type and severity of visitor resource impacts;
- The use or impact relationship limits the effectiveness of visitor use, reduction and dispersal strategies;
- Decision-making frameworks can provide an explicit and flexible means of managing visitor impacts;
- Indirect management strategies are often less costly to implement and are preferred by visitors.

The limits of Acceptable Change Planning process, and its derivative approaches like Tourism Optimization Management Model developed in Australia, represent an effective evolution of problem conceptualization compared to the recreational carrying capacity approach. The models and principles of eco-tourism evolved and implemented in the parks and sanctuaries in Kenya, Brazil, Australia, Malasia, etc. are to be evaluated, reviewed and modified according to Indian conditions, so that these principles may be implemented in India too.

Heritage Tourism

The term heritage tourism refers to tourism in the natural, cultural and built-environment of an area providing the tangible links between past, present and future. It has developed as international phenomenon, based on the historical and cultural resources of tourism destinations. Importantly, heritage tourism has to play a vital role in supporting communities in their quest for sustainable development. Heritage tourism encompasses the live and artistic forms of human expression (painting, sculptures, museums, theatre, folklore) referred to as arts along with historical tourism, ethnic tourism and eco-natural based.

According to Zeppel and Hall (1991), the international tourism industry has of late seen different trends emerge. Heritage and cultural tourism have featured prominently in these developments as the consumer's search for new types of visitor experience focused on the value of cultural heritage. Cultural heritage manifested in monuments, museums, art galleries, historical sites, fairs and festivals, religious places and observations, folk arts and traditions etc. have been panicle sources of tourist attraction over the centuries. In fact cultural heritage is continued to be centre stage of tourism in terms of tourist motivation, tourist attraction, tourist demand, tourist product and tourism supply (Kamra, 2001). There has been tremendous upsurge in tourist demand for cultural attractions in the recent past. In fact, cultural tourism has emerged as one of the major tourist forms of the 19th century. Tourist demand for various art forms, including artichecture, painting, classical and folk dances, instrumental and vocal music and even music instruments has shown an ever-growing trend amongst the domestic and international tourist. Interestingly, religious centres, observances and rituals, religio-socio-cultural fairs and festivals have all become significant globally. India is full of socio-cultural tourism resources since century has been abode of Gods, Goddesses, *Rishis*, and other supernatural powers. A number of religious places, centres of historical importance and cultural heritage as well as folk traditions, arts, and crafts attract domestic and even foreign tourists. In fact, India is a country where the diversity and extent of its heritage underpin much of its appeal and fascination as a tourist destination, cultural heritage i.e. language, customs, performing folk and fine arts etc. combines with a diverse historic and artistic heritage. The festivals and fairs associated with castes, communities and other ethnic groups also attract tourists not only for religious importance but also for enjoyment and enormous cultural values.

Religious Heritage

Pilgrimage or *dharmayatra* is not peculiar to Hinduism. In Islam and Christianity, Buddhism and Jainism, Sikhism and many other religious the same practice is prevalent. The religious faiths are deep rooted in the minds of the Indian people. However, the way of faith, and form worship and social behaviour differ from sect to sect and community to community. The main religions of India are Hindu, Islam, Jainism, Budhism and Christianity. India being an abode of gods, is spread with numerous pilgrimage centres. A brief outlining of such pilgrimage centres is given below:

Budhism: Out of the six great religions of the world. Budhism is one and it belongs to India. Gautam Budha was the originator of it who gave the concept of eight fold path viz. (i) right understanding, (ii) right mindedness, (iii) right speech, (iv) right action, (v) right living, (vi) right effort, (vii) right attentiveness, and (viii) concentration. The important places associated with Budhism are :

- Bodh Gaya (Bihar)
- Sarnath (Varanasi, U.P.)
- Sravasti (U.P.)
- Kushinagar (Gorakhpur, U.P.)
- Vaishali (Bihar)
- Rewalsar (Himachal Pradesh)
- Lahul-Spiti (Himachal Pradesh)
- Laddakh (Laddakh)
- Tawang (Arunachal Pradesh)

Jainism: Vardhaman Mahavira was the 24th Tirthankar or 'Enlightened Teacher' of an ancient religion called Jainism. Jainism gave five main concepts viz. non-violence, truth, not stealing and not owning property as well as chastity. The important Jain pilgrimage sites are :

- Mount Abu (Rajasthan)
- Palitana (Bhavnagar, Gujarat)
- Sauripur (Agra, U.P.)
- Bogipura Sahganj (Agra, U.P.)
- Bhalupura (Varanasi, U.P.)
- Ram Nagar (Bareilly, U.P.)
- Pawanagar (Deoria, U.P.)
- Deograh (Lalitpur, U.P.)

Hinduism: Hinduism is the main religion of India however; it is not identified either with a single teacher or a single book. All major Indian scriptures - Rig Vega, Ramayana, Mahabharat, Puranas and Upnishadas are filled with the accounts of pilgrimages undertaken by the great sages and kings. Pilgrimage is continues to be popular among the Hindus, with its ancient and diverse origins. Hindus believe one supreme Gold but they also believe in many forms of super power called *Devatas,* and *Devis*. They worship Brahma, Vishnu, Mahesh, Parvati, Lakshmi, Durga, Surya, Chandra, Indra, Varuna, Dikpalas, Sesanaga and other various heroes of epics, religious texts. Shaiva and Vaishnava are the two main sects of the religion. It is connected with the concept of mythological content which revolves around gods and goddesses who represent the various forces operating in the universe. At the centre of great are Hindu Trinity represented by Brahma-creator, Vishnu-Persevere, and Shiva-destroyer which is different from the Christianity-father, son and holy spirit (Gupta, 2002).

The important Hindu pilgrimage centres are :

Char Dham (Abodes of God)

- Badrinath (Uttaranchal)
- Rameshwaram (Tamil Nadu)
- Puri (Orissa)
- Dwarika (Gujarat)

Saptapuris (Seven Sacred Cities)

- Mathura (U.P.)
- Ayodhyaya (U.P.)
- Mayapuri (Uttaranchal, Haridwar)
- Kashi (Varanasi, U.P.)
- Kanchi (Kanchipuram, Tamil Nadur)
- Avantipuri (Ujjain, M.P.)
- Dwarika(Gujarat)

Kumbh Fairs

- Prayag (Allahabad, U.P.)
- Haridwar (Uttaranchal)
- Ujjain (M.P.)
- Nasik (Maharashtra)

Twelve Jyotirlingas (Lord Shiva Temples)

- Somnath (Saurastra, Gujarat)
- Malikarjun (Kurnool, Andhra Pradesh)
- Mahakuleshwar (Ujjain, M.P.)
- Omkareshwar (Malva, M.P.)
- Kedarnath (Uttaranchal)
- Vishweshwar (Vishwanath, Varanasi, U.P.)
- Trimbakeshwar (Nasik, Maharashtra)
- Baidyanath (Bihar)
- Nageshwar (Gujarat)
- Rameshwar (Tamil Nadu)
- Ghrishneshwar (Maharashtra)
- Bhimashankar

Panch Prayag (Confluence of Rivers)

- Vishnu Prayag (Joshimath, Uttaranchal)
- Nanda Prayag (Uttaranchal)
- Karma Prayag (Uttaranchal)
- Rudra Prayag (Uttaranchal)
- Deva Prayag (Uttaranchal)

Panch Badris (Uttaranchal)

- Adi Badri
- Yog Badri
- Bhavishya Badri
- Dhyan Badri
- Narsingh Badri

Panch Kedar (Lord Shiva Temples of Uttaranchal)

- Mahabaleshwar
- Tungnath
- Rudranath

- Kalpeshwar
- Kedarnath

Other Hindu Pilgrimage Tourism Sites

- Amarthnath (Jammu & Kashmir)
- Vaishno Devi (Jammu & Kashmir
- Risikesh (Haridwar, Uttaranchal)
- Prayagraj (Allahabad, U.P.)
- Vanasi (Varanasi, U.P.)
- Ayodhya (Faizabad, U.P.)
- Haridwar (Uttaranchal)
- Mathura (U.P.)
- Gaya (Bihar)
- Tripati (Andhra Pradesh)
- Vindhyachal (U.P.)
- Poornagiri (Uttaranchal)

Islamism: Islam is a new religion which was started in A.D. 622 in Arabia only after A.D. 1200 in India. The Prophet Mohammad was the originator of the religion while during Mughal Rule in India, it was patronage. A large number of followers of Islam are converted from Hindu and other religions, therefore acculturate is praising in the rituals, traditions and way of life. Sufi Saint Khwaja Moinuddin Chisti, was the great saint and his associated places are being visited by many followers of the religion. Ajmer (Rajasthan) is main pilgrimage of Muslims in India while a number of Dargah, *Masjids* and *Maqbaras* are being visited by Muslims all over India. Even a number of Hindus and other religion follower pay offer to these places.

Sikhism: Sikhism is one of the great religions whose followers are Hindus in Punjab, Haryana and other important places of India. Nanak was the first Guru (Teacher) of the Sikhs who laid the foundation of Sikhism in India (1469-1539). He preached against hypocrisy in religion. Nanak was followed by nine other gurus in the course of next 200 years. Guru

Govind Singh (1966-1708) gave the Sikh community a clear military orientation was created a new fraternity-*Khalsa*. The important places of Sikh pilgrimage are :

- Golden Temple (Amirtsar, Punjab)
- Anandpur Sahib (Dharmashala, Himachal Pradesh)
- Hemkund Sahib (Uttaranchal)
- Patna Sahib (Patna, Bihar)

Christianity : Christianity is the third major religion of India. Christian missionaries came to India and established their traditions and places of worship (churches) in different corners of India. However, southern states are more influenced by the missionaries. The famous pilgrimage sites are :

- Basilica of Bom Jesus (Goa)
- Secathedral (Goa)
- Convent of St. Monica (Goa)
- Velankanni (Tamil Nadu)

Architecture, Monuments, Sculpture and Paintings

India is rich of varied monuments, architecture, arts and crafts. Temples, stupas, pillars, caves, places, ruins, *chaityas, vihars, tombs, maqbaras*, etc. are some of the important tourist's interests. Arts, crafts and architecture of early Indian history to modern period have been major attraction for the tourists. The monuments may broadly be divided into four categories: (a) Budhist; (b) Brahmanical; (c) Indo-Islamic; and (d) Indo-European. The museums, libraries and academics are also great tourism resources. Some of the monuments have been preserved under the programmes of UNESCO. There are four national museums in the country viz. the National Museum, New Delhi, Indian Museum, Kolkata, Satarganj Museum, Hyderabad and Allahabad Museum, Allahabad which are financially supported by the Government of India. The museums of state importance include Mathura Museum, Allahabad Museum, Anand Bhawan, Bharat Kala Mandir in U.P. Princes of Wales Museum, Mumbai, Tamil Nadu State Museum, Chennai are other regional level museums of India.

Importantly, National Library, Kolkata is the largest library in India. Other leading libraries are Delhi Public Library, New Delhi, Central Secretariat Library, New Delhi, Council of World Affairs, Delhi, NCAER Library, Delhi, IIPA Library, Delhi, Khuda Baksha Oriental Library, Patna, Raja Library, Rampur (U.P.), Sanskrit University Library, Varanasi, BHU Central Library, Varanasi, etc. The main academics include Lalikala Academy, Sangeet Natak Academy, Natinal School of Drama, Sahitya Academy etc. Crafts Museum, New Delhi, Rabindra Sadana, Santhi Niketan, Teen Murthi House, Delhi, Indira Gandhi Memorial Museum, Delhi, Birla Industrial and Technological Museum, Kolkata etc. are also of great importance.

The history of Indian architecture starts from at least 3000 BC with the Indus Civilization. The historical places in forms of monuments, sites, stupa etc. have been great cultural heritage. The stupa of Sanchi and Sarnath are very important for tourists. These stupas were constructed during Maurya and Gupta period. Importantly, templess of South India and North India have great sculpture and art. Some temples were constructed in Gupta, Chola, Chalukyean, and other historical rulers. These temples have been preserved as cultural heritage. Importantly, Mughal architecture such as Gra Fort, Taj Mahal, Fatehpur Sikari, Humayun Tomb, Qutub Minar, etc. are attracting a number of tourists. The monuments of International fame are :

- Ajanta Caves (Maharashtra)
- Ellora Caves (Maharashtra)
- Agra Fort (Agra, U.P.)
- Taj Mahal (Agra, U.P.)
- Sun Temple (Konark, Orissa)
- Mahabalipuram (Tamil Nadu)
- Goa Churches and Convents (Goa)
- Khajuraho (Madhya Pradesh)
- Hempi (Karnataka)
- Fatehpur Sikari (U.P.)

- Pattadakal (Karnataka)
- Elephanta Caves (Maharashtra)
- Brhadisvara Temple (Thanjavur, Tamil Nadu)
- Sanchi (M.P.)
- Humayun Tomb (Delhi)
- Qutab Minar (Delhi)
- Bodh Gaya (Bihar)

Folk Dances, Fairs Festivals and Classical Dances

India has a glorious history of achievements in the fields of paintings, music, architecture, science, literature, etc. The landmarks in music are distinctive stages in development of arts, styles, tunes, tones, and rhythms. The concept of melodies (*ragas*) and their classification, manifestation of different musical phases and compositions, evolution of musical instruments like drum, flute, *vina, mradangas, tabla, sitar, dhole,* etc. are the distinctive features of India music.

Importantly, dance in India has had a long history. It is evidences are available in religious and historical texts. *Natyashastra, Abhinav Darpan, Sangeet Ratnakar* etc. all depict dancing and its related exposition. *Nritta, Nrtya,* and *Natya* are the three main categories of dancing. *Kathakali, Bharat Natyam, Kuchipuri, Kathaka, Odissi, Manipuri,* etc. are classical dances of India and several gharanas (houses) have developed these dances according to new expositions. The folk dances of India are a unique synthesis of music, ritual and celebrations. India presents a varied style of folk and tribal dances. Folk dances are generally spontaneous expressions of the sociological, psychological and historical moorings of rural India (Gupta, et. al., 2002). They are regularly performed on festive and religious occasions in rural India. They differ in colours, costumes, language, music and style. The major folk dances are *Teyyam, Kolattam, Kummi Oatam, Tudal, Kaikotti,kali, and Tappattikkali* in South India; *Kajari, Nautank, Raslila, Karan, Ramlila, Bhangra, Rauf, Khayal,* and *Ghumar* in North India; *Dandia Ra, Garba, Tamasa* in Western India; *Chan* and *Bihin* in Eastern India.

Importantly, ethnic dances such as Kol, Gonda, Naga, *Yak dance*, deer dance, lion and peackock dance of Monipas, *Karma, Magha, Beha, Hero, Andi* dances of Hos, *Jaitra of Oraons, , Jhika, Largren Enec Dhang* dances of Santhals, Kinbhar, Helka and Jabor of Kharias; *Dumhal* of Wattal Elelakharadi of Irulas, etc. are some of the famous folk dances of India.

Celebrations of fairs and festivals in India form a wonderful and joyful series of events. There are festivals and fairs in India which draw millions of people and some of them are

- Kumbha and melas of Nasik, Ujjai, and Allahabad;
- Dasera festival of Mysore, Kullu;
- Dargah of Ajmer, Rajasthan;
- Pushkar and Vaneshwar fairs of Rajasthan;
- Nauchandi fair, U.P.
- Xmas celebrations in Goa;
- Sindhu festival in Jammu & Kashmir;
- Rathyatra of Puri;
- Others

Kinnors, Nags, Asurs, Pischachs, Kiratas, Suras, Yakshas, Gandharvas and Trigartas etc. are the mythological races of the past which are still found in mountains and hills. Fairs and festivals are moments of remembrance and commiseration of the births days and great deeds of gods, goddesses, heroes, heroines, gurus, prophets and saints. Fairs and festivals are accompanied with performances, music dramas, dances and more rugged physical activities.

Tribal's festivals and fairs are associated with

- Agricultural cycle;
- Seasonal changes;
- Huntings;
- Gods and goddesses;
- Ancestral festivals;
- Cattle fuel fire and health;

- Cosmic movements and changes;
- Medicinal practitioners.

Boat race festival, mango festival, garden festival, flower festival, tea festivals, kite festival, elephant festival, desert festival, music and dance related festivals, etc. also attract tourists. National days such as Republic Day (26th January) are celebrted in India with glamorous events. *Lohri, Bhaishakhi, Makar Sankranti, Pongal, Bihu, Vasanta Panchami, Shivratri, Holi, Dwali, Navroj, Mahavir Jayanti, Budh Jayanti, Shab-e-Barat, Idul Fitr, Idul-Azha, Guru Purnima, Nag Panchami,* Independence Day (15th August), *Raksha Bandhan, Ganesh Ghaturthi, Janmasthmi, Muharram, Navrati, Durga Puja, Dashhra, Chistmas* etc. are the ethnic festivals of India in which a large number of persons celebrate and enjoy. These events are full of enjoyment and cultural values which are potential resources for tourism development (Dixit, 2001).

The food and drinks called Indian cuisine also offer varied interest for tourists. A rich variety of regional specialists and fruits and vegetables, meat etc. offer varied meals and drink to tourists who enjoy it very much. Tandoori, *Kabab, Mughalai, Biryani, Prawn Pualo, Navratan Pulao, Chapatis, Puris, Parathas, Idlis, Uppama, Dosa, Sambhar, Dala* are some of the regional cuisine which are popular even among the foreign tourists. *Dashahri, Langra, Alphanso, Gulabkhas* are some of the mango varieties which are liked very much. Jackfruits, *Sitaphal, Lichee,* Pineapples, oranges, melons, are some of the fruits while *gulab jamun, kala kand, jalebis, rasmalai, petha, laddoo, Srikhanda,* are some of the famous sweets. These sweets are very liked by the foreign tourists.

The above analysis simply demonstrates that India has rich and varied cultural heritage and present great potential for tourism development at regional level. Even further promotion of cultural tourism provide avenues for preservation and conservation of folk arts, culture, traditions, crafts, folk songs, dances, theatre, and folklore etc. However, planned development of cultural tourism and management of cultural events- fairs, festivals, occasions etc. should be ensured so that there may be no distortion of cultural values and damage to socio-cultural fabric of India. Culture being a sensitive element of tourism, special efforts is needed to protect our cultural values and heritage.

References

Agrawal, Anil (2002), Sharks and Tourism, *Down To Earth,* July 31.

Bansal, S.P., et. al. (2002), Tourism in the New Millennium, Abhishek, Pub. Delhi.

Bhatia, A.K. (1982), Tourism Development, Sterling Publishers Pvt. Ltd., New Delhi.

Borrie, W. et. al. (1999), Protected Area Planning Principles and Strategies in Eco-Tourism : A Guide for Planners and Managers by (Ed.) K. Lindberg et.al, Natraj Pub., Dehradoon.

Bryden, J.M. (1973), Tourism and Development, Cambridge University Press, Cambridge.

Butler, R.W. (1996) , The Concept of Carrying Capacity for Tourism Destinations: Deal or Merely Buried Progress, *Tourism and Hospitality Research,* Vol. 2.

Chawla, R. (2003), Wildlife Tourism and Development, Sonali Publications, Delhi.

Cleverdon, R. (1979), The Economic and Social Impact of International Tourism in Developing Countries, The Economic Intelligence Unit Ltd., London.

Common Wealth Australia (1998), Commercial Utilization of Australian Nature Wildlife, Reports of the Senate Rural and Regional Affairs and Transport References Committee, Canberra, Parliament House.

Cooperative Research Centre for Sustainable Development (2001), C.R.C. Wild Life Tourism Research, www. cretourism.com.an.

Dixit, Manoj and Charu, Shaila (2001), Tourism Products, New Royal Book Co. Lucknow.

Dredge, D. (1999), Destination Place, Planning and Design, Animals of Tourism Research, 26, (4).

Edington, J.M. (1986), Ecology, Recreation and Tourism, Cambridge Press.

Filion, F.L. et. al. (1992), The Economics of Global Eco-Tourism, Unpublished Report, Canadian Wildlife Service, *Enviroment*, Canada.

Freese C. (1996), The Commercial, Consumptive Use of Wild Species: Managing it for the Benefit of Bio-Diversity, Paper WHOI International.

Freese, C. (1998), Wild Species as Commodities : Managing Markets and Eco-Systems for Sustainability, Washington Islands Press.

Getz, D. (1983), Capacity to Absorb Tourism : Concept and Applications for Strategic Planning, *Annals of Tourism & Research*, Vol. 10, No. 2.

Godfrey, K. and Clarke J. (2000), Tourism Development, Handbook, Classel, London.

Green, R. & Higginbottom K. (2000), The Effects of Non-Consumptive Wildlife Tourism on Free Ranging Wildlife : A Review, Pacific Conservation Biology, 6.

Gupa, S.P. et. al. (2002), Cultural Tourism in India, D.K. Printwell Pub. Delhi.

Gupta, S.K. (2002), Tourism and Heritage Resources in Garhwal Himalaya, Kaveri Pub. Delhi.

Inskeep, E. (1991), Environmental Impact in Tourism Planning on Integrated and Sustainable Approach, Van Nostrand Reinhold, New York.

Jefrey, L.M. & T.A. Farrel (1999), Managing Eco-tourism Visitation in Protected Areas in Eco-tourism: A Guides for Planners & Managers by (ed.) Lindberg, K., et.al, Natraj Pub. Dehradoon.

Johnsingh, A.J.T. (1993), Prospects of Eco-Tourism In National Parks, DWRE, FRI, Dehradoon.

Kamra, K.K. (2002), Managing Tourism Destinations, Kanishka Pub. Delhi.

Kumar, S., Wildlife Tourism in India : Need to Treat With Care (M), Wildlife Institute of India, Dehradoon.

Lascurian, H.C. (1996) , Tourism, Eco-Tourism And Protected Areas, IUCN.

Lindberg, K., et. al. (1997), Eco-Tourism in the Asia Pacific Region: Issues and Outlook, Bennington, V.T., The International Eco-Tourism Society.

Martin, B.S. and U.M. (1960), An Examination of Relationships Between Carrying Capacity and Tourism Life Cycle Management and Policy Implications, *Journal of Environmental Management*, Vol. 31, No. 4.

Mathieson, A. and Wall G. (1982), Tourism : Economic Physical and Social Impacts, Longman, New York.

Negi, A.S., Eco-Tourism, Cheetal, Vol. 34 (1).

Negi, S.S. (1991), Handbook of National Parks and Sanctuaries in India, Indus Publishing Housing, Delhi.

Nigam, Devesh (2000), Tourism Environment and Development of Garhwal Himalaya, Mittal Pub., New Delhi.

'O' Reilly, A.M. (1986), Tourism Carrying Capacity, *Tourism Management*, Vol. 7, No. 4.

Pandey, B.W. (2002), Geo-Environmental Hazards in Himalaya, Mittal Publications, Delhi.

Pandey, B.W. et. al. (1998), 'Population' Urbanization and Tourism in Kullu District in R.B. Singh (Ed.), Sustainable Development of Mountain Environment in India and Canada, Oxford University Press, New Delhi.

Reingold, L. (1993), Identifying the Elusive Eco-Tourist Going Green, A Supplement to Tour & Travel News, Oct. 25.

Rodgers, W.A. and Panwar, H.S. (2000), Planning A Wild Life Protected Area Network In India : A Review, WII, Dehradoon.

Sawarnkar, W. (1999), Conserving Biodiversity in Protected Areas and Forested Landscape (M), LBSN Ltd., Mussorrie.

Shullai, G.F. (1980), A Case Study of Wild Life Tourism in National Parks, DWRE, FRI & C, Derhandoon.

Singh, T.V. et. al. (1986), Studies in Himalayan Ecology, Himalayan Books, New Delhi.

Tribhuwan, R.D. (2003), Fairs and Festivals of Indian Tribes, Discovery Pub. House, Delhi.

Vania, Rustam (2002), Scrambling For Paradise, *Down To Earth*, July 31.

5

Assessment of Tourism Impacts

Tourism has been recognized as a major global industry today. The economic potential of tourism is most important since tourism creates jobs, brings in new money, relatively clean, and has minimum start up costs. Tourism also helps in conservation of national heritage, protecting the environment and contributing in improving in the quality of life and well being of local communication. However, it has affected the socio-cultural value system, heritage and local environment.

Impact is often used as a prejurative term and it is often assumed that impacts are likely to be negative. However, residents of destinations often want tourists to come and want them very much. They do this because they want their life styles to change. They want jobs, higher incomes, increased tax revenues and better opportunities for their children the benefits may be largely economic and may sometimes be illusory, and there may be adverse consequences, often of an environmental or socio-cultural nature, associated with acquiring the benefits (Geoffrey Wall, 1997). Importantly, the impacts of tourism can be viewed as arising from the type or types of tourism involved the characteristics of the communities in which tourism is taking place and the nature of resident visitor encounters. Furthermore, investigations of tourism cycles suggest that impacts in a destination area are likely to change with time as the nature of tourists, the community and resident-visitor interactions also change (Butlar, 1980). Moreover, much change associated with tourism may be cumulative as a number of small enterprises is developed in sequences in close proximity, each having a minor impact when viewed alone, but together having far-reaching consequences. Cumulative impact assessment is a challenging topic which is beginning to attract the attention of those changed with conducting and evaluating impact assessments, although, it has yet to receive much recognition in the tourism literature (Shoemaker, 1994). While environmental impact assessments for specific tourism developments such as resorts and marines have an important place. Thus, in addition to impact assessment, monitoring of change may be required and mitigation strategies may be required to reduce the magnitude of environmental consequences (Nelson et.al., 1993).

Economic Impacts

The key elements of economic change associated with destination tourism include employment local income, and economic diversification and regeneration. Therefore, in order to examine the economic significance of tourism in general, it is necessary to determine tourism contribution to Gross National Product, income levels, employment opportunities, government revenue creation, foreign exchange inflows, economic diversification and regional stimulation (Archer and Fletcher, 1990). The total impacts of tourism consists of the direct plus indirect plus induced effects. The ratio of a change in the levels of expenditure and the effect which it has upon the income levels of the economy is known as the tourist income multiplier. Multiplier values can be derived for government revenue, employment and import requirements. In brief tourism's contribution in economic development may be measured in terms of :

- Tourism's contribution to GDP;
- Tourism's relative position to other economic sectors;
- Creation of jobs of tourism activities;
- Other resources like tax, revenues generated by the tourism industry;

- The tourism's impact on the balance of payments;
- The nature and contributions of tourism's human resources;
- The amount of tourism investment and so on.

Most jobs associated with tourism tend to come in the form of direct service job in tourist related facilities attractions, restaurants, shops selling discretionary goods and travel firms. However, a number of these jobs tend to be (i) low paid; (ii) seasonal; (iii) part time; (iv) having limited career prospects; and (v) having unsociable hours.

Visitor spending not also affects wages and employment opportunities but generates income for both the public and private sector (Godfrey and Clarke, 2000) :

- Tourist enterprises, like all local business, pay taxes to the government and as tourism expends so too do these tax revenues;
- Parking and admission fee collected from public sector facilities also bring in further general revenue resulting from tourism;
- Collected tourist tax can represent further tourism revenue to a destination.

Importantly, tourism is recognized as one industry which can help overcome the difficulties associated with the incumbent economic decline in these places because :

- Towns and cities are natural destinations for visitors;
- Tourism is often complementary to its other functions as a service centre, meeting point and seat of government;
- The tourism labour force is essentially in places;
- Tourism is relatively clean, particularly compared to more traditional manufacturing and extractive industries.

However, tourism may tend to rise in land prices, way demands; and inflation and promotiOn of unethical behaviour of business.

Social Impacts

The rapid growth of tourism in the twentieth century has produced problems, as well as opportunities, on a vast scale for both developed and third world countries. The governments of these countries have come to realise that unrestrained and unplanned tourist development can easily aggravate these problems to a point where tourists will no longer with to visit the destination (Christopher, 2000).

Social impacts of tourism may arise from at least four different situations (Brown, 2000) :

- As residents are faced with unaccustomed behaviour and demands from tourists;
- As residents become involved in changing patterns of employment created by the tourism economy;
- As visitors find themselves spatially distanced from their homes, in the midst of quite different ways of life;
- As residents and tourists interact, both within and outside the context of the tourism industry.

Tourism provides immense scope for interactions leading to social change, while large number of tourists in concentration way create congestion and cause local services to be overloaded in one destination, their presence may also spur thr provision of services that were previously unavailable to local people. Tourism tend to rise in prostitution, drug addiction, alcoholism, loot, robbery and may create problems for maintaining law and order. Importantly, tourism has aided the spread of aspects of different cultures to the generating regions.

The key aspects of socio-cultural change associated with tourism destination development relate to local quality of life and sense of place. Social impacts differ from economic issues for obvious reasons, but also be cause they tend to have a more personal interpretation, take longer to appear are much more difficult to measure. Socio-cultural change can be both real and perceive, and often tourism is but one of many factors which can be linked to this change. Social impacts develop through strength forward direct-indirect or secondary association (Godfrey and Clarke, 2000).

Significantly, tourist spending in destinations often helps to support local facilities and services which are also used by the resident community. Tourism may tend to :

- Affect personal income;
- Help to improve living standards for those more directly involved in the industry;
- Make the difference between a business closing down in the winter or staying open throughout the year;
- Support the diversity of restaurants, theatre and cultural entertainment;
- influence the assortment of goods for sale in many local shops that would not be available in same amount if tourism did not exist to support them.

However, tourism may lead to

- Increased traffic congestion;
- Crowding of public places;
- Longer queues in local shops and facilities;
- Local shops over charging;
- Petty theft from cars and accommodation;
- Pickpockets;
- Serious personal assault; and
- Prostitution and women related crimes.

Significantly, tourism can play a positive role in

- Revitalizing local culture and traditions;
- Enhancing sense of pride in local heritage;
- Reaching local understanding and interest in historical and cultural heritage and monuments;
- Celebrations of cultural and traditional and festivals;
- Promotional of local crafts, arts, traditions, and culture.

Nature of Socio-Economic Impact

Socio-economic impact are identified as positive and negative in different situation as explained below (Nigam, 2002) :

Positive Impact

- Direct economic benefit includes provision of employment, increased income and earning of foreign exchange. This leads to the improved living standards of the local community.
- Increased government revenue through various type of taxation on tourism, that can be used to develop the means of local community and infrastructural facilities. These are beneficial to both tourists and residents.
- In direct economic benefits leading to expansion of trade and manufacturing of handicrafts of the tourist's area. This would directly be of advantage to the residents where tourists are arriving.
- Availability of infrastructural facility and services to the residents of the tourist area which were actually provided for the tourist's need.
- Conservation of important elements of cultural heritage for which the tourist have the attraction. These includes archaeological, historical and religious sites which are presently a unique architectural style.
- Revitalization of traditional art, handicrafts, dance music, drama and other lifestyle.
- Generating larger income in fairs and festivals when the tourists also participate in them with the resident population.
- Creation of a sense of pride in the minds of the resident about the religious and cultural values when they observed the tourists come with the devotion to pay respect for their temples and other important shrines. Such a situation occurs in the case of Garhwal where the people from all over India as well as abroad come with a sense of devotion towards the Char Dham.

Negative Impacts

Although the gains from the tourism outweigh the negative impact but their study is also essential for proper planning of tourism. The negative impact are :

- Financial hardship on the residents because of rising prices of goods, services and land due to greater demand by an ever increasing number of tourists.
- Over crowding in the places of community facilities, shopping centres and transportation points causing inconvenience to the residents.
- Resentment by local people if the migrant worker are brought in greater number to work for the tourist need. When they over stay in those destinations where they are no longer required, it brings cultural conflicts between resident and migrant worker of different cultural background.
- Loss of traditional culture, when sometimes traditional performances based upon dance and music are greatly shortened or changed to the taste of tourists.
- Submergence of local cultural values under the cultural pattern of more affluent tourist's society resulting into a loss of social identity of the tourist destination. Some times it creates wedge and conflicts between different generation of the resident community, when their younger people adopt the cultural trends and lifestyles of tourists without taking into account the financial constraints to the elder generation.
- Conflict between the attitudes of residents and tourists occur when the customs of the two societies widely differ. For example, in churches wearing of shoe is a norm while in Hindu temple it is completely forbidden. However in the context of Garhwal the tourist's coming from abroad even belonging to other religious denomination completely mix up with the

residents of Hindu culture and behave with a great devotion following the cultural norms of the places.

Socio-cultural benefits and costs of tourism are depicted in Chart 1.

Environmental Impacts

The key elements of environmental change connected with tourism development primarily focus on aspects of land and landscape in the built and natural environment (Buhatis and Fletcher, 1995). These physical impacts tend to be the most visually apparent, because the development of tourism. Environmental protection has become a major issue in the recent years. Importantly, tourism as an economic activity has an inevitable effect on the environment, especially at the destination level. Environment is a core feature of the tourist product. Tourists are 'consumers of environment' traveling to producers' locations, the tourist destination, in order to consume the product (Goodall, 1992). However, tourism has responsible for a great number of environmental problems. The major problems arise because the environment is a zero priced public good and subject to excess demand and over utilization (Mathieson and Wall, 1982).

Most of the tourists themselves are becoming increasingly environmentally conscious. The protection, conservation, renovation and transformation of his arrival sites, buildings, heritage and monuments has also been stimulated by tourism activities. In addition, tourism often stimulates the creation of natural parks, man made attractions and marine conservation units.

However, tourism has often been blamed for negative impacts on the environment. The accommodation of increasing tourism demand, especially during the peak tourist period, cannot normally be satisfied by the limited natural resources in a destination. Therefore, a number of problems are generated. The major potential impacts of tourism on the natural environment are illustrated in Chart 2.

Chart 1
Socio-Cultural Benefits and Costs

Benefits	*Costs*
Creates a new medium for social change and multicultural understanding	Physical presence of tourists-saturation, competition for limited resources.
Demonstration effects-encourages adaptation to realities of modern life and works toward improving the host country's environment and lifestyle.	Demonstration effects-inappropriate alien commodities/life-styles; hosts model themselves after tourist behaviour, which is temporary and lacks normal constraints, builds unreasonable economic expectations, youth susceptibility; changes structure of rural life; encourages migration; changes in social structure, roles of women, community cohesion, demographics and institutional membership.
Promotes knowledge and use of language.	Resentments due to expatriate presence - foreign e.g. technology, alien food/drink tastes, foreign managers, specialists, etc.
Improves motivation and conditions necessary for better health disease and sanitation.	Increase in socially disruptive behaviour i.e. crime, prostitution, alcohol and drug congtrol, abuse hawking etc.
Stimulates cultural awareness and exposure through first-hand observation participation (e.g., handicrafts, gastronomy, the arts, history, technology, architecture, social institutions, dress leisure lifestyle, etc.).	Disguised form of colonialism and imperialism - e.g., economic dependency, and multi-national control and manipulation, misuse of local residents.
Opportunity for intercultural communication.	Promotoes immoral behaviour - i.e. sexual liberties, hedonistic behaviour, gambling, loosening of religious traditions.
Renaissance of native craftsmanship, art forms, destinctive lifestyles.	Native language changed or used less.

Contd.

Produces personal benefits for the tourists - i.e. • Psychological • Physical • Interpersonal (between tourists and tourist/hosts). • Cultural • Business and professional development	Tourists induce pollution and transmit disease to the host community.
Provides unlimited opportunities to development authentic attractions, thus enhancing pride in the host's ethnic, artistic and similar cultural origins.	Inappropriate cultural changes - adoption/homogeniztion of 'weak' to 'strong' culture - i..e. strong materialistic, culture and racial drift.
Attracts permanent residents a destination for employment of retirement reasons, thus providing a more stable population base.	Disappearance of traditional art and craft to forms by replacement with mass produced replicas.
	Reduces host culture to commodity status, violates host's cultural rights and creates contrived attractions.
	Promotes cultural arrogance - e.g. manipulate authentic host traditions and events to conform to tourist time schedules, tastes etc.; use of foreign design/furnishing in hotels, restaurants and park spaces.

Source: AFter : Hudman and Howkins (1989).

Chart 2

Some Major Potential Impacts of Tourism on the Natural Environment

Impact Aspect	*Potential Consequences*
Flora and fauna	• Disruption of breeding habits
Species	• Killing of animals through hunting
Composition	• Killing or animals in order to supply goods for the sourvenir trade • Inward or outward migration of animals • Trampling and damge of vegetation by feet and vehicles • Destruction of vegetation through the gathering of wood or plants • Change in extent and/or nature of vegetation cover through clearance or planting to accommodate tourist facilities • Creation of a wildlife reserve/sanctuary or habitat restoration
Pollution	• Water pollution through discharge of sewage, spillage of oil/petrol • Air pollution from vehicle emissions, combustion of fuels for heating lighting • Noise pollution from tourist transportation and activities
Erosion	• Compaction of soils causing increased surface run-off and erosion • Change in risk of occurrence of land slips/slides • Change in risk of avalanche occurrence • Damage to geological features (e.g. tors, caves) • Damage to river banks
Natural Resources	• Depletion of ground and surface water supplies • Depletion of fossil fuels to generate energy for tourist activity • Change in risk of occurrence of fire • Depletion of mineral resources for building materials • Over-exploitation of biological resources (e.g. overfishing) • Change in hydrological patterns • Change in land used for primary production
Visual Impact	• Facilities (e.g. building, chairlift, car park) • Litter • Sewage, Algal blooms.

Source: Modified from Green and Hunter (1992).

The visual pollution as environmental impact of tourism may result from several sources (Inskeep, 1991) :

- Poorly designed hotels and other tourist facility buildings that are not compatible with the local architectural style and scale or well integrated into the natural environment;
- Use of unsuitable building materials on external surfaces;
- Badly planned layout of tourist facilities;
- Inadequate or inappropriate landscaping;
- Use of large and adventuring signs;
- Overhead utility lines and poles;
- Obstruction of scenic view by development and
- Poor maintenance of buildings and landscaping.

Tourism has in many places provided both the means and justification for the conservation of our built or man made heritage. Tourism has helped (Godfrey and Clarke, 2000) :

- To stimulate funds for, and the practice of, conservation and rehabilitation of historical buildings, sites and monuments all over the world;
- Reestablish and present individual buildings and places of important events to reflect their former significance;
- Encourage the regeneration, redevelopment and landscaping of town and city districts which no longer serve their original functions having become derelict or rundown;
- The renovation of many redundant industrial and commercial sites into new shops and services, visitor attractions, hotels, apartments and exhibition space which would not likely exist if it were not for the tourist interest;
- Lead to a renewed interest in transport systems and infrastructure from an earlier era, railways, trams, and river boats, both as on attraction in themselves and as an actual means of transport;

- The creation of 'development control' policies legislation, designed to provide a more active approach to maintaining environmental quality when new tourism development takes place.

However, the lack of planning or a strategic approach to the development of tourism has caused (Godfrey and Clarke, 2000) :

- Problems of architectural pollution, where new buildings are somewhat at old with the original character of an area;
- The creation of 'strip' or 'ribbon development' and urban sprawl particularly on the approach or access to destination areas;
- The training of local service infrastructure, causing breakdown in the supply of fresh water, sewerage systems and electricity;
- Traffic congestion and parking problems leading to local aggravation, noise and environmental damage.

The summary of selected impact of tourism on mountain environment is illustrated in Chart 3. These impacts are ecological, environmental, socio-cultural and economic.

Krippendrof has proposes 10 principles for achieving a tourism development in harmony with nature (Lancquer, 1990):

- Recognize the need to take action;
- Support weak element/destinations/communities
- Set the objectives of development in a restive way;
- Exercise control over property and land and pursue on active policy towards land ownership and land development;
- Adopt a policy of restrictions on materials and facilities according to integrated objectives;
- Protect nature and the countryside effectively by managing it dynamically in a way in which nature can evolve primarily;
- Strengthen agriculture and forestry and use as allies;

Chart 3
Summary of Selected Impact of Tourism on Mountain Environments

Negative Impact

Ecological/Environmental	*Socio-cultural*	*Economic*
Destruction of • Forests (Energy) • Fauna (poaching) • Grazing land (camping) *Pollution* • Water • Air • Noise • Trash, garbage, etc. trails *Degradation of* • Landscape • Scenic appeal • Promotional of throwaway mentality • Congestion/overburdening • Hygiene problems	• Cultural loss • Alienation • Xenophobia • Vandalism • Selling antiques • Imitation of western culture *Changes* • Lifestyles • Native architecture • Settlement pattern • Folk traditions • Customs *Promotes* • Moral laxity • Crime/gambling • Prostitution • Beggar mentality *Disturbs* • Religious practices • Indigenous style • Social cohesion • Promotes neocolonialism	*Encourages* • Inflationary trends • Conspicuous consumption • Demonstration effect • Impact for tourism/ leakages • Privileged treatment of tourists • Withdraws labour • Overburdened communal services • Uneven economic development • Tourist enclaves • Seasonal dependence • Dependence on tourism • External domination (city) • Drug addiction • Inferiority (local)

Contd.

Positive Impacts

Ecological/Environmental	*Socio-cultural*	*Economic*
Encourage • Ecological awareness • Conservation Measures • Measures to hold pollution • Cleanliness in campgrounds /parks/trails/woodlands *Help* • Maintenance of scenic landscape • Retreat from marginal hillside farming	*Preserves* • Cultural monuments • Folk traditions • Cultural properties • Art or history *Responsible* • Tourist • Space organization • Urbanization • Increased communication • Modernization of facilities *Encourages* • Education • Training of craftsmen/ expedition • Rediscovery of lost traditions • Fund mobilization	*Creates* • Job opportunities • Foreign exchange • Additional income/tax • Better multiplier effect • Diversification of economy • Jobs for unskilled/ semi-skilled *Improves* • Infrastructure • Local afts/crafts • Regional development • Standards of living • Contract with outside work • Speedy knowledge

Source: Singh, T.V. The Kulu Valley : Impact of Tourism Development in the Mountain Areas. Study Supported by ICIMOD; Himalayan Books, 1989.

- Widen the range of economic activities;
- Help pressure local architecture, traditions and cultural and folk heritage;
- Put tourism marketing and promotion at the service of integration.

The possible mitigation of negative impacts of tourism are depicted in Chart 4. Overall strategic planning and management of tourism resources can mitigate the negative impacts of tourism.

Chart 4
Managing Negative Impacts

Factor Involved	*Negative Impact on Environmental Quality*	*Possible Mitigation or Corrective Action*
Overcrowding	• environmental stress on humans • changes in animal behaviour	• limit visitor access • expand carrying capacity in wildlife areas • disperse visitors to other areas and attractions
Overdevelpment	• creation of rural slums • habitat loss • destruction of vegetation • land scars and watershed interference • nesthetic impact of power lines	• upgrade and rehabilitate • apply land use planning and zoing regulations • conduct awareness campaign • establish regulations • limit visitor access
Noise pollution	• irritation to wildlife, local residents and visitors	• conduct awareness campaign • establish regulations
Litter	• wildlife depends upon garbage • aesthetic clutter • health hazards	• provide litter containers at appropriate places • conduct awareness campaigns • establish regulations • increase surveillance
Vandalism	• multilation and destruction of facilities • loss of irreplaceable historic and cultural treasures	
Overcrowded roads Off-road driving	• environmental stress to humans and animals • Soil, vegetation and wildlife damage	• increase availability of public transportation • limit access • establish or improve enforcement regulations
Fishing	• competition with natural predators • resource depletion	• restrict access • implement environmental education programme

Source: Nigam, Devesh, 2002.

References

Archer, Z. & Fletcher, J. (1990), Tourism : Its Economic Importance in Handbook of Tourism by (Ed.) Miles Quest, McMillion Press, London.

Brown, Frances (2000), Tourism Reassessed: Bright or Blessings? Butterworth, New Delhi.

Buhalis, D., and Fletcher, J. (1995), Environmental Impacts on Tourist Destinations: An Economic Analysis, in Sustainable Tourism Development by Coccossis and Nijikamp (Ed.), Avanbury Astgate Pub. Ltd., London.

Christopher, H. (2000), The Business of Tourism, Longman, London.

Godfrey, K. & Clarke, J. (2000), Tourism Development Handbook, Casell, New York.

Goodall, B. (1992), Environmental Auditing for Tourism, in Cooper, C. and Lackwood, A. (Ed.) Progress in Tourism, Recreation and Hospitality Management, Vol. 4 (London) .

Inskeep, E. (1991), Tourism Planning : An Integrated and Sustainable Development Approaches, Van Nostrand, New York.

Krippendrof, J. (1987), The Holiday Makers: Understanding the Impact of Leisure and Travel, Heinemann, London.

Lanquer, R. (1990), Integration of the Environment in Tourism Planning for the Meditererrarian Coast, Tourism Reports, Vol. 2.

Mathieson, A & Wall, G. (1982), Tourism : Economic, Physical and Social Impacts, Longman, London.

Nigam, Devesh (2002), Tourism Environment and Development of Garhwal Himayala, Mittal Pub. Delhi.

6

Tourism Profile of Karnataka

The Karnataka State, a region inhabited predominantly by Kannada speaking people, is situated in the west-central part of peninsular India. It consists of a narrow elongated belt between the Arabian sea and the Western Ghats with strikingly exquisite and enchanting coastline of about 400 km., the hilly track of Western Ghats with its magnificent ranges of scenic beauty and ever-green forests, a broad undulating terrain in the south, the tank country of Karnataka representing the core of erstwhile Mysore state and a broad but less undulating country in the north covering with a landscape of monotonous, seemingly endless crystalline plateau with black and rich cotton soil and large open treeless fields. The contrast between the coastal plain and the central plateau is striking. The eastern part of Karnataka is in general, a rolling plateau which is traversed by several isolated ridges and a series of quaint, awe-inspiring rockey out corps and gigantic boulders giving rise to a aerie atmosphere. Several chains of hills running chiefly north and south subdivide the whole country into numerous valleys with differing shapes and sizes.

Karnataka, called a Karunadu (elevated land) in ancient times. The course of Karnataka's history and culture takes us back to prehistoric times. The earliest find of the Stone Age period in India was a land axe at King Asugur in Raichur district. The Ashoka's rock edicts found in the state indicate that major parts of Northern Karnataka were under the

Mauryas Chandra Gupta Maurya, the great Indian emperor abdicated the throne and embraced Jainism at Shravanabelagola. The Hoysala's who ruled from the 11th to the 13th century chiseled their way into the pages of glory by building more than 150 temples, each one is a master piece in its own way. Vijayanagara, the greatest of all medieval Hindu empires and one of the greatest the world over, fostered the development of intellectual pursuits and fine arts. "The eye of the pupil has never seen a place like it and the ear of intelligence has never been informed that there existed anything to equal it in the World" is what Abdur Razaaq the Persian ambassador had to say about Krishnadevarya's time.

The Vijayanagara Empire with its capital at Hampi fell a victim to the marauding army of the Deccan Sultan in 1565 A.D. As a consequence of this, Bijapur became the most important city of the region. The Bahmani Shahis and the Adilshahis of Bijapur have played a notable part in the history of Karnataka by their contribution to the field of art and architecture and also by their propagation of Islam in the state. Hyder Ali and his valiant son Tipu Sultan are notable figures in the history of the land. Tipu was a great scholar and lover of literature. Tipu Sultan "Tiger of Karnataka" was killed in 1799 A.D. and the Mysore throne was handed over to Wodeyar's. The new state was named as new Mysore and the Maharaja of Mysore was appointed Governor by Independent India. This unified State was renamed as Karnataka on November 1, 1973.

Location and Boundaries

The Karnataka State is situated between 11° 31′ and 18° 45′ worth latitudes and 74° 12′ and 78° 40′ east longitudes and lies in the west central part of peninsular India. Its maximum length from north to south is about 700 km. and from east to west 400 km. It is bound on the north by Maharashtra State, on the north-west by Goa, on the east by Andhra Pradesh, on the South and south east by Tamil Nadu, on south-west by Kerala and on the west by the Arabian Sea.

Area

Karnataka state covers an area of 1,92,204 Sq.km. or occupies 5.35 percent of the total geographical area of the country. Among the districts of the state, Bijapur occupies the largest area of the geographical area of the State with 8.89 percent and Kodagu district has the smallest area with only 2.14 percent.

Mansoons and Rainfall

The state can well be called the land of two mansoons, because both the south-west and north-east monsoons give the major part of rainfall to the State. There is some, though small, quantity of rainfall in the other two seasons (winter and summer) also. In the coastal region of Dakshina Kannada district, rainfall increased from the cost eastwards towards the Ghats, whereas in the coastal region of Uttara Kannada district, rainfall decreased from the coast eastwards.

Temperature

It is lowest in the beginning of January and increases thereafter gradually at first and rapidly after the middle of February or beginning of March.

Forest

The total forest area of Karnataka state is 36,384.06 sq.km. as against the geographical area of 1,91,791 sq.km. The percentage of forest area to geographical area is 20 as against the all India average of about 23 percent and 33.33 percent prescribed in the National Forest Policy. The Forest Survey of India (FSI) in its state of forests report 1999 says Karnataka has 32,467 sq.km. of forest cover.

The Uttara Kannada district is increasingly losing its forest cover because of the various projects. After 1947, Uttara Kannada district lost about 84,000 hectares of forest land. The district will lose another 1,304 hectares of fores area with the Ankola–Hubli railway line project. In all Rs.260.88 crores worth green trees will be cutdown to pave the way for this railway line.

Rivers

Karnataka is blessed with water wealth in its numerous rivers and streams and to a limited extent in its groundwater. The rivers of the coastal belt are west-flowing. The Sharavati, the Kalinadi, the Netravati, the Varahi, the Bedti(Gangavali) and the Aghanashini are the more important rivers all of which have considerable hydro-electrical potential.

Coastal Region

The coastline has a length of about 400 km. and there is a gradual transition between the Konkan coast in the north and the Kerala coast in the south. The coastal region is further broken into three districts Uttara Kannada, Udupi and Dakshina Kannada. Near South of Karwar, the crest of the Ghats breaks down before rising to over 1800 metres at Kudremukh. The valleys are deep gorges and are three to five Kilometers broad and over 300 km. deep. The most spectacular water falls with a straight leap of 220 metres, is on the Sharavati river.

Language

One of the three coastal district of the state, Dakshina Kannada whose people are industrious and enterprising, enjoys a more vibrant economy than the other part of the Kanara coast-Uttara Kannada and Udupi, a major part of which is under forest than any other districts with the native tongue of a large of people in the district being Tulu and Kannada.

Jainism

A part from the district especially Udupi is being the bastion of Dwaitha Philosophy. It was also under the influence of Jainism, which flourished for long. For people from the Jain community the Jaina Basadis at Moodabidre popularly known as Jain Kaashi have been a top draw. History goes to state that Jainism was introduced in South Kanara in the 9th century. Many part of the undivided Dakshina Kannada particularly Karkala, Venoor, Moodabidri which combined together is referred to as the Jain Kashi.

Christianity

The contribution by Jesuits have impacted Dakshina Kannada too and left an indelible mark on the culture of this region. The beautiful paintings on the walls and ceiling of the St. Aloysius College Chapel have been declared a national monument and attract tourist from distant lands. The St. Lawrence Church near Karkala is regarded by the local people as a healing centre.

Islam

The influence of Islam is obvious in coastal region and especially in Dakshina Kannada too and one of the famous places that pilgrims flock is the Syed Madani Darga at Ullal, 13 kms. from Mangalore.

Banking

The outstanding contribution of coastal regions to the banking industry and its pioneering efforts to build the beedi, tiles and cashew units are a testimony to the enterprising nature of the people. The Dakshina Kannada district got its first branch of a modern bank through the Presidency Bank of Madras in 1868.

Territorial Changes

The erstwhile State of Mysore came into being in 1799A.D. after the fall of Tipu. In 1881, it consisted of seven districts only, viz., Bangalore, Mysore, Kolar, Kadur, Tumkur, Chitradurga and Shimoga. In 1886, Hassan was carved out as the eighth district with seven taluks and in 1939, Mandya, the ninth district of the State with seven taluks. In 1950, there was an exchange of enclave areas between the old State of Mysore and the then province of Madras under the Provinces and State (Absorption of Enclaves) Order, 1950 and these exchanges resulted in an increase in the area of the State from 76,296 sq.km. (28,458 sq. miles) to 76,376 sq. km. (29,489 sq.miles).

FAUNA

Karnataka has a rich and most colourful heritage in respect of wild life. It is favourable location for species of large and small animals, including large vertebrates. The natural distribution of animals, especially of mammals, is governed by vegetation. Animals as hetrotrophs depend upon primary production which should be able to maintain a biotic diversity in the ecosystem. A study of the feed-potential in the various vegetation types reveals that ever-green forests are eminently suited to many species of arboreal animals like the monkeys, while the deciduous forests offer a more congenial habitat for the larger herbivores, such as the gaur, the elephant and the deer. Bats are flying mammals and can be easily identified. The Indian fruit bat or flying fox is destructive to garden fruits. The insectivorous bats like Pipistrella are rapid fliers and play a useful role in insect control. A species like the antelope which can withstand drought considerably is suited for open-dry scrub forests. Our forests and their fauna can be a perennial source of inspiration and can considerably boost tourist traffic. The forests in the State offer good habitat for larger grazing animals like the gaur and the deer.

Karnataka's Coastal Circuit

Karnataka has everything that a tourist loves. The state has historical treasures, ancient sculptures, unspoilt beaches, hill stations, wild life, pilgrim centres, adventure sports, silks, antiques, handicrafts and pubs.

Karavali or coastal Karnataka stretches along the length of Uttara Kannada, Udupi and Dakshina Kannada districts from Karwar in the north to Mangalore in the south. A fertile belt, sheltered by the Western Ghats on the east and bounded by the Arabian Sea on the west, Karavali is a paradise of unspoilt beaches. Warm blue seas fast flowing rivers green forests, colourful rituals and the buoyant Yakshagana dance form.

Tourist Desintations

Bangalore

The capital city of Karnataka is a veritable melting pot of various races and cultures. The Garden city has well-laid out parks, gardens, long avenues of blossoming trees and salubrious climate. Emerging as the hi-tech capital of India, it still retains a charm that is totally Indian. Founded in 1537 by a local Chieftain Kempe Gowda, Bangalore has changed dramatically over the years. There are numerous 'not-to-be-missed' sights in Bangalore like the magnificent Vidhana Soudha, Sprawling Cubbon Park, Colourful Lalbagh etc. and the convenient and exciting way to explore these sights is to take the KSTDC conducted Bangalore Sight-seeing tour.

Biligiri Hills

120 kms from Mysore and 247 kms. from Bangalore, the Bilgirirangana range of hills are picturesquely situated between the Cauvery and Kapila rivers. At a height of 5,091 feet above sea level, this hill stretches from north to south for about 16 kms. All rounds are deciduous trees. A roaming amidst the long grass and tall tress are animals. Plenty of them! So if you are looking for a cool time with a little bit of wild excitement thrown in welcome to B.R. Hills. Wake up to the chirping of birds and humming of bees. Breathe in fresh, clean air. Take a stroll through the sylvan surroundings. And let the cool breeze blow your cares away.

Kemmanagundi

215 kms. from Bangalore is Chickmangalur town 55 kms. North from Chickmangalur town is Kemmanagundi, a scenic hill station on the Baba Budan range of hills. It is also called K.R. Hills after Wodeyar King, Krishnaraja Wodeyar who had made it his favourite summer camp. Kemmangundi at a height of 1,434 meters, is surrounded by thick forests and a salubrious climate the year.

Kudremukh

95 kms. from south-west of Chickmangalur town is KUDRE-MUKH (Horse face) range, so named because of the unique shape of the kudremukh peak. Overlooking the Arabian Sea the broad Hills are chained to one another with deep valley and steep precipices Situated at 1,894.3 meters above sea level,

Kudremukh is rich in iron ore deposits. The Kudremukh Iron ore company conducts mining operations, benefaction and transportation of the ore as slurry through pipelines to the post at Panambar near Mangalore.

Madikeri

Mdikeri is the district headquarters of Kodago (formerly Coorg). Dubbed as the Scottland of India, Kodagul is the home of the colourful robust martial race–the Kodavas. Said to be the descendants of the Greeks (Alexander's soldiers), the Kodavas are fiercely independent. They were never conquered by either Tipu sultan neither the British. And so on this day all Kodavas retain the privilege of carrying firearms without a license. Kodagu is famous for the generals it has produced for the Indian Army. The women are known for their beauty.

Nandi Hills

It is 65 kms. from Bangalore and 1,478 meters above sea level is Bangalore's own hill station. It was Tipu Sultan's summer retreat and Tipu's fort walls still stand as testimony to history. The rivers Pennar, Palar and Arkavati originate from these hills. A flight of 1175 steps lead from the base of the hills to the top. a popular hill resort of the Bangaloreans. The Tipu's Drop, a 600 meter high cliff, where prisoners were hurled down the precipice is an awe-inspiring sight.

Jog falls

The most thrilling spectacle in the entire western region of Karnataka is the Jog Falls. It is situated at a distance of 100 km. from Shimoga. The wondrous sight is that of the river Sharavathi taking a spectacular leap into the Chasm from a height of 900 ft. to form the highest waterfalls in India. The river Sharavathi hurtles in 4 distinct cascades is the 'Rocket', Roarer, Raja and Rani.

Achakanya Falls

It is a small fall in Hosanagar Taluk. The river Sharavathi takes a spectacular leap here.

Abbe Falls

Venake-Abbe, a small waterfall, 4 kms. away from Agumbe is an ideal picnic spot and the serene surrounding is a flourishing brush stroke to an already rich picturesque frame.

Bhadra Dam

The dam, which is constructed across the river Bhadra is 194 ft. in height. Adjacent to the dam is the electricity generating station. Aqua farms have been set up near the dam.

Bhadravathi

The Lakshminarasimha temple, built by the Hoysalas in the heart of the town and the Rameshwara temple built on the banks of the river Tunga attract pilgrims from all parts of Karnataka and other states. Also famous is the sacred Heart Church, built in Roman Gothic style and considered to be the Second tallest church in India, 18,000 sq. ft. with prayer hall which can accommodate 5,000 people. It is also the most prominent Industrial centre in Shimoga district. The renowned sir M. Vishweshwaraiah Iron and Steel factory, the Mysore Paper Mills and Sugar Factories were harbingers of Karnatak's industrial development.

Bijapur

The Chalukyan Rulers of Kalyana laid the foundation of Bijapur City, naming it "Vijayapura" or "City of victory". Bijapur came under Muslim influence, first under Allauddin Khilji, Sultan of Delhi and then under the Bahmani Rulers of Bidar in 1347. Yusuf Adil Shah, Governor of Bijapur in 1481, declared his independence in 1489, establishing the Adil Shahi dynansty.

Archaeological Museum

Located in the building in front of Gol Gumbaz, the museum preserves arts from the Chalukyan as well as Adil Shahi periods.

Gol Gumbaz

Dominating the Sky line of Bijapur city for miles around is the Gol Gumbaz, of the Indian(1626-1656) as a mausoleum for himself, it boasts of the second largest dome in the world, after St. Peter's at Rome. A square hall, 205 ft. in length and breadth is enclosed by four lofty walls rising to a height of 100 feet, buttressed by octagonal towers, surmounted by a hemispherical dome on a petal led base.

Mehtar Mahal

An ornamental gateway, leading to a mosque and garden. Mehtar Mahal is a small, beautiful monument built by Ibrahim Adil Shah.

Jod Gumbaz

The twin domes of the Jod Gumbaz, built on an elevation by Aurangzeb are tombs of Khan Mohammed who betrayed the Sultan and Khawaskhan, who betrayed Sikandar during the time of Ali-II.

Siddeshwara Temple

This temple, housing the deity of Siddeshwara (Shiva) draws thousands of devotees.

Sri Prasanna Ganesha Temple

This is new temple that has carvings by Shyama Ramachar, a national award winning sculptor of Karkala.

Bagalkot

Bagalkot earlier a part of Bijapur district, was carved out as a separate district in 1997. This area is home to some of the finest examples of temple architecture in the world.

Aihole

Aihole was the capital of the Chalukyan kings, between the 4th and 6th century A.D. You will see Hindu temple architecture in its embryonic stage from simple shrines, like those in the Konthigudi group and the Lad Khan temple to the more complex edifices, such as the Meguthi temple. The oldest temple here is perhaps the Lad Khan dating back to the 5th Century A.D. The Hutchamalli temple, the Ravalphadi Cave temple, the Konthi temple complex, the Jain Meghuthi temple and Buddhist temple are the sites worth visiting.

Pattadakal

Twenty two km from Aihole, on the left bank of the Malaprabha river is Pattadakal, second capital of the Chalukyas, used mainly for coronations of Kings. Pattadakal, declared by UNESCO as a World Heritage Site was an experimentation ground for temple architecture. One therefore see two main types of temple architecture side by side. On the one hand you see the curvilinear (Spires) of the Kashivishweshwara, Jambulinga and Galaganatha temples. On the other side you see the temples of Mallikarjuna, Saugameshwar and Virupaksha with their square roofs and receding tiers.

Ilkal

Thirteen km. from Hungud, this town is an important commercial centre. It is famous for its hand-woven Ilkal sarees and a variety of red granite. The Venkateshwara and Shankarlings temples and the Vijaya Mahanthesha Math draw many visitors.

Hassan

Hassan is 180 km. from Bangalore and a useful transit point if you are visiting Belur, Halebid and Shravanbelagola. Hassan district which adjoins the north western region has a scenic skyline with grasslands, wide stretches of woods and coffee plantations. The mercury reading on climate says "cool" for most of the year.

Sharavanbelagola

Shravanbelgola town is a renowned centre of Jain pilgrimage and abounds in monuments. What put Shravanbelagola on the tourist map was the gigantic statue of gomateshwara–a Jain Saint and an idol of worship for centuries. The symmetry in stone was created around 983 AD. by Chamundaraya a General and Minister of the Ganga King, Rachamatta. The 17 meter 1000 year old statue is among the tallest and most graceful sculptures in the world. A flight of 600 steps cut into the rocky surface of Indragiri hill elevates you right up to the foot of the statue.

Dattatreya Peetha

Situated on the Baba Budan Giri is the Dattatreya Peetha venerated by Hindus and Muslims alike. A laterite cave here is believed to have been sanctified by the residence of Dattatreya Swamy as well as Hazarat Dada Hayat Mir Khalnder. The worship is led by a Fakir. Annual jatra/Urus is celebrated by both Muslims and Hindus with great aplomb.

Sringeri

A charming town on the banks of river Tunga, 90 km.s west of Chikmagalur town is one of the most celebrated pilgrimage centres in Karnataka with epic associations. Named after Rishyashringa from Ramayana. Adi Shankaracharya established the Sharda Peeta and propogated advaitha, the philosophy of non-dualism. Sureshwacharya was the first head of the peeta. Shankaracharya installed an image of Sharda Devi made of Sandalwood which was replaced with a golden replica in the 14th century.

Hampi

It is situated on the banks of the river Tungabhadra in the region of Bellary, is a vast site of monuments and ruins, a mute witness to an er of glories, triumphs and tragedies. The ruins of Hampi are so majestic and imposing that they leave the visitor totally dumb founded, awestruck and humbled.

Founded by Hukka (also called Harihara) and Bukka in 1336, the famous capital of the kings of Vijayanagara has now become the focal point as it attracts attention and great admiration of a arthitects,historians and archeologist and of course the innumerable tourists who visit these monuments from all over the world.

Vidhana Soudha

A magnificent building of the Neo-Dravidian style, houses the state Legislature. It was conceived and executed by Kengal Hanumanthaiah, the former Chief Minister of Karnataka in 1956.

Cubbon Park

This beautiful park which spreads over 300 acres in the heart of the city, serves as the lung space of the evergrowing Bangalore city. Designed by Lt.General Sir Mark cubbon in 1864 is dotted with beautiful statues, flowering trees, fountains and a library in its midst.

Vishveshwaraya Industrial & Technological Museum

This museum is a tribute to Sir M. Vishweswaraiah the Architect of modern Kanrnataka, a must see for students and Science buffs, which presents the amazing wealth of modern science.

Tipu Sultan's Fort and Palace

A very small portion of the mud fort built by Hyder Ali and his son Tipu Sultan, stands to this day, which is far cry from the originl. But the summer Palace of the great hero, Tipu sultan, built in wood and ornately decorated, remains untouched by the vagaries of time.

Bannerghatta National Park

Located appropriately 22 kms. away from Bangalore, this park has a mini zoo, Elephant ride, Lion and tiger Safari and Corcodile farm.

Community Lift

The Hindus have several religious holidays, occasions of festivals and fasts throughout the year while all Hindus have a few common festivals, some sections have their own exclusive ones, the Brahamans claiming many more than the rest. The two seasons into which the year is equally divided are Uttarayana and Dakshinayana. The following is a chronological enumeration of more important festivals, and of holy days observed by different sections of Hindus in the State.

Yagadi, the first day of Chaitra month, is the New Year day of Shalivahana Shaka and is observed by all castes. The day is considered as one of the most auspicious days in the year. On this day, the priest reads the New Year's Panchanga or the Hindu almanac. Ramanavami, the ninth day of Chaitra is celebrated as the birthday of God Rama, the seventh incarnation of Vishnu. Devotional musical programmes Harikathas and cultural programmes are the special additional recent features during the festival arranged by several Sri Rama Seva Mandalis which are voluntary bodies. The festival in these cases is held for a month or so. Hanuma Jayanti, the birthday of Hanuman is observed on the full moon day of Chaitra in north Karnataka area.

On every third or fourth in the month of Vaishakha of each year, a special festival is held in honour of Goddesses Dynamavva and Durgavva (village deities) in several rural places of Belgaum area. During the festivals of village Deities, the Kodavas Kodagu has special dances in the temples. The performers who are in their national costume form a ring, in the centre of which stand the musicians. A song on God Mahadeva is sung.

Basava Jayanti (Akshayatritiya) the birthday of Basaveshwara who led momentous Sharana(Veerashaiva) movement is celebrated on the third day o Vaishakha Sudhh (Rohini nakshtra). Now-a-days the festival is taking a social turn and lectures on the life and teachings of Basaveshwara and other social and cultural programmes are arranged. On the day of Basava Jayanti, the Lingayats of certain parts of the State visit Basavakalayna, Kudala Sangam, Basava Bagewadi and other places, to pay homage to him.

Shankara Jayanti is conducted for 5 days from Vaishakha Suddha Padyami with Shankara Vijaya Parayana (recitation) at sharada Peetham, Sringeri and other places. Akshayatritiya, the third lunar day of Vaisakha is considered as one of the luckiest days of the year. Most of the cultivators start their spade work on this day and in general people begin on this day anything new they wish to do.

Narasimha Jayanti, the full moon day of Vaisakha is observed as the birth day of god Narasimha, the fourth incarnation of Vishnu by a section of Brahmans. Kara Hunnime is the full moon day of Jyeshta. It is celebrated in all pomp by cultivating class of North Karnataka area. Ashadha Ekadashi, the eleventh day of the bright half of Ashadha is observed by several sections of Hindus. If some sections fast on that day others feast. Many devotees visit Pandharapur in Maharashtra on the day.

On all Mondays in the month of Sharavana, religious-minded Hindus fast part-time and enjoy a feast in the evening. Nagapachami, the fifth day of Sharavana is one of the important festivals observed by almost all sections. The serpent in the form of stone or earthen images is worshipped. Gokulashtami, the eighth day of the dark fortnight of Sharvana, the birthday of Krishna is observed by Hindus, as a day of fast. An idol of Him is worshipped. The whole night is often spent in singing devotional songs.

Ganesh Chaturthi is one of the popular festivals falling on the fourth day of the birght half of Bhadrapada. It is the festival which lasts for one, three five or 11 days and during which Ganesha is worshipped. The schools, colleges and several voluntary associations of the Staste organize Ganesha festival on a large scale with music, Harikatha, cultural programmes and lectures.

Navaratri or Dasara is one of the most important festivals and it being has now-a-days assumed importance as Nadahabba. Literary and cultural programmes are arranged throughout Karnataka. It is observed in Karnataka from the days of the Puranas and nowhere else is this ancient ritualistic festival held so scrupulously and elaborately and with such pomp and splendour as in Mysore City. During Dasara dolls' display in homes is an expression of joy. In Dakshina Kannada people impersonate as tiger, bear, etc. and dance. Other kinds of impersonation to entertain people are common. It takes the shape of a fancy dress festival for nine days. Throughout the nine days, Chamudeshwari is worshipped in the Mysore Palace. On the seventh day, Sharada Puja is performed. People worship books in their houses on the day. Sharada Puja is observed in educational institutions too of the State. Durgashtami and Mahanavami are also observed. On the Ayudha Puja day (ninth day) household utensils, writing materials, domestic animals, agricultural implements, vehicles, tools, machineries, etc. are worshipped.

At Mysore, on Vijayadashmi (the victorious tenth) day a colourful procession is taken. It contains tableaux giving the spectators a thrilling glimpse of historical episodes. In the evening the statue of Goddess Bhuvaneshwari is taken in procession on the tastefully caparisoned elephant,

Suggi Habba (harvest festival) is popularly celebrated for 10 days in about April and May in the rural parts of Chikamagalur district. The main deities worshipped are Parvati, Shiva and Kumaraswami. Kumbars officiate as priests during the festival. Kolata, Salu-kunita, Suttu-kunita, Bete-kumita and Raja-kumita are some of the dances performed during this festivity. Fire walking is also practiced during this festival.

Udupi-Location and Area

Udupi is one of the smallest districts in the state and is located in the western belt. Being a coastal district, the Arabian sea forms the natural boundary on the west. It is bound on the north by Uttara Kannada district, on the north east and east by the districts of shimoga and Chikmangalur on the south east and south by its parent district i.e. Dakshi Kannada dist. and on the west by the Arabian Sea. Total area of this district is 3852 sq.km. and the district Head Quarters is located at Udupi town.

History

The district of Udupi came into existence on 15th August,1997 while carving out this new district the Dakshin Kannada district was bifurcated and as a result of the said division, three taluks namely Karkal, Kundasur and Udupi were detached from the Dakshin Kannada district to form the present Udupi district. After the creation of this new district, all the said three taluks were kept under the administrative control of Kundpura sub-division.

They are comprising the present district formed a composite district known as Kanara and belonged to the Madras presidency. The bifurcation took place in 1860 and in 1862 while South Kanara was retained in the Madras presidency. North Kanara was transferred to the Bombay Presidency. This name remained unaltered till 1977 even though the country and the state there in witnessed tremendous changes in the politico-administrative sphere. In January, 1977 the name of the district was changed to Dakshin Kannada. This change does not, however, implay any material alteration. The area of Dakshin Kanada remained unchanged till the year 1997 when this was bifurcated and formed yet another district.

The coastal district of Udupi, with its palm fringed coastline dotted with bays and estuaries, sheltered by the soaring Western Ghats, is studded with spots of great scenic beauty. It has aptly been described by Sarojini Naidu, India's eminent poetess, as "Nandanavana", "Garden of Pleasure." It is also renowned for its pilgrimage centres, as well as its literary traditions and rich cultural heritage.

It was ruled, since the early period of the Christian era, till the end of the 14th century, by the Alupa Kings. From the 14th to 16th centuries the area came under the governance of the Vijayanagar dynasty. But the strongest influence was that of the Portuguese, who arrived on the coast in the 15th century. Haider and Tipu Sultan held sway until 1799 when the British forces defeated Tipu Sultan. The district is well known for its fabulous costumed, musical dance drama form, Yakshagana and Kambala-Buffalo Race, a sport popular among the community of cultivators of wetlands.

Languages and Religion

Main language spoken in the district is Kannada. The other languages spoken in the district are Malayalam, Konkani, and Hindi but speaker of these languages is less in comparison to Kannada.

Geography and Physical Features

The district comprises a long strip of territory running parallel to the west coast and it is endowed with a coastal line. The coastline is low and sandy and is indented by numerous bays and creeks which have been formed by river estuaries. The landscape forms a broken low plateau spreading out from the foot of the western ghats towards the Arbian Sea and is characterized by several water courses and numerous valleys contining rich alluvial soils.

Rivers, Canals and Water ways

Gangolli, Situanadi and Swarna are the main rivers of this district. Gangolli River is formed by the union of several streams such as Kollur, Haladi, Chakra etc. which is rather small from the point of view of distance covered but carry large quantities of water drained from the mountain ranges. This river is joined by other smaller streams enroute and finally forms a broad estuary to the north of Kundapura town. Sitanadi and Swarnanadi originate in the hills situated respectively in the north eastern and the south eastern covers of Udupi taluk.

Towns Villages and Amenities

The district is comprised of one sub-division and three taluks. It has 13 towns and 277 villages. Community development blocks are coterminus with taluks in jurisdiction but exclude the statutory towns.

Udupi District's Places of Interest

Udupi

Located 60 km north of Mangalore, Udupi is one of the most sacred sports in India, visited by pilgrims from all over the country. The importance of the place dates from the time of Madhwacharya the 13th century religious leader, who is said to have founded the temple and placed the image of Krishna in it. Madhavachary lived and preached here and established eight mutts in the area. The eight mutts take turn in administering the temple and the famous "Parayya Festival" held once in two years in January, marks the handing over ritual. It is colourful spectacle drawing thousands of pilgrims from far and wide.

Malpe

7 km. West of Udupi at the month of the Malpe river is the natural harbour of Malpe, an important port on the Karnataka coast, with a fine beach. It is also an important fishing centre. Malpe has the Balarama temple as well as the oldest tile factory set up by the Basel Mission.

St. Mary's Island

Close to Malpe, this island is said to be the site where Vasco Da Gama first landed in India, which he called "El Padron de Santa Mria". The island is noted for its unique basalt rock formations and is a popular excursion for locals and day-trippers.

Manipal

Located 5 kms. to the east of Udupi, Manipal is today an important, progressive educational and medical centre. The Academy of education, founded in 1942 runs the numerous education institutions. Manipal has a modern temple dedicated to Venugopalkrishna, whose structure has features of a Church and a mosque. The M.G.M. College here has an institute of Yakshagana, a musical dance, drama form, with elaborate colourful costumes.

Udyawara

Located 5 kms. north west of Udupi Udyawara was the seat of the ruler of Alupa , about the 8th century. The Palace and Fort area contain some of the earliest monuments of the district. The Bhairava Temple built on a large rock, containing ten pillars is the main attraction.

Barkur

About 16 kms. north of Udupi, Barkur was once the capital of the Alupa Rulers and a province of the Vijayanagar Empire.

Remnants of the two forts built by these rulers are still visible. Amongst the many temples built over the years are the Panchalingeshwara Temple, Bette vinayaka Temple and the Ganapathi Shrine of Mudukeri.

Saligrama

20 kms north of Udupi, this has been a religious and cultural centre for a long time. The temple of Yoga Narasimha is believed to be 1000 years old.

Kollur

80 kms. north of Udupi, the Mookambika temple located at the foothills of the Kodachari Hills, is one of the most important centers of Shakti worship in South India. Adi Shankaracharya is said to have consecrated the deity, Mookambika, Slayer of the demon, Mookasura on a Sri Chakra, which is installed in a copper roofed, gold crested temple that is said to be 1000 years old.

Kodachadri Hills

These hills (4411 ft.) constitute one of the largest forest areas in Karnataka and part of this region is designated as the Mookambika Nature Reserve. Kollur is an ideal base to explore the hills. The Mookambika Nature Camp, a park 4 kms. South of Kollur, is a tranquil place, from where one can go on rambles into the forest.

Thrasi

9 kms. to the north of Kundapur, situated near the national highway is a fine beach.

Maravanthe Beach

About 12 kms. north of Kundapur and 50 kms. of Udupi, this is one of the most beautiful spots of the district. A drive along the west coast highway at sunset, bordered by the Arabina Sea on the west and the Sauparnika River to the east, with the Kodachadri Hills in the background, is an unforgettable experience.

Kaup

12 kms. south of Udupi, Kaup has a lovely beach as well as an old 100 ft. light house, that is the guiding star for all navigators.

Karkala

35 kms. south east of Udupi and 52 kms. North-east of Mangalore is Karkala, a important Jain pilgrimage centre. The towering 42 ft. monolith of Gommateshwara, completed in 1432 is the major attraction. The chaturkukha Basadi, completed in 1586, has four identical entries from all sides, life size statues of three Teerthankaras and several smaller images. The Mahamastabhisheka held once in 12 years to Gommateshwara.

Ottinane

40 kms north of Kundapur, 2 kms. from the national highway, this is a scenic spot on a beach to view sunsets.

Padubidri

26 kms. south of Udupi, Padubidri has a Mahalingeshwara Temple, a Mahaganapathi Temple and a Brahasthana. A religious festival called "dakke bali" is held once in two years.

Perduru

20 kms. east of Udupi is an ancient centre with the Sri Anantha Padamanabha Temple. This area is well known for the Yakshagana dance drama form, which is here also known as Perduru Mela. The Vandaru Arasi Kambala (Buffalo Race) held annually on 12th December, is a popular event.

Attur

8 kms. from Karkala is the St Lawrence Church, built in 1845. People from all religious participate in the religious function held every year in January. The village has a fine temple of Mahalingeshwara with a copper plated garbhagriha (sanctum).

Bajagoli

The Jodukere Kambala also known as the Lava Kusha Kambala (Buffalo race) started in 1970 at Bajagoli in Karkala taluk, taken place on the first Sunday of February, every year on the fields of Bettu Gadde, which are 140 meters and 15 meters wide. A modern gallery has been built for spectators.

Dakshin Kannada

Location & Area

It is one of the two coastal districts of the state and is located in the western belt. This area is separated from the rest of the south Indian peninsula by the Western Ghats which form the natural boundary of the district on the east. On the west, the Abrabian Sea forms the natural boundary. On the north the district is bounded by Uttara Kannada district on the north east, east and the south east by the district of Shimoga, Chikmangulur, Hassan and Kodagu, on the south by Kodagu district, on the south west by Cannanore district of Kerala state. The district covers a geographical area of 8441 sq.km. lies between the latitudinal parallels of 12o 27′ N and 13o 35′ E and 75o 40′ E. the district head quarters is located in Mangalore.

History

For more than a century and a quarter in all the official records,the district was known as South Karwar as distinguished from its northern counterpart which was called North Kannada. Both the Kanara districts at one time formed a composite district and belonged to the Madras presidency .The bifurcation took place in 1860 and in 1862 while South Kanara was retained in the Madras Presidency. North Kanara was transferred to the Bombay presidency. This name maintained unalrtered till 1977 and in January 1977 the name of the district was changed as Dakshin Kannada.

Sheltered by the soaring Western Ghats on the east and bordered by the blue waters of the Arabian sea, Dakshina Kannada is blessed with abundant rainfall, fertile soil and lush vegetation. Prestine beaches, picturesque mountain ranges, temple towns and a rich, vibrant culture make it a sought after tourist destination. Dakshina Kannada is well known for

Yakshagana, a fabulous costumed dance drama form and Kambala, the sport of buffalo racing by farmers.

Geography and Physical Features

Geographically, this small district is seen to consist of six natural divisions. The coast line which is low and sandy in indented by numerous bays and creeks has been formed by river estuaries. The landscape forms a broken low plateau spreading out from the foot of the Western Ghats towards the Arabian Sea and is characterized by several water courses and numerous valleys containing rich alluvial soil. The most interesting of the mountains here is the Kudremukh group which consists of three peaks–Mukha Head (1881 meter.) with a magnificent precipice of over 300 meters Midge Point (1883 meters) and the Funk Hill. The other important hills are Kodachadri, Ballalarayana. Durge, Kattegudda, Subrahnmanya and Sisalkal. The slopes of Western Ghats are in particular, clothed with dense vegetation. The chief timber trees are the teak, rose wood, benteak, Karalbhogi matti, marvu and Kada halasia.

Dakshin Kannada's Places of Interest

Mangalore

Located 347 kms. fom Bangalore on the coast, Mangalore, the district head quarters of Dakshina Kannada, has been a trading centre for several centuries. It was, since the early period of the Christian era till the end of the 14th century, the capital of the Alupa Rulers. From the 14th to the 16th centuries the area came under the governance of the Vijaynagar dynasty. Conquered by Hider Ali in 1763, Mangalore became the Chief part of Mysore. When Tipu Sultan's Fort fell in 1799 to the British, they made it the district headquarters of Kanara. With an important port, this once coastal town has become a bustling commercial centre.

Ullal

It is tuated on the south bank of the Netravati River, at a distance of 8 kms. from family of Puttige. The ruins of the area indicate that it was a kingdown ruled with pomp and splendour. Abbakkadevi, a fiery, brave queen of the 17th century is said to have defeated the Portuguese and the Uchil Fort was probably her strong hold. The Somanatha Temple has beautiful sculptures and bears a district Italian influence. The Dargah of Syed Mohammed Shereeful Madani, who is said to have come to Ullal from Madina, 400 years ago is famous. An urus is held once in five years here.

Pilikula Nisarga Dhama

Located 12 kms. from Mangalore, this is an integrated park for tourists. Spread over 300 acres of land the park has a lake with boating facilities, a wild life safari, a mini aquarium and science centre.

Dharmasthala

75 km. east of Mangalore, set in Sylvan surroundings on the lower slopes of the Western Ghats; this well known pilgrimage centre is an interesting amalgam of faiths. The Manjunatha Temple is a prominent Shaivaite Centre that has Madhawa Vishnavaite priests and is administered by a hereditary Jain family, the Heggades. The jain influence can be seen in the 39 ft. statue of Bahuballi, erected in 1980 on the hill near the temple. Charity is a way of life here and pilgrims that throng the temple are given free food and lodging for three days. During the annual festival, Laksha Deepotsave held in November-December and religious discourses held.

Moodabidri

This is an important Jain pilgrim centre, known as the Kashi of Jain pilgrim located 35 kms. north east of Mangalore. The 18 basadis in Moodabidri were built between the 14th and 16thg centuries. The Guru's basadi and the Sri Bhuvana Tilaka Choodamani basadi are the architectural delights. The largest of them is the 15th century Chandranatha Basadi also known as the 1000 pillar basadi, built by Jain devotees, under the direction of Devaraya Wodeyar, Vijayanagar governor of the "Mangalouru Rajya."

Venur

54 kms. from Mangalore is the Venur where 38 ft. high monolith of Bahubali located on an elevated terrace on the south bank of the Gurpur river. Sculpted by Janakacharya the statue was installed by the Jain ruler, Veer Thimanna IV Ajila in 1604.

Kukke Subrahmanya

Nestled between hills, this pilgrim centre, 104 kms. from Mangalore is famous for the temple of kukke Sri Subrahamanya. The epics narrate how the divine serpent Vasuki and other snakes took refuge under God Subrahamanya in the Caves. Here God Subrahmanya is worshipped as a snake which is the god's divine power. A ritual dane called Nagamandala is performed during the worship, where the dancer wears the attire oif Ardhanarishwara (hjalf man, half woman), Symbolising the concept of female (prakruthi) and male (Purusha) forces being one.

Jamalabad

Forty kms. from Mangalore, the Jamalabad Fort was built in 1794 by Tipu Sultan, the Tiger of Mysore, in meory of his mother Jamalbee.

Kateel

20 kms. east of Mangalore, is the Durga Parameshwari Temple, located on an island in Nandini river. The Chief deity is in the form of an udhbhava linga. The pillars of the temple bear beautiful sculpturers.

Mulki

Twenty nine kms. south of Mangalore is the ruined fort and palace of Venkatappa Nayaka Savanth of Bindanur, built in 1608. The Duyrga Parameshwari Temple, Venkataramana Temple and the twin temples of Somnatha and Narayana are well known.

Uppinangadi

48 kms. west of Mangalore at the confluence of the Netravati and the Kumaradhara rivers is the Sahasra Linga, the Thousand Linga Temple. The "Makhi" fair takes place here when thousands come to make offerings to their ancestors.

Uttar Kannada District

Bounded by the Kravali coast to the West, the Deccan Plateau to the East and the Sahyadri ranges of the Western Ghats (Malnad) to the south, Uttara Kannada is a district of immense natural beauty-an eco tourist's paradise. As a tourist destination, Uttara Kannada offers diverse attractions, like pristine beaches, water falls, wild life sanctuaries, scenic views, adventure sports like River Rafting, Mountain Biking, Rock climbing and trekking as well as religious shrines.

Karwar

The district headquarters of Uttara Kannada is a charming port town, situated at the mouth of the Kali River. The Kali river bridge situated at the confluence of the river and the Arbian Sea, dominates the town's landscape. The Sadashivgad Hill Fort with its dargah (tomb) of Peer Shah Shamsuddin Kahrobat and the Naganath Temple are the other attractions of the town. The Baithkola beach on the northern outskirts of Karwar is one of the most beautiful natural beaches of the coast. Nobel Laureate Rabindranath Tagore has described the tranquil beauty of the Karwar Coast thus:

"The sea beach of Karwar is certainly a fit place in which to realise that the beauty of nature is not a mirage of imagination, but reflects the joy of the infinite and thus draws us to lose ourselves in it."

Dev Bagh Beach Resort

Run by the Jungle lodges and Resorts Ltd. This resort can be reached by a 10 minute boat ride from the boat pier next to the kali bridge. Log huts on stilts, set amidst casuarinas groves offer deluxe accommodation to tourists. Swimming off private beaches, beach sports, boat cruises on the river, jungle treks and traditional coastal cuisine ensure an idyllic getaway holiday.

Kudle Beach

This lovely beach can be reached by a 20 minute walk from Gokarna. The track takes you to the top of a barren headland with magnificent sea views and then descends to the curving sandy balance .

Om Beach

Om beach (So named because it resembles the auspicious Om sign) is a near deserted beach, which is accessed by a 20 minute walk over a dirt track near the south end of Kudle beach.

Gokarna

60 Km. south of Karwar, this Coastal town has, among other things, an ancient temple with the Atmalinga. Gokarna is also a famous centre for Sanskrit learning.

Kumta

Seventy km. from Karwar, this town houses the Kumbheshwara temple, earlier known as Kumteshwara. It is well known as a centre for the production of beautiful carved sandalwood handicrafts.

Yana

Set in the midst of green forest, 50 km. from Gokarna and 45 km. from Sirsi are the unique rock formations of Yana. The tiny Shrine of Shiva is an attraction, where a perennial stream bathes the Shiva linga continuously.

Honnavar

This town is an important railhead of the newly constructed Konkan railway that connects this coastline. Six km. from Honnavar are the "Apsara Konda Falls" (Pond of the Celestial Nymphs) set in a picturesque setting and a fine beach that offers glorious sunset. Fifteen km. Away is the well known Ganapathi temple at Idagunji.

Sirsi

It is a tranquil town, dotted with terracotta tiled houses, Jain Basadis and ancient Hindu temples. The 16th Century Marikamba Temple enshrines a wooden deity that is believed to have been found in a tank. The temple has a car festival once in two years.

Banavasi

Capital of the Kadamba Kings who established the first Kannada Empire in 345 A.D. Banavasi town is the site of an annual cultural festival-Kadambotsava held in December.

Siddapura

The waterfalls nearby, known as Unchalli Falls or Keppa Jog or Lushington Falls are worth of a visit.

Dandeli

117 km. fom Karwar and just 75 km. from the railhead Hubli lies Dandeli, gateway to 834 sq.km. Dandeli Game Sanctuary. It is home to rare species of animals like barking deer, sloth bear, civet cat, panther, Flying squirrel and Malabar Squirrel, Woodpeckers and Hornbills are some of the birds sighted. Take in the jungle experience by staying at the Kali Wilderness camp, located on the edge of the Kali River or at the Bison River Resort.

Magod Falls

About 20 km. from Yellapur, is the Magod Falls where the river Bedthi, cascades from a height of 650 ft. into a rocky ravine. Nearby are scenic spots like Jenukallugudda (honey rock hillock) where one can view memorable sunsets and Kavadi kere, a large lake built by Bhima that he is said to have crossed carrying a Kavadi.

Sathodi Falls

26 km from Yllapur this is one of the most picturesque sports in the region.

Attiveri Bird Sanctuary

15 km. From Mundagod is the Attiveri bird Sanctuary, which has a bird life of about 79 species, including migratory birds from 22 countries, best seen between November and March. The Tibetan university near Mundgod offers study and research facilities in Buddhist Philosophy to students from all over the world. The Ayurvedic Dispensary, run by Tibetans is renowned. Also famous are the Tibetan carpets and rugs woven by the community.

Tourism Development in Karnataka

There has been lot of investment from private sector and also lot of changes have taken place ever since the policy came into being. However, many representations about various provisions are received. The following items justify the revision of the policy.

- *Thin Spread of Benefits:* The package of inventive has been thinly spread all over the State. Impact of investments has not been felt in thrust areas identified by the Department, more particularly in Northern parts of Karnataka.
- *Further Investment from the Private Sector Needed:* Lot of facilities is yet to be created. More investment has been there in Southern parts of the State, specially Bangalore, Mysore and surrounding areas. There has been little investment in Northern sector. More investment is required in these areas in addition to the Southern sector. Attractive package of incentives need to be continued.
- *Massive Investment:* During last Tourism Policy, the Department succeded in attracting massive investments of over Rs.900 crores in 280 approved projects. This needs to be continued in order to achieve the goals.
- *Master Plan:* The Department has prepared a master plan that envisages massive investment of Rs.4500 crore (approx.) in tourism sector. Three-fourths of it

is expected from private sector and quarter of it from Government sector.

Definitions of Tourism Service Providers

Tourism Unit: Tourism Units are those units which are commercial establishments open to public in Karnataka providing facilities/services to the tourists and will include the following:

- Accommodation Units including Hotels, Resorts, Dormitories, Choultries, Wayside Facilities, Heritage Hotels etc.
- Wayside facilities with hotel, motel and restaurant and other facilities like telephone, kiosks, toilets, rest spots, parking etc.
- Tourism Resorts
- Amusement Parks and Adventure Sports
- Lakes and River Cruises and House Boats
- Tourist Villages

Hotel : Hotel means a boarding and lodging unit providing a minimum of 40 fully furnished beds in double or single rooms, each attached with sanitary fitted toilets and bathrooms, with adequate dining, reception and public areas or a cluster of huts with similar attached facilities in each hut and located in a tourist resort, each cluster equipped with adequate dining, reception and public areas or a permanently fixed tented tourist camp with all modern amenities including sanitary fitted common bathrooms and toilets, one after every four beds, with adequate dining, reception and public areas or a lodging unit providing a minimum of 40 fully furnished beds in rooms with a capacity from 2 to 6 beds, provided with sanitary fitted bathrooms and toilets, one for six beds with adequate dining, reception and public areas.

Tourist Resorts: Tourist resorts are those units which have 20 double rooms with sanitary fitted toilets and bathrooms and at least any eight or more of the following activities/ facilities/characteristics:

- Health club facilities e.g. sauna bath, Jacuzzi, steam bath, gymnasium, etc.
- Water sports eg. White water rafting, canoeing, kayaking, water skiing, yachting, wind surfing, rowing, pedal boating etc.
- Swimming pool
- Aero sports e.g. power flying, hang gliding, para gliding, para sailing etc/
- Sports like Table Tennis, Tennis, Badminton, Billiards, Bowling Alley
- Golf
- Angling
- Nature cures facilities eg. Naturopathy, Yog, Ayurvedic /Herbal cures
- Beauty parlour including barber shops and massage facilities
- Children's corner including crèche, park, indoor games and other recreational facilities.

Heritage Hotels: Heritage Hotels are hotels run in heritage buildings built prior to 1950 and approved by the Department as per its guidelines.

Amusement Park: Amusement Park means an open area developed for recreational facilities for people of all ages. It should contain various kinds of fun joy rides. It should also contain facilities for entertainment activities permissible under law, magic shows, science fiction(sci-fi) shows, meals, toilets, telecommunication, first-aid, adequate parking, etc. It should also curtain residential accommodation of 10 single or double rooms attached with sanitary fitted toilets and bathrooms.

House Boats: House Boat means a boarding-cum-lodging facility available on a water body such as lake or river system having at least two properly furnished bedrooms with attached sanitary fitted bathrooms and toilets and independent dining and drawing rooms, served by a separate kitchen boat.

Adventure/Recreation Activity Centre: Adventure/ recreation activity centre means a facility for learning as well as undertaking various adventure activities such as rock-climbing, para-sailing hand-gliding, hot air-ballooning, rafting, kayaking, yachting, water skiing, angling, golfing etc. The centre must provide complete technical equipment, expert instructions and rescue arrangements for the activities which it offers. The Activity Centre should be operated in accordance with international safety standards and regulations for these activities. It may provide in-house boarding and lodging facilities for at least 20 persons.

Any registered organization involved exclusively in such adventure activities is eligible for the incentives towards building and infrastructural facilities. The investment subsidy would be 30% subject to a maximum of Rs.30 lakhs. These projects should also have 5 cottages for accommodation.

Tourist Village: The Cultural Heritage Village would have several features, prominent of which are :

- It would attract a large number of tourists, as it would provide those glimpses of the rich heritage and culture of the State.
- It would satisfy their desire to know more about Karnataka in a shortest possible time.
- It will be quite educative for students as well as public.
- It is an innovative idea. If successful, it can be replicated elsewhere in State and country. Karnataka could be a role model in this direction.
- It will have low budget and would have a wealth of information about life style of people, their culture etc.
- Integration of various components like handicrafts, crafts, etc. is possible.
- Sales counters could also be an added advantage.
- This village could also be used as a training centre for people involved in tourism industry.

Choultries: Choultries are boarding units constructed by Muzarai Institutions and Trusts at important pilgrim centres that attract large number of tourists/pilgrims.

Dormitory Accommodation: It is a Boarding and Lodging unit with necessary facilities constructed for tourists.

New Unit

New Unit means a tourism unit which commences execution of the project on or after 1.6.1997 with prior approval in writing of the Director-Tourism, Government of Karnataka.

Eligible Units

Only projects approved by the Department of Tourism after 1.6.1977 and before 31.5.2002 would be eligible for incentives and concessions.

Validity of Existing Incentive Rules

The existing projects and projects under execution will, however, continue to be governed by existing incentive rules sanctioned vide Government Order No. ITY TTT 89 dated 30.5.92. The package of incentives as envisaged in the Tourism Policy will be available to the private investors setting up new tourism projects in the State. It would also be applicable for expansion of projects provided the total ceiling amount is not exceeded by an investor.

Penalty for Default

Entrepreneurs of tourism projects/units who violate the terms of the agreement entered into with tourism Department will be liable to refund the amount taken by them in the form of subsidy in one lump sum along with penal interest @ 18%. Such entrepreneurs who do not refund the money to the State Government on the issuance of notice by the Department of tourism will be liable for being proceeded against under the provision of Karnataka Land Revenue Act and the arrears shall be recovered as arrears of land revenue.

World Heritage Centres in Karnataka

For Karnataka it is a matter of pride tohave two world heritage centres. It is necessary to give special status to these.

- Hampi Hospet taluk and Anegundi Gram Panchayath Area
- Pattadakal Badami taluk and Aihole Gram Panchayat

Special Tourism Areas

District	*Area*
Bijapur	Bijapur Taluk Hungund taluk
Bidar	Bidar taluk, Basavakalyan taluk
Chitradurga	Chitradurga Taluk
Chitadurga	Chirtradurga Taluk
Hassan	Hassan taluk, Belur Taluk, Channarayapatna taluk, Arakalgud talk
Mandya	Srirangapatna taluk
Mysore	Mysore taluk except Mysore Corportion Limits. Gundlupet taluk, T. Narasipur taluk, Kollegal Taluk, Yelandur Taluk.
North Kanara	One km. width of entire coast line from hightide line
Shimoga	Sagar Taluk
South Kanara	One km. width of entire coast line from the high tide line except the area covered by Mangalore City Corporation limits.

The tasks of the district Level Committee under the Tourism:

- To work as a Single Window Committee under the Tourism Department in relation to tourism related projects.
- Monitoring the on-going projects of the tourism Department.
- Regularly convene the monthly meeting and co-ordinate other tourism projects.
- To suggest long-term and short-term plans for the development of tourism in the district. To formulate such suggestions/projects for each place of the district.
- To formulate special and innovative projects to develop major tourist centres.
- To give due publicity about the tourism development processes and also the tourist attractions. Also to co-ordinate and organize seminars and other related activities.

- To mobilize resources and subscriptions to maintain and develop the tourist attractions of the district.
- To invite associated MPs and Legislative Members to the meetings of the Committee.

Investment Proposed for all Circuits in Karnataka (1997-2002)

(Rs. in lakhs)

Circuits	*Government*	*Private*	*Total*
Northern Circuit	85,878	20,305	1,06,183
Southern Circuit	21,210	2,06,130	2,27,340
Coastal circuit	10,225	73,830	84,055
Hill Resort circuit	7,371	7,820	15,191
Wild Life Circuit	1,475	1,950	3,425
Total	126,159	3,10,035	4,35,194
Human Resource Development	600	1,400	2,000
Sculpture Promotion	100	-	100
Marketing Strategy	5,000	-	5,000
Incentives & Subsidies	2,500	-	2,500
Total	8,200	9,600	
Crand Total	1,34,359	3,11,435	4,45,794

Karnataka Tourism Policy

Karnataka was among the first state in the country to bring out a progressive Tourism Policy as early as June 1992. This had the twin objective of promoting tourism related activities and enhancing employment and income-generation among all sections of the society to further promote tourism in the State. The Government is giving new thrust to promote tourism in the State All bonafide tourism related enterprises are duly recognized and given special incentives and concessions. Areas that need rapid development have been identified. Infra-structural facilities need considerable investment ad the private sector is invited to participate in such areas. They are encouraged to invest in hotels, beach resorts, eco-friendly resorts, wayside facilities, adventure/recreation centers like golf courses, aero sports, amusement parks and other tourism related activities. Tourism being a major engine of economic growth, the State Government constituted a sub committee of the Cabinet to make suitable recommendations for comprehensive development of tourism in Karnataka dated 16th November, 2000. The Cabinet Sub-committee met several times and held discussions with the ministers and secretaries of all departments connected with tourism. All the recommendations of the Sub-Committee were approved by the Cabinet at its meeting held on 18th April, 2002 with certain modifications. A preliminary Government order was issued in 2002. In continuation of this, a final and detailed government order was issued on dated 20 January, 2003. After careful consideration, the government is pleased to order the following priorities for the State government Department and concessions and incentives to the private sector with a view to enhance tourism potential and attract more private investment into the tourism sector in the State :

- Tourism is heavily dependant on the coordinated performance of many departments and agencies. Hence, a State Tourism Council headed by the Chief Minister, with all stakeholders represented in it, to take decisions on policy and strategy, is hereby constituted.
- A State Level Co-ordination committee under the Chairmanship of the Chief Secretary with Secretaries of tourism-related departments as members, is set up for effective implementation of the Tourism Policy.
- The District Tourism Councils headed by the Deputy Commissioner are reactivated with General Manager, District Industries Centre and the Assistant Director of Tourism assisting the Council.
- The department of Tourism, to prepare comprehensive development plans for the development of major tourist spots in a phased manner and also assign activities which have to be taken up by the Government as development plans for the following key destinations: Nandi Hills, Brindavan Gardens, Kemmannagudi, Jog Falls, Badami, Aihole, Pattadakal, Belur, Halebid, Sharavanbelagola, Bijapur, Hampi, Gokarna, Karwar, Mysore, Hesaraghatta, Agumbe and Nehruloka.

- The department of Tourism shall prepare and implement a comprehensive infrastructural plan for providing connectivity and common facilities at major tourist destinations in the State with an initial out lay of Rs.125 crores. The funds for this plan are to be availed from financial institutions after getting the projects prepared and vetted by professionals and agencies. The major components of this infrastructural plan are :

Air Connectivity

Airports: Providing new airstrips/improving existing airstrips to increase accessibility the to following places: Hampi, Mysore, Hassan, Bijapur, Shimoga, Belgaum, Hubali, Bidar, Bellary, Gulbara, Raichur Mangalore, Karwar, Shimoga And Kodagu.

Heli Services: Identify locations and prepare plans for potential areas where heli services are possible and provide landing and other facilities.

Encouragement to Private Air Operators: In order to encourage private air operators for reaching out to various tourist destinations, *the* tax on aviation turbine fuel is reduced to 4% and underwriting 50% tickets of private airlines for an initial period of three years.

Roads: In order to improve the road connectivity to tourist destinations, the roads leading to such destinations which are neither National nor State Highways, a plan would be prepared by the Department of Tourist on priority basis and implements them with needed signages and wayside faculties.

Public and Civic Amenities: Prepare a comprehensive plan for providing common public and civic amenities at important tourist destinations and implement general up-keep of their surrounding.

Preparation of Comprehensive Plan and Acquisition of Land: The Department of Tourism, with the assistance of experts, will identify the requirement of tourism facilities in major tourist destinations and prepare comprehensive plans. The Department will also identify the locations where these would come up and acquire lands through KIADB to make them available to they are to be offered to private entrepreneurs at 50% of its market value.

To encourage private sector participation in the various facts of tourism, the following Department are mandated to streamline their polices and procedures. This is to ensure concerted efforts upgrading infrastructure and making available better opportunities for the private sector in the filed of tourism.

- *PWD, RDPR and Urban Development:* Departments the Departments of PWD, RDPR and UD are mandated to invest and improve roads leading to identified important tourist destinations, which has already been done by the Department of tourist. These three Departments shall devil these roads on priority basis in the coming financial years through appropriate budgetary allocations.
- *Forest Department:* Extensive tree planning in all tourist spots to be taken up by the Forest Department. The Forest Department is to have a clear policy, based on carrying-capacity studies of forest areas for private investors wishing to set up resorts, with access for their guests into forests.
- *Ecology and Environment Department:* Implementation of Costal Zonal Regulation to be simplified with more delegation of powers to the State environment department authorizes a quick processing by the Department. Zonal mapping on scale is to be completed to facilitate private investors. Permission to be given for some beachfront activates requiring temporary structures.
- *Finance Department:* Finance Department will augment the budgetary allocations to the Department of Tourism keeping in view the enhanced activities in the current policy period. To further augment the resources of the Department of Tourist, 50% of the revenue generated thorough gate and other collection sin important tourist destinations are to be deposited

in a find and used for maintenance and development of those facilities.

- *Transport Department:* A separate queue for tourist vehicles at the time of checking by Transport Department at State borders is tobe ensured.
- *Home Department:* Facilitate new concept of multiplexes by having a policy that provides for:
    1. Cinema hall beyond the first floor.
    2. Multi-entertainment activities in same building.
    3. Any number of shows within a 15 hour time span.
    4. Exemption from having a middle aisle in I-Max theaters.
    5. Entertainment tax exemption of 100% for the first 3 years and 75% for next 2 years for I max theaters only.
- *Tourism Department*

(i) The existing accommodation and other facilities of both Government and Karnataka State Tourism Development Corporation are to be usefully and optimally utilized by inviting private sector partner's management of these properties in a phased manner.

(ii) The Department of Tourism is to provide land for following facilities.

1. Food Craft Institute
2. Tourism Complex
3. Information centre

(iii) Take up the following specific projects :

1. Palace on Wheels
2. Night safari in Bannerhatta National Park
3. Develop Badamo, Aihole and Pattadkal circuit
4. Develop a Coastal Circuiting North Canara
5. Provide world class facilities in Brindavan Gardens though private participation
6. Comprehensive developments of Job Falls area

7. Develop area around important ancient and historical monuments
8. Private management of Government accommodation

(iv) Develop Bangalore as a major tourist destination through adventure sports and high end accommodation in Nandi Hills with private sector participation. Make available tanks like Ulsoor, Sankey, Madiwala, Bellandur etc., to private parties for boating and maintenance plant tress extensively to beautify Bangalore, Civic amentias to be given for maintains to corporate houses. Motor racing track outside Bangalore, city walks, lighting up heritage buildings, craft bazaars etc.

(v) Trained tourist guides are tobe made available at al major tourist locations.

(vi) The department will avail the help of consultants, whenever necessary, in order to prepare design and implement tourist projects.

1. To encourage private sector participation in al tourist related activities I the State, the following incentives an concession are offered in the policy period:
   a. All concession offered under the Industrial policy of the State (2002-07) are made available for private investment in the tourism sector.
   b. Luxury Tax to be charged only or room tariff above Rs. 400 (Ruppes Four Hundred) and to be charged only on actual tariff collected A cap of 10% to be placed on it.
   c. Additional state excise duty of 66% on imported liquor to be reduced to 25% or levied on basic rate.
   d. Motor Vehicle Tax levied on tourist vehicle plying between States to be rationalized on a reciprocal basis.
   e. 50%, 100% stamp duty exemption for investment below/above Rs. 50 9 Rupees Fifty) crores.

f. Concessional registration charges of Rs. 1 (Rupee One) per Rs. 1000 (Rupees One Thousand)

g. Waiver of Conversion Fee

h. Entry tax exemption during implementation of project for a period of three years.

i. Entertainment Tax exemption of 100% for first three years and 75% for next two years for I-Max theatres only.

j. Tax on aviation turbine fuel is reduced to 4% and underwriting 50% of tickets of private airlines for an initial period of three years.

k. Government land will be offered at 50% of its market value to entrepreneurs.

The state provides enormous scope for tourism development. The state tourism policy also emphasizes on public private participation in tourism development and managing tourism destinations and services. Moreover, coastal and eco-tourism destinations of the state highlight the growing importance of tourism industry while they also demand for strategic planning and measures for management of tourism resources.

7

Management of Tourism in Karnataka

Development of 'Tourism' as an industry in India has evolved through a series of successive stages of growth. At the authoritative level the development of tourism was taken up in a schematic manner in 1956 coinciding with the second five year plan. For further expansion tourism requires better planning, investment and scientific appraisal of the subject, with this target in view more and more educational institutions are offering tourism as a subject in their educational curriculum. Since time immemorial India has been a great source of attraction to the world, but the scope of tourism industry has not been exploits so far to its full potential.

Karnataka is known for many historically elegant monuments, scenery, exquisite natural renowned religious places etc. Therefore, if the Government of Karnataka exploits the available resources, it could develop and prosper tourism as an industry to a very large extent. The exotic and natural charm offered by places like Brindavan Garden in Mysore, Maharaja Palace, Tipu Sultan Palace Vidhana Soudha, Cubban Park, Lal Bagh, Utility Building in Bangalore etc. should be turned to a feast for the tourists.

Pilot study conducted reveals that ample opportunities are exist in the coastal region of Karnataka to develop tourism industry. A few people have undertaken the study regarding it, but they are piecemeal and isolated in nature. There is the need to make an integrated study on tourism industry in the region and hence the subject entitled "A Study of Problems and Prospects of Tourism Industry in Coastal Region of Karnataka State" has come up for further in-depth study.

Objectives of the Study

The present study is undertaken with the following main objectives:

1. To study the conceptual background and related aspects of tourism industry.
2. To study and examine:
   - the nature and extent of tourism industry in the coastal region of Karnataka state.
   - the policies adopted by the Government of Karnataka for the development of tourism industry.
3. To review the working of selected tourism business units n the coastal region of Karnataka and to ascertain the problems and prospects for tourism industry in general and in particular for coastal region of Karnataka.
4. To assess the quality of services experienced by tourists in the coastal region of Karnataka state.
5. To study the contribution of tourism industry in the coastal region of Karnataka state.
6. To present, analyse and interpret the necessary relevant data, put-forth constructive suggestions for better performance of tourism industry.

Hypothesis

- There is no significant difference in the attitude rating for various concessions among the respondents.
- There is no significant difference in the attitude rating for travel vehicle (buses) among the respondents.
- There is no significant difference in the attitude rating for punctuality aspect among the respondents.

- There is no significant difference in the attitude rating for accommodation facilities among the respondents.
- There is no significant difference in the attitude rating for cleanliness and hygiene among the respondents.
- There is no significant difference in the attitude rating for first aid and medical facilities among the respondents.
- There is no significant difference in the attitude rating for guide arrangement at tourist spot among the respondents.
- There is no significant difference in the attitude rating for Karnataka as a tourist place among the respondents.
- There is no significant difference in the attitude rating for first meeting experience with travelling agency among the respondents.
- There is no significant difference in the attitude rating for quality of food among the respondents.
- There is no significant difference in the attitude rating for general entertainment during the tour.
- There is no significant difference in the attitude rating for shopping facilities among the respondents.

Methodology Adopted

The present study is based on both primary as well as secondary data. Stressing the prime importance on survey method, the data were collected by personally visiting a good number of tourist spots, various libraries and government offices. The methodology basically adopted comprises of survey method and observation method.

Sources of Data Collection

The survey method was carried out by personally visiting all the selected tourist spots of the coastal region of Karnataka state.

Primaty Data

These were collected through the use of structured questionnaire, through informal discussions, personal observations and formal interview.

Questionnaire

A detailed and comprehensive questionnaire was prepared, pre-tested and then suitably amended. The questionnaire was then administered by personal visits to the selected hotels, travel agencies and tourists. While preparing the questionnaire care was taken to develop a Likert type scale for certain questions where the

- Objective response was of more importance than the subjective response. To achieve the given objective in all, three sets of questionnaires were administered to the travel agencies. tourists and hotel owner/ managers.
- Informal discussions, structured and unstructured interviews were conducted to elicit data from the respondents.

Table 1
Details of Sample Design

Tour & Travel Agencies	*Tourist*	*Hotels*	*Total*
108	560	23	691

After the administration of questionnaire it was felt necessary to have a detailed investigation of certain issues which could not be adequately covered in the questionnaire. The questionnaires were taken up and the information was solicited through informal discussions and through structured and unstructured interviews with officials of the department of tourism, Government of Karnataka, Karnataka State Tourism Development Corporation, hotel managers/owners, tour operators etc.

Secondary Data

For the theoretical framework, review of the past literature and statistical data in respect of the present study, secondary sources were made use of for this purpose and data has been collected through secondary sources.

Office Document

Regular documents of various departments were used for day to day transactions, different reporting forms and also considered to generate information related to the set objectives of this study.

Office Records

Various official records related to tourism industry, tourist arrivals, conditions for establishment of hotels etc were taken from the official records

Visit to Libraries

To clarify theoretical concepts published sources in various libraries were utilized.

- Chh-Shahu Central Institute of Business Education & Research-Kolhapur
- Padmabhooshan Vasntraodada Patil Institute of Management Studies and Research-Sangli
- Barr khardekar Library-Shivaji University
- Mangalore University Library-Mangalore
- Karnataka University Library-Dharwad
- Divakar College of Commerce-Library Karwar
- Karwar District Public Library-Karwar

Various journals, periodicals, paper clippings, hand-cuts and government publications, trade journals, research and dissertations reports, annual reports of tourism corporation of India, annual reports of Karnataka State Tourism Development Corporation, (KSTDC) and the reports of ministry of tourism, have been considered.

Computer Analysis

After the collection of data it was scored and analyzed with the help of a computer for the purpose of arriving at various statistical inferences. This was achieved with the help of computer package office 2000, at a private computer center.

Sample Design

The sample for the present study has been refered under three phases. The first phase constitutes of the selection of tourists while the second phase deals with the responses from the managers/owners of the hotel industry. The final phase indicates the selection of tours and travel agents (Table 1).

Phase I

The researcher visited the government offices and the department of tourism ministry to take cognizance of the total number of tourists arriving in a given period at study area. It was brought to the notice of researcher that no authentic statistical data was maintained. However the officials in these departments stated that ranging between 45000 to 50000 tourists, representing 11000 to 11500 families arrived at the coastal region of Karnataka every year. Accordingly it was thus decided to have a 5% sample size of the above stated number of families. Thus 560 respondents were contacted and the pre-tested questionnaire was administered. Care was taken by the researcher to have a representation of one respondent representing one family, similarly equal case was taken to have a representation of the broad spectrum of social stratification.

While selecting the 560 respondent's convenience sampling techniques was adopted. The researcher visited the hotels, tourist spots and collected the data from those respondents who were willing to take part in the study.

Phase II

The list of hotels was procured from the concerned authority of government department, and it was noted that appropriately 230 hotels inclusive of all varieties were existing. A proportion of 10% of these hotels were considered as a sample for the study. Therefore in all 23 hotels were visited and their owners/ mangers were contacted and the data was elicited. While selecting hotels, care was taken to ensure representation of all types of hotels such as star hotels, deluxe hotel etc.

Phase III

There are more than 1000 tour operators in the study area of which 108 respondents have been considered for the study which constitutes of 10 to 11 % of the universe. Thus 108 tour-operators were approached by the researcher and the data required for the study was collected. The precautionary measures borne in mind was the spread of respondents (tour operators) in the study area. Therefore the respondents thus selected represents the area of study.

In this chapter the primary data collected from the tour and travel agencies, tourist and hotel owners/managers has been analysed with the help of simple percentage tabulation and the same has been analysed and interpreted. In order to validate the data the hypothesis set forth has been tested with the help of Kolmogorov Smirnov Test.

Section A
Tour and Travel Agencies

In tour industries location of the office plays a vital role in marketing their services. Tourist offices near bus stand, city, railway station, near airport, centre places in the city becomes convenient from marketing point of view. In survey researcher found 11% near central places of city, 63% near bus stand, while 20% near railway station and rest of 6% found near airport (Table 2).

It is observed from the table that majority of the tourist prefer to purchase the packages/tickets from the agencies which is near to the bus station and rest near to the railway station (Table 3).

A package tour is designed to fit a particular group of travellers This falls in the category of special interest tours such as mountain tours, museum tours, shopping or governmental tours. Package tours are often advertised in the form of broachers, listing terms and conditions, price, type of accommodation and other services provided. The institution of package tour is going to gain momentum in near future owing to its innumerable advantages for such tours saves time and unnecessary correspondence it succeeds in reducing the

Table 2

Location Wise Set-up of Tour and Travel Agencies

Location	Uttar Kannada		Udupi		Dakshin Kannada		Total	
	No.	%	No.	%	No.	%	No.	%
Near Centralplace & city	02	11.12	02	08	08	12.30	12	11.11
Near Bus Stand	04	22.22	22	88	42	64.63	68	62.96
Near Railway Station	12	66.66	01	04	09	13.84	22	20.37
Near Airport	–	–	–	–	06	9.23	06	5.56
Others	–	–	–	–	–	–	–	–
Total	18(16.66)	100	25(23.15)	100	65(60.19)	100	108(100)	100

Note: Bracket figure indicates percentage.

Table 3
Package Tour

	Uttar Kannada		Udupi		DakshinKannada		Total	
Package Tour	*No.*	*%*	*No.*	*%*	*No.*	*%*	*No.*	*%*
Yes	16	88.88	24	96	60	92.30	100	92.59
No	02	11.12	01	04	05	07.70	08	7.41
Total	16	100	25	100	65	100	108	100

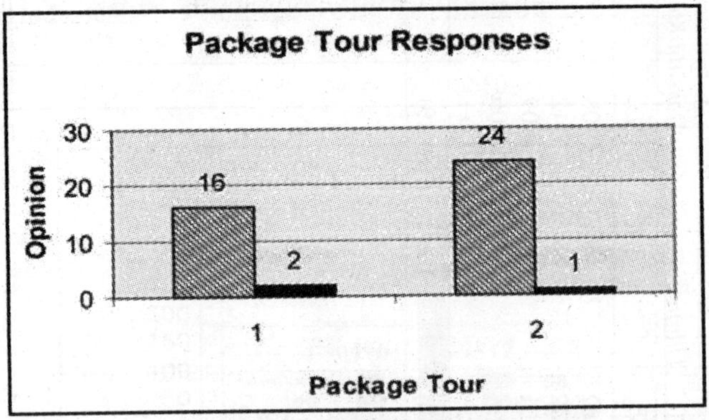

real prices of travel, it succeeds in reducing the real prices of travel, its comparatively cheap and much earliest to operate. The survey also substantiated this fact. Survey in Uttar Kannada revealed that of the total 18 tours and travel operating agencies 16 of them organised tour packages (88.88%). In Udupi also the response towards package tour was highly positive 96% of tour and travel operators conducted package tours. In the Dakshin Kannada district also the demand for package tours was found to be note worthy i.e. of 60.18% of tour operating agencies 92.3% arranged tour packages.

Table 4
Nature of Tour

	Responses		
Nature of Tour	*Yes*	*No*	*Total*
State Tour	98(91)	10(9)	108(100)
All India Tour	24(22)	84(84)	100(100)
International Tour	04(3)	104(97)	108(100)

Note : Bracket figure indicates percentage.

The pleasure seekers often depend on readymade facilities provided at the easiest convenience. Past surveys reveal that the tourists rely upon these agencies even in the choice of their tour destination. Hence a wide range of tourist trips has to be made available to create variety and demand.

During survey, researcher observed that in the coastal region of Karnataka, the agencies give more priority in organising State tours 91%, the tour conducted to localities outside the state was limited to 22%. Where as international trips were given little importance with just 3%. Hence to build in better demand for all India and international tours besides state tours, economical packages and other adequate provisions has to be furnished (Table 4).

The researcher found that 83% of tour operators conducted tours through bus and 21% through railway. So it shows that the majority of the tourist prefer to travel through coach instead of railway. The reason for this can be contributed to the railway

Table 5
Mode of Transport

	Response from Agencies		
Media	*Yes*	*No*	*Total*
By Bus	90(83)	18(17)	108(100)
By Train	23(21)	85(79)	108(100)
By Air	00(00)	108(100)	108(100)

Note: Bracket figure indicates percentage.

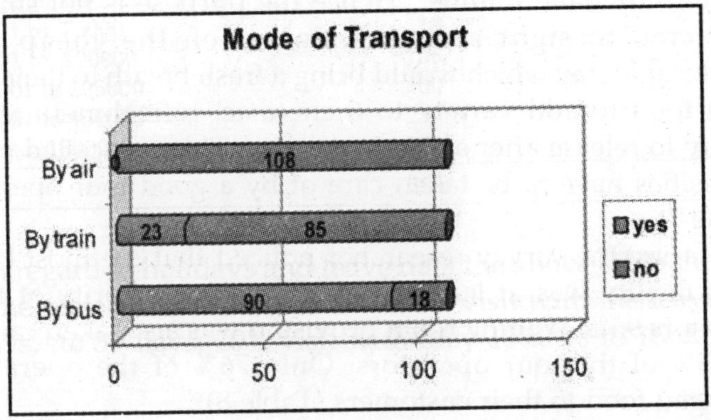

authorities, their negligence in providing first hand means to the tourists - Our railway fail to provide healthy and hygienic environment, easy and comfortable rooms are lacking luggage loading facilities are poor and even the supply of beverages and refreshments are inadequate and lack in variety. The railway has co-operate with the tourism industry by way of providing concession in railway fair to encourage the use of as a mode of transport. (Table 5)

Duration of tour depend upon the economic condition of tourist, if he is of high class he could even prefer the one month tour. The figures in the table shows that majority of tour operators i.e. 57% are preferring to organize one week tour, 50% fortnight, 35% one week and the rest 13% one month. (Table 6)

Table 6
Duration Wise Tours

Tour Duration	*Yes*	*%*	*No .*	*%*	*Total*	*%*
One day	62	57	46	43	108	100
One week	38	35	70	65	108	100
Fortnight	54	50	54	50	108	100
One month	14	13	94	87	108	100
Any other	–	–	–	–		

The major motive of a tourist in undertaking a journey is pleasure seeking, they wish to have respite from the drudgery of their mundane routine. Hence the purpose is not simply restricted to sight seeing; they search the cheap and comfortable stay which would bring a fresh breath to their life, good food to add variety to their taste, refreshment room facility to release after a tough journey. These so called basic necessities have to be taken care of by a good tour operator (Table 7).

During the survey researcher noticed that the most basic toilet facility was at least provided by the majority of tour operators 96%. Waiting room provision was also taken care of by 85% of the tour operators. Only 76% of the operators arranged food to their customers (Table 8) .

Table 7
Unique Features of Tours

Unique Features	*Yes*	*%*	*No.*	*%*	*Total*	*%*
Catering units	83	76	25	24	108	100
Waiting room Facilities	92	85	70	15	108	100
Sulabh toilet	104	96	5	4	108	100

Lack of enthusiasm of the tour operators in seeing to the comforts and convenience of his customers is definitely contributing to the slow pace of growth of this industry in the region.

Table 8
Moderate Needs of Tourism Business

Moderate Needs of Tourism Business	*Yes*	*%*	*No.*	*%*	*Total*	*%*
Trained staff by IATA	37	34	71	66	108	100
Baggage Insurance	13	12	95	88	108	100
Health requirement	27	25	81	75	108	100
Computers forOffice administration	21	19	79	81	108	100

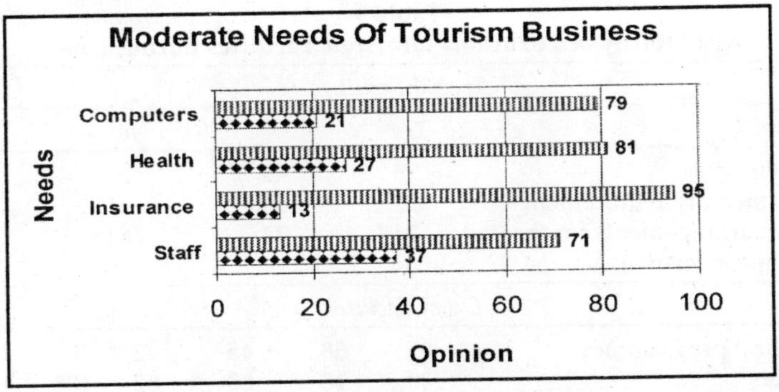

In this era of competitive and co-operative tourism in which a high level of services and other facilities are the need of the hour both service and efficiency should be the motto of this pioneering body of tourism trade. It has to cater to every requirement of the tourist. Safety, security, Health and hygiene, Systematic administration etc. are name of the moderate needs to be taken care of trained staff with the right understanding about the needs and aims of tourism trade can develop the industry to heights.

Through the survey it was obvious that Health and Security of the tourists was not a matter of much concern. For only 12% of the operators assured baggage insurance facility. Basic requirements as a full fledged first aid box were maintained by only 25% of them. Registration and other documentation were manually managed by the majority with only 19% using computers for maintaining records. Trained staff from Information Technology contributed 34% of the administrative staff, the rest were without any pre-service or pre-entry training. (Table 9)

It seems from the table that appointment of the staff is based upon well net parameters of the tourism trade. Pre service and post service training is essential. Candidates with prior experience from the Directorate of tourism or with a background of Art and Culture can be given preference. Tourism agencies have to offer insurance policies to death, disablement, loss or damage of baggage.

Table 9
Availability of Luxurious Life Style Facilities during Tour

Special Facilities						
Features	*Yes*		*%*	*No .*		*%*
Television set	73		68	35		32
Documentary requirement	57		53	51		47
Ticket arrangements for theater and music festival	24		22	84		78
Other Facilities						
Cultural programmes	63	58	45	42	108	100
Porters	20	18	88	82	108	100
Foreign currencyexchange	03	02	105	98	108	100

Tourists are always on the look out for fun and frolic. More ever the considerable proportion of the tourists are accompanied by their Kith and Kin, these people want a variety of activities and entertainment programmes to make their trip enjoyable. Keeping this in view researcher made an analysis of the entertainment programmes arranged by the tour operators. Researcher noticed that about 68% of the tour programmer provided the luxury of television set. Documentary requirements were equipped by 53% of the tour programmers.

Since majority of the tourist belong to the pleasure seeking category, KSTDC authorities should create more facilities to generate pleasure and fun to be synchronised with traditional cultural heritage of the region. Folk dance programmes traditional and regional festivals, religiously associated programmes has to be organised to arouse the interest of pleasure and having section both domestic and foreign. Another major problem encountered by a foreign tourist is the issue of currency exchange. If the tour and travel agencies would deal with the provision of foreign currencies, travellers cheques etc it can save a lot of time and energy of the tourist in waiting regular banking channels covers of my study, Researcher observed the 58% of the operators made arrangement for cultural programmes. The problem related to the currency exchange was tackled by only 2% of the operators and porters were supplied by 18% only. (Table 9)

To set any business an entrepreneur has to procure a licences and then he is liable to pay tax to the government. In tour operating agency they pay four types of taxes sales tax, commercial tax, municipal tax, and other taxes like state entry tax, octroi etc. During this study the researcher found 20% operators pay sales tax, 89% pays commercial tax, 95% pays municipal and rest of 3% pays other taxes like state entry tax, Octroi etc. To encourage the industry the government has to liberalize some of the policies related to the payment of taxes by the tourism trade. (Table 10)

Table 10
Tax Payment by Tour Agencies

Types of Tax Payment	*Yes*	*%*	*No .*	*%*	*Total*	*%*
Sales Tax	22	20	86	80	108	100
Commercial tax	96	89	12	11	108	100
Municipal tax	103	95	05	05	108	100
Other	04	03	104	97	108	100

Wander thirst is latent in every individual to promote the trade this dormant thirst has to be propelled out and nourished.

Media and advertisement has a crucial role to play in this field. Right formulas and strategies adhering to the requirements of the different sections of the population have to be formulated and specified in the advertisement to attract the curiosity and arouse the interest in them.

T.V. is a very powerful media in this modern era which supplies information to every sections of the society. It has its advantages over other experience to the colourful dimensional frictions etc. hence this media has to be exploited to arouse the interest in the public.

Researcher found in this study only 81% of tour operators are advertising their package tours in local news papers, 87% in magazines, 28% in modern media like T.V or through local cable operators, 17% through the professional journals and 5% through information broachers, hand bills, banners and pamphlets (Table 11).

Table 11
Use of Advertisement Media for Sales Promotion

Advertisement Media	*Yes*	*%*	*No.*	*%*	*Total*	*%*
New Papers	88	81	20	19	108	100
Magazines	94	87	14	13	108	100
Modern media (Cable media)	30	28	78	72	108	100
Professional Journal	18	17	90	83	108	100
Others	06	05	102	95	108	100

Until and unless the problems of tourism industry are taken note of the prospectus of tourism promotion will remain dim and low. The problems confronting the tourism industry could be grouped into many stages. These are promotional functional and factual problem. In this survey researcher found that 29% of the operators faced the problems at promotional level i.e. procurement of loans and 42% faced the problem of selection of location (Table 12).

Table 12
Financial & Location Constraints for Travel Agencies

Problems	*Yes*	*%*	*No .*	*%*
Procurement of loans at high rate of interest	31	29	77	71
Location	45	42	63	58

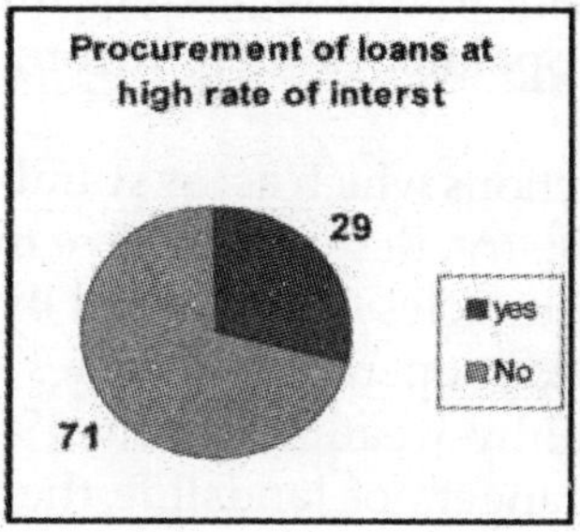

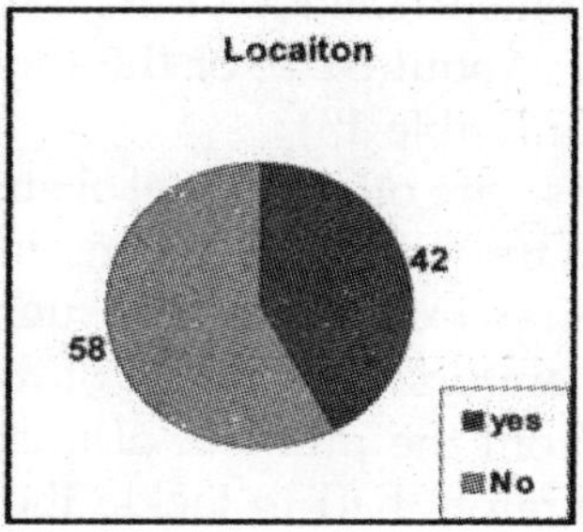

At the functional stage also tour operators encounter a number of obstacles which can be tackled and resolved only by the co-operation of department of tourism and the encouragement of the government. Tourism is not an solitary industry, it can work efficiently only by the assistance and co-ordination of a large chain of hospitality industries like hotels, motels, various types of excursion resorts, restaurants, hospitals etc.

Table 13
Functional Operational Problems during Tour

Operational Problems During Tour	*Yes*	*%*	*No .*	*%*
Water scarcity	74	69	34	31
Purchasing for catering units	39	36	69	64
Accommodation	54	50	54	50
Medical	96	89	12	11
Expansion of tourist activities	63	58	45	42
Generation of new tourist sites	40	37	68	63
Providing basic amenities	67	62	41	38
Promotion of tourist activities in the off season	90	83	18	17

The researcher come to realise that, the principal problem confronted by majority of the tour operators was water scarcity (69%) non availability of suitable accommodation at the tourist spots and the problem of arranging the basic amenities was also severe with 50% and 62% respectively. About 58% of the tour operators encountered difficulty in expanding their programmes in the course of journey. Generation of new sites to make use of the spare time was also tedious about 37% of the operators found this difficult to tackle. Another major issue was the insufficiency of medial care in remote area of tourist interest. About 89% of the tour operator suffered from this problem (Table 13).

These are other factual obstructions which act as stumbling block in the promotion of this industry. Researcher have made a thorough examination of such obstacles encountered by the tour operators. About 95% of the tour operating agencies had to confront the problem of unhealthy weather. About 19% of the operators had to tackle the dangers of landslide the hill station. Other unavoidable problem was the payment of high state entry tax i.e. (92%). Other miscellaneous technical problems and problems related to Road Transport Office was faced by 62% and 76% of the operators respectively. (Table 14)

Table 14
Factual Problem to Tour Agencies

Factual Problems	*Yes*	*%*	*No .*	*%*	*Total*	*%*
Unhealthy climate	103	95	05	05	108	100
High state entry tax	100	92	08	08	108	100
Harassments fromtourist &governmentofficials	73	68	35	32	108	100
Land sliding at hill Station	21	19	87	81	108	100
Road TransportOperator problems	83	76	25	24	108	100
Technical problems	67	62	41	38	108	100

Reputation and experience of the tour operating agencies plays a vital role in enhancing the market value of the product. During researcher found that about 30% of the agencies had the reputation of being established for a period more than 21 years. 38% of the agencies were established with in the past 11 to 20 years. About 18% of the agencies passed the life span of 6 to 10 years and 14% of the agencies were recently established less experienced. (Table 15)

Table 15
Age wise Classification of the Tour Operating Agencies

Age(in Years)	*Number*	*%*
1 to 5 years	15	14
6 to 10 years	19	18
11 to 20 years	41	38
Any other	33	30
Total	108	100

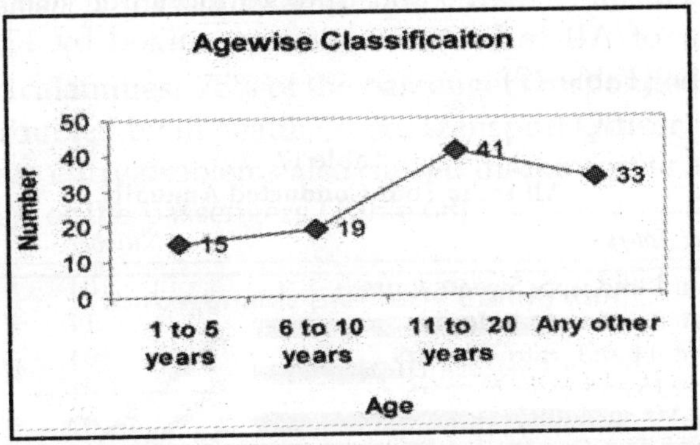

So as to make an estimate of the total percentage of state tours organised by these agencies both seasonal and off seasonal per year analysis was undertaken. Researcher perceived that the maximum number of tours more than 6 and up to 15 tours conducted by majority of the tour operators come up the to 65%. About 22% of the operators organised more than 11 and up to 15 tours per year. The highest number of tours i.e. more than 16 and up to 20 tours were reported by only 2% of the operators. About 7% of the operators were found to be organising the least number (Table 16).

Table 16
Tour Conducted with in Karnataka State

Number of Tour Per Year	*Number*	%
More than 1 and upto 5 years tours	06	7
More than 6 and upto 10 tours	52	65
More than 11 and upto 15 tours	18	22
More than 16 and upto 20 years	02	03
Any other	02	03
Total	80	100

Regarding All India Tour researcher found that the highest number of tours was (more than 16 and up to 20 tours) organised by only a minimum of 4% of the operators, 17% of the operators stood second in conducting more than 11 and up to 15 tours per year. Majority of the tour operators (58%)

organised more than 6 and upto 20 tours per year and least number of All India tours was organized by 17% of the agencies. (Table 17)

Table 17
All India Tour Conducted Annually

Number of Tours	*Number*	%
More than 1 and upto 5 years tours	04	17
More than 6 and upto 10 tours	14	58
More than 11 and upto 15 tours	04	17
More than 16 and upto 20 years	01	04
Any other	01	04
Total	24	100

Regarding international tours the performance of the agencies was found to be in need of more encouragement. 50% of agencies conducted the highest number of tours (more than 6 and up to 10 tours per year) No agencies organised more than 10 tour per year. The least number of trips (more than 1 and up to 5 trips per year.) was conducted by 50% of the operators (Table 18).

Table 18
International Tour Conducted Annually

International Tour	*Number*	%
More than 1 and upto 5 years tours	02	50
More than 6 and upto 10 tours	02	50
More than 11 and upto 15 tours	–	–
More than 16 and upto 20 years	–	–
Any other	–	–
Total	04	100

An analysis was made on the different mode of conveyance provided by the tour operator. 83% of the operators dealt only with bus services Railway service was found to be almost neglected in tourism industry, only 14% of the operators took care of arranging railway as conveyance. 6% of the operators gave priority for both railways and roadways. Airways as means of conveyance was provide by none.

Private and governmental sectors has to work in collaboration for the upliftment of this industry. Karnataka State Tourism Development Corporation (KSTDC) has to formulate policies and terms with the railways and airways by way of concessions in the fare and provisions of packages to enhance the product value (Table 19).

Table 19
Means of Tour

Means	*Number*	%
By Bus	90	83
By Train only	15	14
By Both	06	06
By Air	00	00

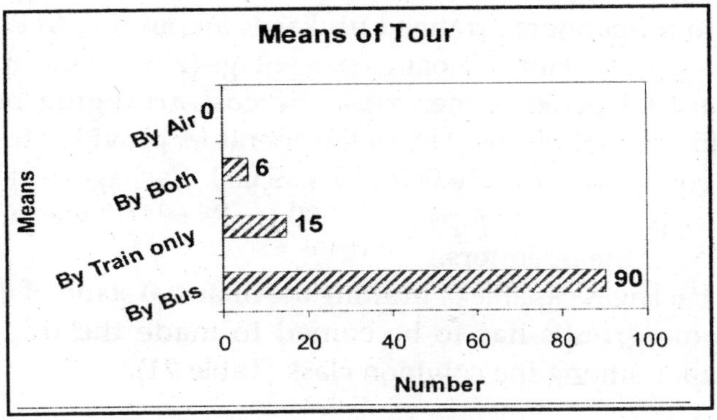

In the recent past the tourist traffic has not only changed in magnitude but its characteristics have also undergone complete change. In the past, the bulk of tourists were from richer class who would go around in luxury coaches and air conditioned hotels. Now a days majority of the tourist belong to middle income group. Hence cost efficient packages catering to the economic standard of the middle class has to be given precedence.

In survey researcher come to know that the minimum cost earn by the operators for a single one day tour was Rs.8000 to Rs.10,000 i.e. 85% of the operators arranged such packages. Cost between Rs.10,000 to Rs.12,000 was encountered by about

10% of the operators. The packages of highest amount with an expense of Rs.12,000 to Rs. 14,000 mostly catering to the high income group was provided by only 5% of the tour operators (Table 20).

Table 20
Cost of One Day Tour with 50 Persons Bus Capacity

Cost of One Day Tour (Rs.)	*Number*	%
8000 to 10000	53	85
10001 tc 12000	06	10
12001 to 14000	03	05
Any other	00	00
Total	62	100

The table shows that in the case of one week tour 55% of the tour operators arranged packages amounting to Rs.40,000 to Rs.45,000. Only half of this percentage (29%) of the operators organised programmes with the cost arranging between Rs.45,000 to Rs50,000. 11% of the operators provided trips with the cost price of Rs.50,000 to Rs.55,000. Packages catering to the high income groups Rs.55,000 to Rs.60,000 was arranged by 5% of the operators.

Packages capable of meeting the financial stand of different income groups has to be coined to made the trade more popular among the common class (Table 21).

Table 21
Cost of One Week Tour With 50 Persons Bus Capacity

Cost of One Week Tour (Rs.)	*Number*	%
40000 to 45000	21	55
45001 to 50000	11	29
50001 to 55000	04	11
55001 to 60000	02	05
Any other	00	00
Total	38	100

When an analysis of the fortnight tours conducted by the respective tour operating agencies was made, the researcher found that 63% of the agencies organised tours for net cost ranging between Rs.70,000 to Rs.75,000 Only 20% arranged programmes for an amount ranging from Rs.75,001 to Rs.80,000, 11% and 6% of the operators had packages of a higher range expenses ranging from Rs.80,001 to Rs.85,000 and Rs.85,001 to Rs.90,000 respectively (Table 22).

Table 22
Cost of Fortnight Tour with 50 Persons Bus Capacity

Cost of Fortnight Tour (Rs.)	*Number*	%
70000 to 75000	44	63
75001 to 80000	11	20
80001 to 85000	06	11
85001 to 90000	02	06
Any other	00	00
Total	54	100

The table revealed that the tours of one month duration was also arranged, though not of much range. About 64% of the tour operators gave priority for trips ranging in the expenses between Rs.2,50,000 to Rs,2,60,000. 14% of the operators conducted tours of two categories i.e. cost ranging from Rs.2,60,001 to Rs.2,70,000 and Rs.2,70,001 to Rs,2,80,000. Only 8% of the operators took care of tours ranging between Rs.2,80,001 to Rs,2,90,000 (Table 23).

Table 23
Cost of One Month Tour Tour with 50 Persons Bus Capacity

Cost of One Month Tour (Rs.)	*Number*	%
250000 to 260000	09	64
2600001 to 270000	02	14
270001 to 280000	02	14
280001 to 300000	01	08
Any other	00	00
Total	14	100

There is always a positive correlation between ones income and the urge for Travelling. Hence the charge allotted by these agencies has to be affordable and price worthy to the varying income classes in general and middle class in particular. When the researcher examined the charge allotted by these agencies per person, Researcher came to the conclusion that the price charged was quite affordable and lenient enough to meet the economic standard of middle income groups. Rs. 350 per person was the highest charge assigned, it was assigned by over 21% of the tour operators. Closely following were 8% of the agencies which allocated Rs.325/- per person. 19% and 8% of the agencies came down in the price and has commissioned Rs.300 and Rs.275 per person.

For encouragement, family concessions can be given to those who are traveling with Kith and Kin. Fare of Kith and teenagers can be made lenient by allocation of different categories of travel fare (Table 24).

Table 24
Charges for One Day Tour Per Person

Charges of One Day Tour (Rs.)	*Number*	%
Up to 250	00	00
Up to 275	04	06
Up to 300	12	19
Up to 325	05	08
Up to 350	13	21
Any other	28	46
Total	62	100

In the case of one week tour researcher found that the least amount charged was Rs.1000 per person. It was commissioned by only 10% of the tour operators. 18% of the operators raised their charge by Rs.250 and came with Rs.1250 per person. 26% and 24% of the operators had packages charging Rs.1500 and Rs.1750 per person respectively. 11% of the operators allocated the highest amount Rs.2000 per person (Table 25).

Table 25
Charges for One Week Tour Per Person

Charges of One Week Tour (Rs.)	*Number*	%
1000	04	10
1250	07	18
1500	10	26
1750	09	24
2000	04	11
Any other	04	11
Total	38	100

When researcher observed the charges allocated for fortnight tours, researcher noticed that-Packages of varying frequencies were arranged with charges ranging from Rs.2000 to Rs.4000 per person. About 19% of the operators come up with packages of Rs.4000 per person. Little behind was 15% of the agencies which had packages for Rs.3500 per head. Among these operators 28% charged Rs.2500 per head. Only 6% of them had trips for Rs.2000 per person (Table 26).

Table 26
Charges for Fortnight Tour Per Person

Charges for Fortnight Tour (Rs.)	*Number*	%
2000	03	6
2500	15	28
3000	14	24
3500	08	15
4000	10	19
Any other	05	08
Total	54	100

Charges allotted for one month tour was also found to be quite affordable provided quality is assured by all means. Packages of different category was found to be lacking in this category–for 29% of the operators offered packages of Rs.10,000 per person, 14% offered packages of Rs.14,000 per person. Packages of intermediate charges was found to be missing (Table 27).

Table 27
Charges for One Month Tour Per Person

Charges of One Month Tour (Rs.)	*Number*	%
8000	00	00
10000	04	29
12000	00	00
14000	00	00
16000	02	14
Any other	08	57
Total	14	100

The table reflects that the highest number of tour operators 69% are earning only 10 to 15% profit from tourism. Whereas the lowest number of operators or agencies i.e. only 6% are earning highest profit of 26 to 30%. This very fact reveals the poor condition of tourism in our country (Table 28).

Table 28
Average Profit Earn

Average Profit Earn (Rs.)	*Number*	%
10 to 15 %	69	64
16 to 20%	14	13
21 to 25%	13	12
26 to 30%	07	6
Any other	05	5
Total	108	100

Transport is the primary service needed by the tourist in order to reach the destination, and further to move around at the destination. Provision of adequate, safe, comfortable, fast, convenient and economical transport is a pre-requisite for mass marketing tourism. The tourist agencies has to be self sufficient in their supply, adequate and appropriate means of transport. But pathetically researcher found that only 32% of the tour agencies possessed their own bus service; 68% of the operators were hiring buses on lease or rental basis (Table 29).

Table 29
Ownership of Bus

Ownership of Bus	*Respondents*	
	Number	%
Yes	35	32
No	73	68
Total	108	100

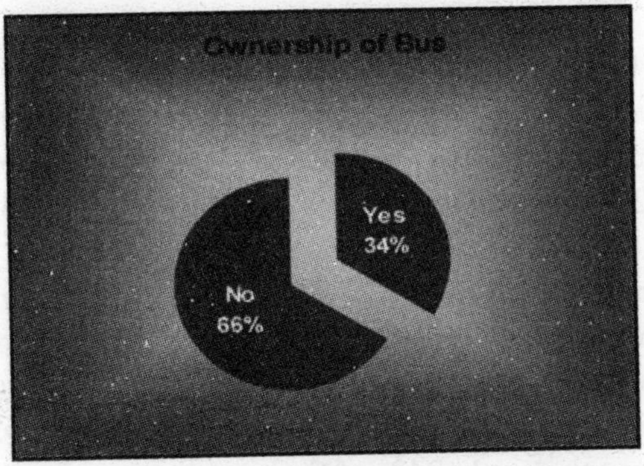

Researcher found that only 14% of the operators could afford to possess bus on their own funds. Majority (66%) depended on loans from financial institutions to purchase the means of transport. 20% of them hired buses on lease basis. Government can provide subsidy and loans on interest basis to and them in the procurement of means of transport (Table 30).

Table 30
Financing of Bus Purchases

Purchase of Bus	*Responses*	
	Number	%
By own funds	05	14
By loan from financial Institutions	23	66
By lease basis	07	20
Total	35	100

The response of 71% operators shows that the hiring of buses on rental basis is the common tradition in tourist agencies. The reason may be that of finance which is not easily available (Table 31).

Table 31
Availability of Buses on Rental Basis

Rental Basis	*Respondents*	
	Number	*%*
Yes	52	71
No	21	29
Total	73	100

In order to motivate the travellers and to make their journey memorable and unforgettable, some token of remembrance and gifts can be offered by the companies. In survey it was found that about 52% of the operators initiated to present some forms of gifts and tokens, where 48% replied in negative.

Number of strategies, methods of approach and tactics appealing to the public has to be evolved to make the industry attractive and magnetic. Researcher made a study of whether these agencies provided any cash discounts to their clients, researcher saw that only 24% of the operators were giving any discount in price, whereas 76% of the operators denied of providing any relaxations.

An efficient agency foresees all obstacles which will be likely to be in store during the course of a journey and take maximum precautions to assure satisfaction to the customers. Researcher wanted to affirm whether the operators were prompt and punctual in maintaining their time of departure. Respondents of which 33% were very particular in maintaining the exact schedule of departure, where as the majority of 67% replied that they failed to be punctual.

Sometimes some families cannot spare bulk amount at a stretch for touring–especially so in the case when they wish to travel in more number. In such cases if credit facility is provided by the agencies these facilities can plan their journey beforehand without the botheration of financial hurdle. During research, researcher saw that only 29% of the operators were capable of providing credit facilities where as 71% believed in direct settlement of cash (Table 32).

Table 32
Adoption of Motivational Techniques

Motivational Practices	*Responses*		
	Yes	*No*	*Total*
Offering Gift	56(52)	52(48)	108(100)
Offering cash discount	26(54)	82(76)	108(100)
Punctuality in departure	36(33)	72(67)	108(100)
Credit facility	31(29)	77(71)	108(100)

(Bracket Figure indicates percentages)

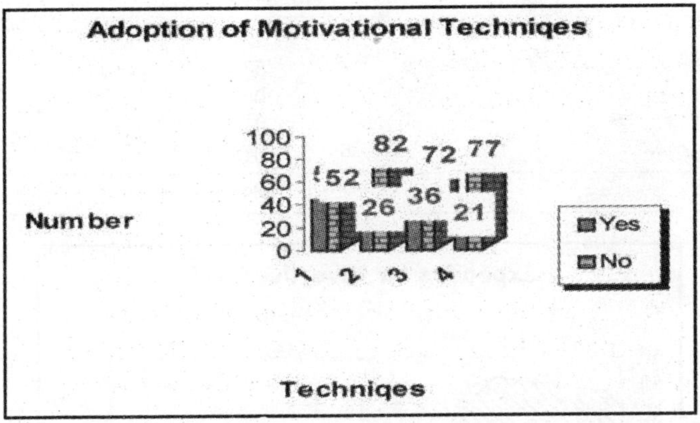

About 58% of the operators responded positively when questioned about charging penal interest on delayed payment, the other 42% replied in negatively and objected to harassing the travellers by charging them additional interest for delayed payment (Table 33).

Table 33
Charges Panel Interest on Delayed Payment

Charges Panel Interest	*Number*	%
Yes	63	58
No	45	42
Total	108	100

It was expectant to estimate the expense set aside by each company to pupularise their industry among the public. It was found that very little fund was spent by these companies for advertising their firm 5% of the agencies spent as much as 15,000 to 20,000 for advertisement annually. Of the total, about 5% of the agencies allocated per year Rs.,15,000 for advertisement expenditure, where as 50% of the agencies spent Rs.10,000 annually on advertisement, and 44% agencies Rs.5000 per year on advertisement (Table 34).

Table 34
Expenses on Advertisement

Expenses on Advertisement	*Number*	%
5000	47	44
10000	53	50
15000	06	05
20000	01	0.50
Any other	01	0.50
Total	108	100

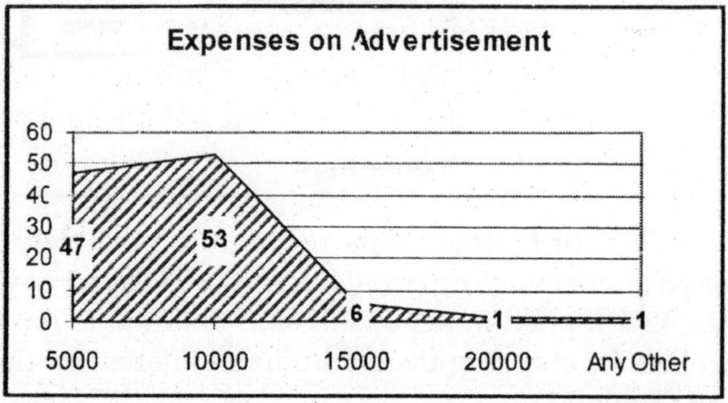

When questioned on whether the Tour operators maintained a strict schedule and punctuality in taking them to various tourist spots, of the total, 18% respondents replied in affirmative, while 82% of them were rather unrestrained in keeping up with the schedule.

Customer satisfaction is of utmost important for the success of any kind of industry. It is not only necessary that facilities be provided but the prompt and in time delivery facilities enhance the market value and demand. The researcher found that 39% of the operators were prompt in arranging suitable accommodation and other facilities. 64% of the operators found it quite easy to arrange tea and snacks in time. Only 31% of the operators were successful in providing lunch facility in schedule and only 16% provided dinner promptly (Table 35).

Table 35
Adoption of Motivational Tools

Motivational Practices	*Responses* Yes	No
Tours Schedule	19(18)	89(82)
Accommodation	42(39)	66(61)
Tea	69(64)	39(36)
Lunch	33(31)	75(69)
Dinner	17(16)	91(84)

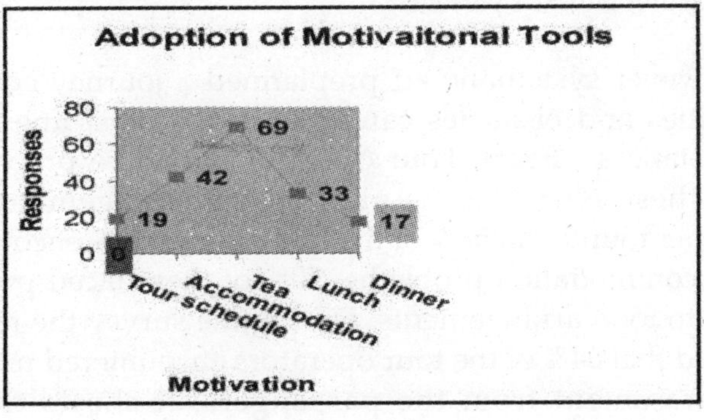

A tourist guide is an important person who acquaints the tourists with our historical and cultural background relating to various spots of tourist interest. A guide with a second communication knowledge of the history, archeology, literature, facts of a place is an inimitable part of a tourist group. He should also have thorough communicative knowledge of the language spoken by the tourists especially so in the case of foreign tourists ignorant in English. Researcher observed that only 24% of the tour operators took the botheration of providing guide service, 76% failed to provide any guide.

On examining whether additional entertainment programmes came under the priority of these tourist operators, researcher found that 43% of them entertained the tourists by arranging cultural programmes in the evening where as 57% provided no such facility of entertainment.

When questioned on whether they are successful in providing immediate alternative arrangement, 26% of the tour operators only answered affirmatively (Table 36).

Table 36
Various Arrangements during Tour

Various Arrangements During Tour	*Responses*	
	Yes	*No*
Guide	26(24)	82(76)
Cultural programming	46(43)	62(57)
Substitute arrangement during emergency	28(26)	80(74)

Bracket figures indicates percentage

However systematic ad preplanned a journey could be, difficulties and obstacles can arise in the most unexpected circumstances. Every Tour operator has to be prepared to tackle these obstacles by alternative arrangements. The researcher found that 58% of the tourist operators encountered with accommodation problems. 70% of them faced problems related to food arrangements. During the survey the research observed that 64% of the tour operators encountered problems like harassment from the passengers. It shows that the operators should be also prepared to face the circumstances. The table reflects that 89% of the operators agreed on encountering R.T.O. problems during the transit of tourists. A curse of our country is the lack of any definite government policies and the frequent amendments of the existing policies, the definitely cause inconvenience to the public. About 95% of the Tour operators replied affirmatively to this question.

There was also lack of experienced and trained staff in the field. About 81% of the operators complained about the non-availability of efficient and trained staff. It is time to realise that there ought to be well formulated policies about recruitment in the vital tourist body and this exercise is to be done by experts on the subject. Pre-service and post entry training has to be made a requisite, more promotional avenues need to be created so that the employees may be able to continue with dedication and given their best for the development of tourist trade (Table 37).

Table 37
Problems in Transport

Problems	*Respondents* Yes	No
Accommodation	63(58)	45(42)
Food arrangement	76(70)	32(30)
Harassment by passengers	69(64)	39(36)
R.T.O. problems	96(64)	12(11)
Problems due to unawareness towards changing R.T.O. rules	103(95)	5(5)
Problems due to inadequacy of experienced staff	87(81)	21(19)

Bracket figures indicates percentage

There is no denying the fact that our consumer formed their opinion from the treatment they received from the service staff. Naturally, if better treatment is accorded to the tourist, more tourists would be motivated to undertake tour to the region. Adequate number of service staff is necessary to see through the requirements of the tourists. Researcher observed that 69% of the agencies maintained a staff of 15. About 13% of the agencies had a staff group of 20, while 13% of the agencies maintained a staff strength of 10 and 3% agencies had an elaborate staff 25 in number (Table 38).

Table 38
Staff Members

No. of Staff Members	*Responses* Number	%
10	14	13
15	74	69
20	14	13
25	04	3
Any other	02	2
Total	108	100

The survey revealed that about 58% of the tour operators maintained staff with an expenditure of Rs.15,000 per month. 14% of them had a staff with an overall expenditure amounting to Rs.20,000 per month. 7% and 3% of the operators spent Rs.10,000 and Rs.5,000 per month respectively on payment of the staff (Table 39).

Table 39
Avg. Monthly Expenditure

Avg. Monthly Expenditure in (Rs.)	*Number*	%
5000	04	3
10000	08	7
15000	63	58
20000	15	14
Any other	18	18
Total	108	100

Researcher found that no fixed rules were followed in the appointment of staff. Most of them recruited staff on temporary basis, only 26% of the operators maintained permanent staff (Table 40).

Table 40
Number of Permanent Staff

Number of Permanent Staff	*Responses*	%
Yes	24	26
No	84	74
Total	108	100

On the question of frequency of staff, the researcher got the response that, the 67% of the operators are having the medium frequency of staff and only 22% high (Table 41).

Table 41
Frequency of Staff

Frequency of Staff	*Responses*	%
Low	12	11
Medium	72	67
High	24	22
Total	108	100

During survey it was evident that majority of the employees were recruited either directly or through adver-tisements, hence they did not have any kind of pre-entry training. About 77% of the recruitments were by adhoc appointments, only 23% were from the internal source. So the need for pre-entry training is indeed very genuine and it should be followed by past entry training in various stages (Table 42).

Table 42
Sources of Recruitments of Staff

Recruitments of Staff	*Number*	%
Internal Sources	25	23
External Sources	83	77
Total	108	100

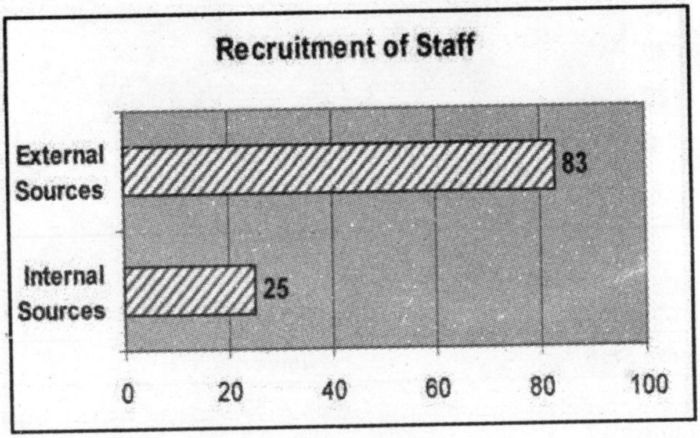

Some of the agencies had a combination of both trained and untrained staff. About 70% of such agencies were identified in this area; while 12% maintained only trained staff, 18% of them did not follow any fixed criteria for recruitment (Table 43).

Table 43
Recruitment of Trained & Untrained Staff

Staff	*Number*	%
Trained	13	12
Untrained	20	18
Both	75	70
Total	108	100

The researcher found that 70% of the staff has undergone through a post-entry training. 30% of the agencies did not provide any kind of training (Table 44).

Table 44
Training to Staff

Training to Staff	*Number*	*%*
Yes	76	70
No	32	30
Total	108	100

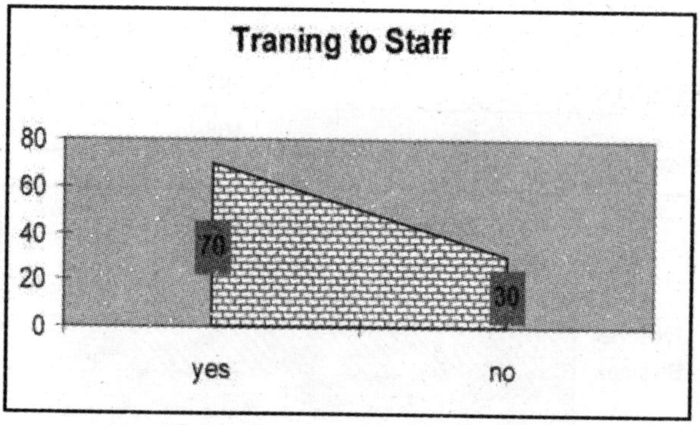

Table 45
Motivation to Staff

Motivation to Staff	*Number*	*%*
Monetary	32	30
Non-monetary	13	12
Both	10	9
No.	53	49
Total	108	100

When the respondents were asked whether they provided any motivation avenues, 30% of the respondents agreed saying that they provided monetary benefits. 12% of the employers sanctioned non-monetary benefits to their employees, 9% provided both monetary and non monetary incentives. Where, 49% denied of having providing any incentives or benefits (Table 45).

On enquiring whether they possessed any authorized ticket reservation agency, 78% of them responded negative. Only 22% ran authorised firm (Table 46).

Table 46
Possession of Authorized Ticket Reservation Agency

Ticket Reservation Agency	*Number*	%
Yes	24	22
No	84	78
Total	108	100

For the question whether other reservation makes ticket reservations at their travel agency on commission basis, 69% of them replied in negative and 31% responded in affirmative (Table 47).

Table 47
Ticket Reservation on Commission Basis

Commission Basis Ticket Reservation	*Number*	%
Yes	34	31
No	74	69
Total	108	100

The rate of commission received by the travel agencies for seat reservations, ticket transit etc. varied in percentage from agency to agency. 80% of the agencies received a common of 10%, 3% of the agencies charged 7% as commission, and 1.5% of the agencies charge 9% and 5% as commission respectively (Table 48).

Table 48
Rate of Commission

Rate of Commission	*Number*	%
5%	2	1.50
7%	4	3
9%	2	1.50
10%	87	80
Any other	13	14
Total	108	100

50% of the agencies reserved as such as 70% of tickets, Far behind was 17% of the agencies which reserved 50% of tickets. 13%, 6% and 11% of the agencies reserved a high percentage of 80%, 90% and 60% respectively. 1% and 2% of the agencies reserved as much as 100% and 40% of tickets (Table 49).

Table 49
Ticket Reservation for Tour Operator

Ticket for Tour Operator	*Number*	%
10%	–	–
20%	–	–
30%	–	–
40%	03	2
50%	19	17
60%	12	11
70%	53	50
80%	14	13
90%	06	6
100%	01	1
Total	108	100

An analysis was made on the total investment born by the agencies to establish the agency. 17% of the respondents said that the net investment was Rs.41,000 to 45,000. 11% of the operators replied that their net cost to start the agency was Rs.46,000 to Rs.50,000. 4% and 2% of the operators managed with Rs.36,000 to Rs.40,000 and Rs,30,000 to Rs.35,000 respectively (Table 50).

Table 50
Investments

Investments	*Number*	%
30000 to 35000	02	2
35001 to 40000	04	4
40001 to 45000	19	17
45001 to 50000	12	11
Any other	71	66
Total	108	100

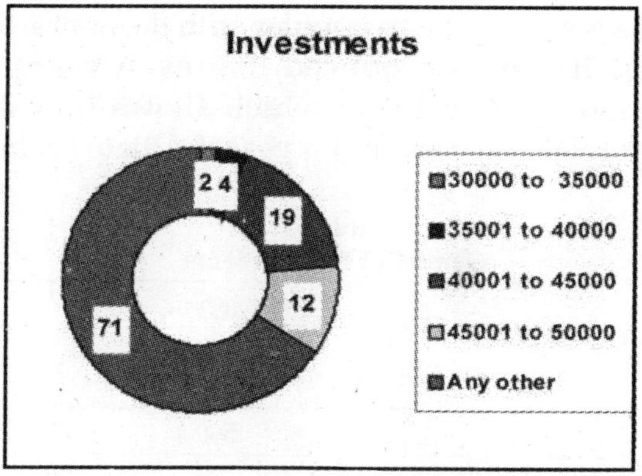

Section B
Tourist

The table shows that the tourist have been classified on the basis of their age into 8 categories. The table shows that most of the tourist i.e. 30% belong to the age group of 21 to 25 years, while the next 16% tourist were in the age group of 26 to 30 years, 14% identified themselves with the age group of 36 to 40 years and the 11% of tourist belong to the age groups of upto 20 years and 46 to 50 years was 11% each. Tourist up to 51 and above were only 1%. (Table 51)

Table 51
Agewise Classification of Tourists

Age group	*Number*	*%*
Upto 20 years	60	11
21 to 25 years	166	30
26 to 30 years	92	16
31 to 35 years	73	13
36 to 40 years	81	14
41 to 45 years	20	04
46 to 50 years	60	11
51 and above	08	01
Total	560	100

In regard to the sex of tourist it shows that out of 560 tourist 61% were males and 39% were females. It indicates that tourist in Karnataka is slightly more popular with the males, than with the females. It was also noticed that even young women travelled alone to Karnataka which shows that they find Karnataka a relatively safe and a peaceful state (Table 52).

Table 52
Gender of Respondents

Gender	*Number*	*%*
Male	344	61
Female	216	39
Total	560	100

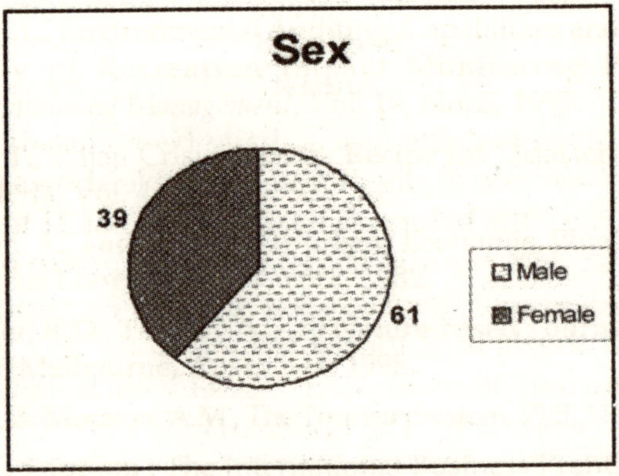

This table show that it is the younger generation of tourist from all party of the world who want to go around and see India in all its mood. It is for them that most of the infrastructure and potentials are to be geared up. In study researcher interviewed 66% of married tourist and 34% unmarried ones (Table 53).

Table 53
Marital Status

Marital Status	*Number*	*%*
Married	367	66
Unmarried	193	34
Total	560	100

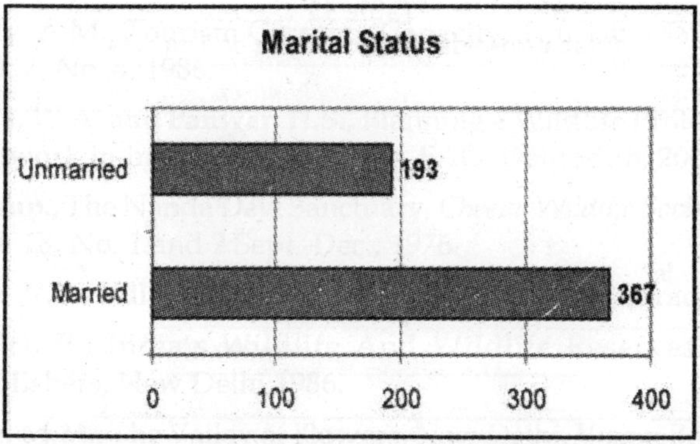

The table shows that the tourist have been classifieds on the basis of members in the family into five categories. The table shows that most of the tourist 39% is accompanied by Kith and Kin of the age group 3 to 5, 34% reveals that they have the members in the family of the age groups 6 to 10, while the next 20% tourist mentioned that their members in the family were below 2 (Table 54).

Table 54
Members in the Family

Members	*Number*	*%*
Below - 2	113	20
3 to 5	219	39
6 to 10	188	34
10 and above	40	07
Total	560	100

To identify the preferences of tourist it is important to know their education background. Hence they are classified into six groups viz non matric, matriculate, intermediate , Graduate, Post graduate and Others. About 45% tourist were graduate which is the highest among tourist, while 20% each belonged to categories of intermediate and post-graduate. Thus tourist planners must take note of the fact that since most of the tourist are highly qualified, the tourist guide and staff ought to be well informed, gentle and suave, so that they may be able to deliver the good befitting to their clientele (Table 55).

Table 55
Education wise Distribution of Tourists

Education wise	*Number*	*%*
Non matric	06	01
Matriculate	20	04
Inter mediate	110	20
Graduate	254	45
Post graduate	112	20
Others	58	10
Total	560	100

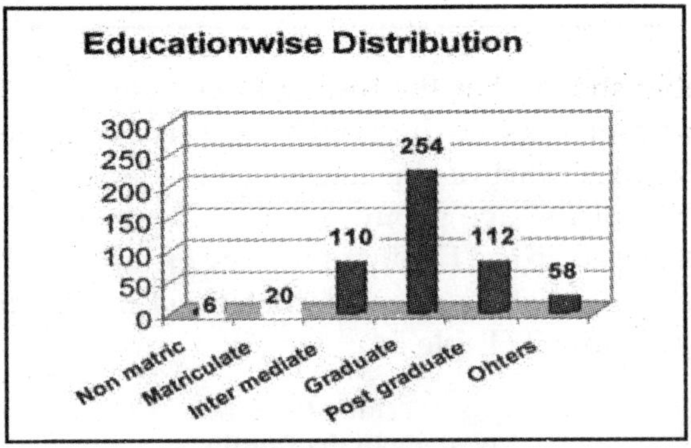

The table shows the nature of job of the tourist, 38% of the tourist which is the highest, come from the self-employed businessman, 29% from the government organisation, 21% from the private organisation and 12% of the tourist falls in other categories such as professionals etc.

Socio economic profile of tourists affects the use pattern to greater extent. It gives an idea of their liking and disliking according to their education , occupation etc. (Table 56).

Table 56
Nature of the Job

Job	*Number*	*%*
Employed government organisation	165	29
Employed Private organisation	119	21
Self employed businessman	213	38
Other professionals	63	12
Total	560	100

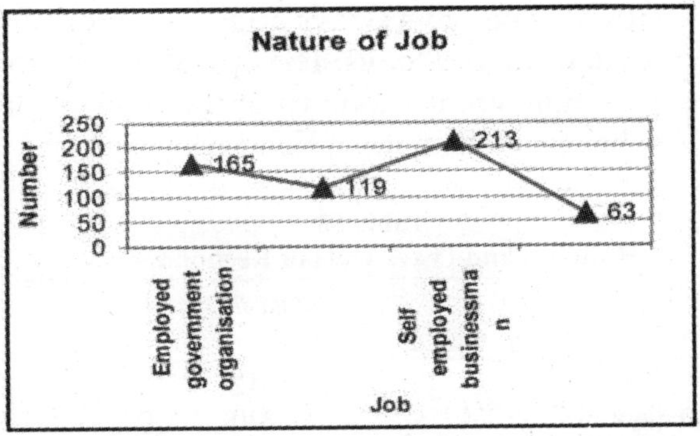

The response to the question on income was quite revealing in regard to the availability of funds for travel. The tourist were classified into 6 categories on the basis of the stated incomes. This will help in planning tourist programmes and facilities. The above table shows that 34% tourist come from the income group of Rs. 75001 to Rs. 100000, 42% from the group having income above 10000 and below 125000, 1% tourist come from the income group of up to 50000 since they fall into the category of students, housewives etc. this table further demonstrates that the Karnataka State Tourism Development Corporation (KSTDC) providing services mainly to the highest start of society (Table 57).

Table 57
Annual Income

Annual Income	*Number*	%
Upto Rs. 50000	9	01
Rs 50001 to. 75000	12	02
Rs 75001 to 100000	188	34
Rs 100001 to 125000	100	18
Rs 125001 to 150000	237	42
More than 150000	14	03
Total	560	100

In regard to holidays and leave data the above table shows that the majority i.e. 59% of the tourist visit with the leave of 16 days, to 30 days, 20% visit with only 10 days to 15 days ,

19% visits with 31 days to 45 days and the minority i.e only 2% visits with 46 days to 60 days. The operators has to realize that in order to motivate the tourists at the time of planning, the operators have to take note of holidays (Table 58).

Table 58
Holidays and Leave Data of Respondents

Number of Holidays and Leave	*Number*	*%*
10 days to 15 days	112	20
16 days to 30 days	330	59
31 days to 45 days	104	19
46 days to 60 days	14	02
More than 60 days	–	–
Total	560	100

One of the objectives of survey was to find out how tourist are motivated to undertake an excursion, to assess whether the role played by travel agencies were adequate enough or not. The survey revealed that only 36% of the tourists depended on the travel for tour agencies. A high majority of 64% made their own arrangements for excursions.

The survey reveals that the functioning of travel information leave much to be desired there has been a lack of co-ordination between department of tourism structure and private sector travel agencies, which has to be evolved and established. The travel agencies should be active and must be well equipped by the Karnataka State Tourism Development Corporation (KSTDC) authorities with all kinds of tourist literature. Travel agencies should serve as a center of publicity to promote tourist. (Table 59)

Table 59
Arrangement of Tours

Arrangement	*Number*	*%*
By own arrangement	359	64
By approaching travel agency	201	36
Total	560	100

In regard to the leave travel allowance out of 560 respondents 31% of the tourist responded affirmative while majority i.e. 69% answered in the negative this table shows that the majority of the tourist are deprived of the leave travel allowances (Table 60).

Table 60
Leave Travel Allowance

Facilities	*Number*	%
Yes	176	31
No	384	69
Total	560	100

In order to ascertain the degree of interest of the population for touring, a questions was asked about their preferred duration of tour. A majority of 52% wanted to engage themselves in one week tour. There was a percentage of 21 who preferred touring for a fortnight. One and more than one month tour was fund to be less popular with only 4% and 11% opting it. One day was also seen to be too lower a duration, for it was opted only by 11% of the tourist population (Table 61).

Table 61
Tour Duration Preferences

Tour Duration Preference	*Number*	%
One day	70	12
One week	293	52
Fortnight	116	21
One month	21	04
More than one month	60	11
Total	560	100

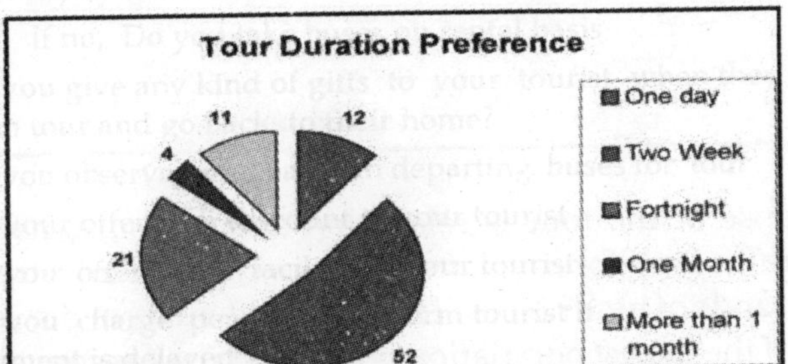

Man's drive to navigate the unknown is inherent in him, history gives us an account of mans urge to cross the boundaries and uncover the hidden. Human being wants to explore his surrounding and unravel the mysteries behind it, this impulse was also evident in our tourists population. Among the 560 respondents, 57% of tourists group wanted to cross the boundaries of their state and see the nook and corner of India and its brightness. 37% confined their taste to exploring their own state, while only 6% believed in navigating the world. Hence more spots of tourist attraction has to modified and amenities be provided adequately (Table 62).

Table 62
Types of Tour

Type	*Number*	*%*
State tour	210	37
All India tours	317	57
International tours	33	06
Total	560	100

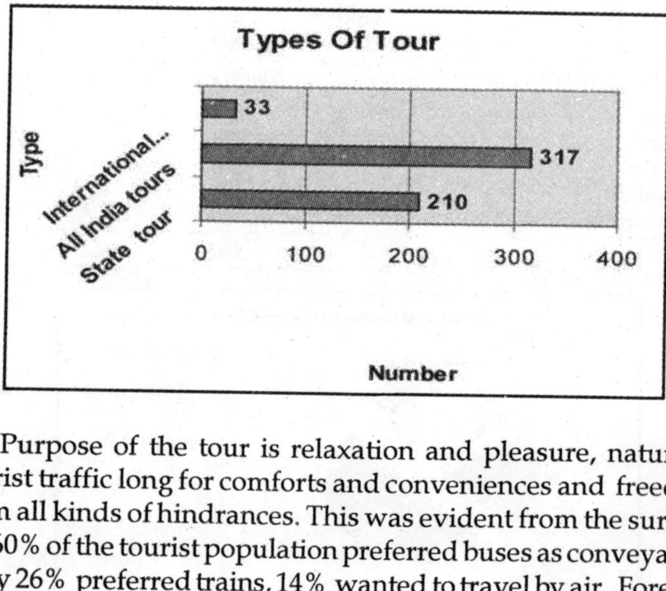

Purpose of the tour is relaxation and pleasure, naturally tourist traffic long for comforts and conveniences and freedom from all kinds of hindrances. This was evident from the survey, for 60% of the tourist population preferred buses as conveyance. Only 26% preferred trains, 14% wanted to travel by air. Foreign, tourist should receive considerable attention in the planning of tourist development. They have more to spend on recreation and vacation activities and expect more luxurious and sophisticated facilities. Railways has to come forward and gear up their facilities to meet the requirements of tourist traffic (Table 63).

Table 63
Types of Journey

Preference for Types of Journey	*Number*	%
By bus	334	60
By train	143	26
By air	83	14
Total	560	100

The table shows the uprising popularity of the tourist trade among the public. Among the 560 respondents 39% spent as much as 15% of their income on touring. Closely following was 31% of the respondents who claimed that their expenditure set aside for holidaying come up to 20% of their income. 16% and 2% of the respondents kept aside a larger percentage of 25 and 30% on tourism. In the recent years there has been an increase in the percentage of population, notably from the middle income group, who set out on tours. This large percentage of holiday seekers emphasis the need to provide cheaper and adequate hotel accommodation and the development of tourist resort areas (Table 64).

Table 64
Proportion of Income Spent on Tour

Income Proportion	*Number*	%
10% of Income	68	12
15% of Income	219	39
20% of Income	173	31
25% of Income	87	16
30% of Income	13	02
Total	560	100

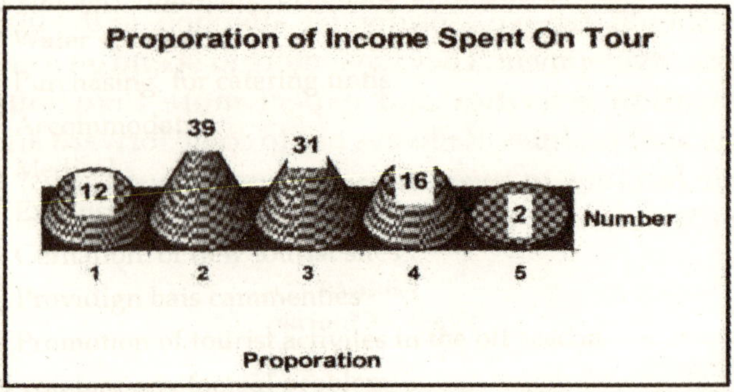

Travel agencies has a significant role in organising executing tourist trips. It is a supplies of services (Transport, accommodation, food etc.) It is its duty to ensure that the services supplied are first rate and meet the normal requirements of tourist traffic. It is its function to make known to the market the change in tastes, needs and new tendencies of travellers. It represent all aspects of the market. An analysis was made on the rising influence of such agencies on the public. Among the 560 of the tourist traffic 79% (445 numbers) replied that they approached travel agencies for tour purposes and a minority of 21% denied of having any contact with agencies (Table 65).

Table 65
Travelling with Travel Agency

Travel with Travel Agency	*Number*	*%*
Yes	445	79
No	115	21
Total	560	100

In the era of rapid urbanization and industrialization, when man is engulfed by fatigue and varying kinds of tensions, the need for leisure and recreation is all the more vital. Recreation gives relaxation peace, sound mind and body, pleasure etc. This intimately results in more efficiency in work and better living. Modern man has now realised the importance of recreation and tourism is a feasible solution. When researcher met the tourist in person it was crucial to make an evaluation of the time they spent in touring, researcher questioned about the frequency of their experience with the travel agencies. 47% of respondents had only single experience with a travel agency was for the record time. 20% of the travellers had 3 times experience with the agencies where as only 4% of the travellers traveled about 4 to 5 times with these agencies. Those who traveled for more than five times were nil in number. The vital role of travel agents in the growth and promotion of tourism is now established. The Govt. has to work in collaboration with them to plan a organise package tour to various destination both India and abroad. More incentives and awards has to sanction to motivate the tour operators ad travel agencies to attract more and more tourist to India (Table 66).

Table 66
Average Travelling Experience with Travel Agency

Travelling Experience	*Number*	%
One time	211	47
Two time	112	25
Three time	88	20
Four time	19	04
Five time	15	04
Five time	00	00
Total	445	100

In order to make an evaluation of the various health problems encountered by the tourists during the journey, it was important to collect their viewpoints. Some of the common problems was ailments resulting from the change in climate, water, food, air pollution etc. A high percentage of 93% faced health problem resulting from the change in climate. Contaminated or unhygienic food and water contributed to 89% to 71% of ailments. Sickness relating to air pollution was also found to be common with 67%. Continuous journey also caused fatigue and sickness to some of the travellers with 62% replying positive (Table 67).

Table 67
Health Problem During Tour

Problems	*Yes*	%	*No.*	%
Change in water	315	71	130	29
Change in food	397	89	48	11
Change in climate	413	93	32	07
Daily travel	276	62	169	38
Air pollution	297	67	148	33
Water pollution	273	61	172	39

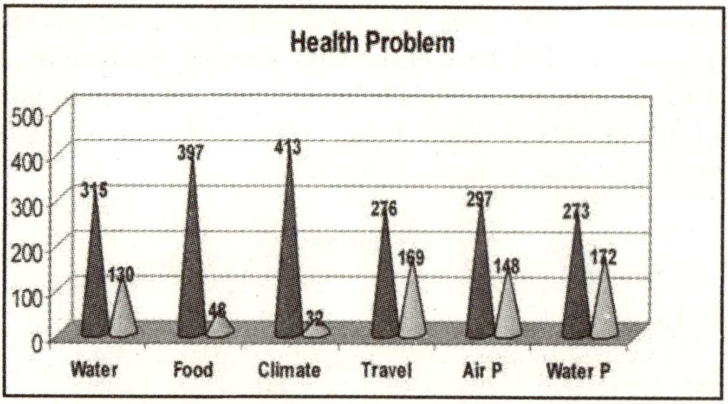

The tourists were questioned about other difficulties they faced during the course of the journey such as technical problem, Road Transport Officer problem, state entry problem, natural calamities, health of other passengers, late arrivals of passengers etc. which might have caused hindrances to their pleasure trip. 72% of the respondents claimed that they encountered a number of technical problems. 25% of the respondents said that they faced inconvenience owing to

Table 68
Unreasonable Problems During Tour

Problems	*Yes*	%	*No.*	%
Technical problems	319	72	126	28
R.T.O. problems	140	31	305	69
Other state entry problems	217	49	228	51
Natural climates	113	25	332	75
Health of passengers	334	75	111	25
Late arrivals of passengers	173	39	272	61

natural calamities. 75% of the passengers responded that they were troubled by ill health, Road Transport Officer problems and state entry problems also caused discomfort to about 49% and 31% of the passengers (Table 68).

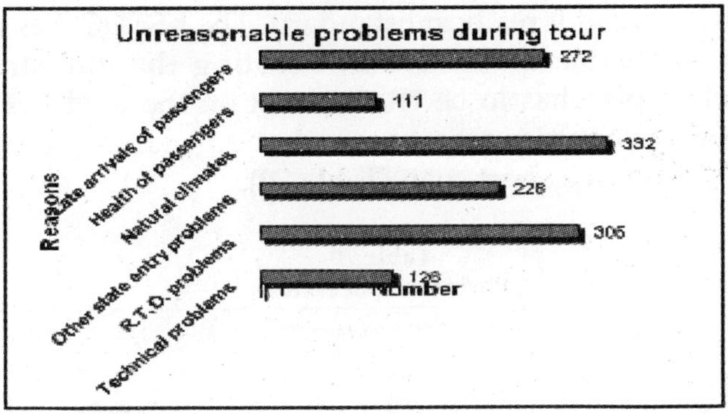

From the survey it evident that the tourists were indeed put to a lot of discomfort, the tour operators were ill equipped to tackle a number of problems which sprung up in course of the journey. Of all the travellers researcher spoke to each one of them acknowledged that they had to encounter one or the other kind of problem. 73% stated that they were put to inconvenience owing to the lack of professional knowledge of the operators. 61% faced difficulty because of the non-availability of language study material. 37% mentioned that found the charge of traditional handicrafts unreasonable. 56% faced pollution problems, 35% faced trouble owing to the lack of tourist guide, 39% of the travellers encountered encashment problems (Table 69).

Table 69
General Problem During Tour

Problems	*Yes*	*%*	*No.*	*%*
Lack of professional knowledge of tour operators	326	73	119	27
Encashment problems of travellers cheques	174	39	271	61
Non-availability of language study material	273	61	172	39
Unreasonably charges for traditional handicrafts	163	37	282	63
High pollution	249	56	196	44
Lack of tourist guide	156	35	289	65

Regarding the various concessions available from the Karnataka State Tourism Development corporation(KSTDC) researcher saw that only 22% of respondents found it sufficient and satisfactory. A majority of 69% did not have much high opinion but termed it as average. There was a small minority of 1% who found it really substandard. The KSTDC has to be more responsible in its role in boosting the industry. A perspective plan has to be chalked out on the model of our neighboring countries who has made tremendous growth in this field with in a short span (Table 70).

Table 70
Various Concessions

Facilities	*(N)Number*	*Percentage*	*(W)Weightage*	*(NxW)Rating*
Excellent	08	2	7	56
Very good	13	3	6	78
Good	38	8	5	190
Average	307	69	4	1228
Satisfactory	77	17	3	231
Bad	02	1	2	04
Atrocious	–	–	1	00
Total	445	100		1787

Mean score= N x W / N = 1787 /445 = 4.01

Experience With Regard To the Tour

Comments from the tourists were also invited on the qualitative aspect of the various facilities and provisions provided. The conveyance facility arranged was utilised by majority of the respondents 71% of the tourists commented that the bus service provided was just average. 26% found it satisfactory in performance. There was only a minute percentage of 3% which termed the vehicle very good in condition. 4% of the respondents found the vehicle to be bad in condition. Though the mean score is 3.78 between satisfactory and average (Table 71).

Promptness and punctuality aspect of the bus service also was received by varying responses from the travellers. 71% of the travellers responded that the punctuality of services was average 16% of the respondents did not appreciate the promptness and services but expressed that they were satisfied 5% of the respondents complained it as bad. Only a meager percentage of 3% and 5% said that the service was very good. A good impression created in the tourist can persuade them to avoid the service. Again and again, this can be done by rendering them on efficient and savour service (Table 72).

Table 71
Travel Vehicle(Buses)

Experiences	*(N)Number*	*Percentage*	*(W)Weightage*	*(NxW)Rating*
Excellent	00	00	7	00
Very good	14	03	6	84
Good	26	06	5	130
Average	237	61	4	1092
Satisfactory	116	26	3	348
Bad	16	04	2	32
Atrocious	–	–	1	00
Total	445	100		1686

Mean score = N x W / N = 1686 /445 = 3.78

Table 72
Punctuality Aspect

Experiences	*(N)Number*	*Percentage*	*(W)Weightage*	*(NxW)Rating*
Excellent	–	–	7	00
Very good	12	03	6	72
Good	22	05	5	110
Average	317	71	4	1268
Satisfactory	73	16	3	219
Bad	21	05	2	42
Atrocious	–	–	1	00
Total	445	100		1711

Mean score = N x W / N = 1711 /445 = 3.84

Of the many and diverse element of the tourist industry, accommodation constitute one of the important segment. Without an adequate development of accommodation resources, neither the national scenery, nor a good climate nor even all the sporting and recreational facilities will suffice to sustain a good volume and tourist trade. Accommodation constitute not only magnificent and elegant infrastructure but number of factors like good service, cleanliness of environment, good location etc. During survey researcher questioned travellers about the quality of accommodation provided to them. 50% of respondents found the facility neither too good nor too bad but average in nature. 41% of my respondents claimed the facility to be fairly good. On the extremes were a minor percentage of respondents (0.5%, 4%, 0.5%) who termed the accommodation as excellent, very good and bad respectively (Table 73).

Table 73
Accommodation Facilities

Experiences	*(N)Number*	*Percentage*	*(W)Weightage*	*(NxW)Rating*
Excellent	02	00.50	7	14
Very good	16	4.00	6	96
Good	183	41	5	915
Average	219	50	4	876
Satisfactory	23	04	3	69
Bad	02	00.50	2	04
Atrocious	—	—	1	00
	445	100		1974

Mean score = N x W / N = 1974 /445 = 4.43

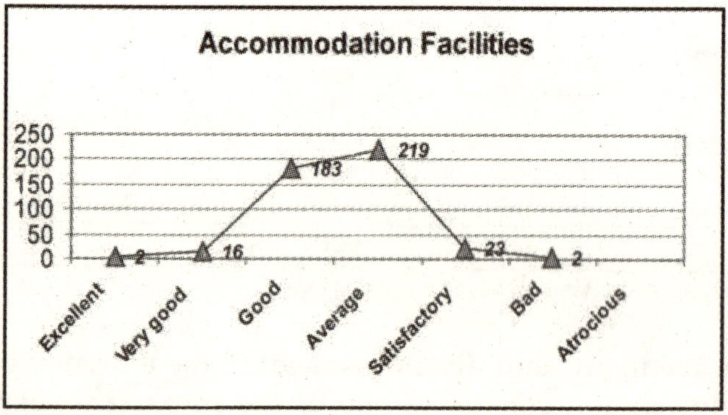

In survey researcher wanted to find out whether the cleanliness and hygiene maintained was up to the mark. Once again researcher got diverse responses. To researchers disappointment there was only a minor percentage of 2% and 1%

who really admired the facility provided remarking it as excellent and very good there was 22%, 24% and 17% of passengers who did not have nay complaints but remarked the facility as average satisfactory and good respectively. 5% of respondents utilised the facility (Table 74).

Table 74
Cleanliness & Hygiene

Experiences	*(N)Number*	*Percentage*	*(W)Weightage*	*(NxW)Rating*
Excellent	04	1	7	28
Very good	09	2	6	54
Good	259	58	5	1295
Average	25	06	4	100
Satisfactory	67	15	3	201
Bad	73	16	2	146
Atrocious	08	02	1	08
	445	100		1832

Mean score = N x W / N = 1832 /445 = 4.11

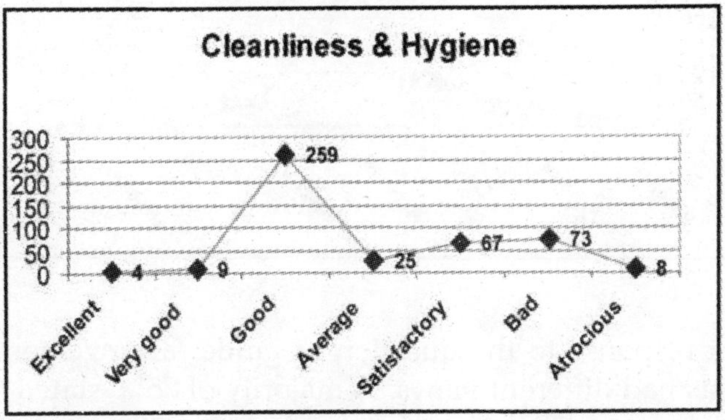

Regarding the first aid and medical facilities majority of the travellers opined that it was (59%) average. 10% and 19% of the respondents exclaimed that it was satisfactory and good respectively. 11% and 2% found it quite atrocious. Mean score is 4.30 which means that first aid and medical facilities are above average. Shortage of medical centers and the lack of even the primary equipments in such centers is a sad truth regarding our villages and remote areas, renovation of medical centers and dispensaries is a must (Table 75).

Table 75
First Aid and Medical Facilities

Facilities	*(N)Number*	*Percentage*	*(W)Weightage*	*(NxW)Rating*
Excellent	13	1	7	91
Very good	36	8	6	216
Good	83	19	5	415
Average	263	59	4	1052
Satisfactory	44	10	3	132
Bad	02	0.50	2	04
Atrocious	04	2.50	1	04
	445	100		1914

Mean score = N x W / N = 1914 /445 = 4.30

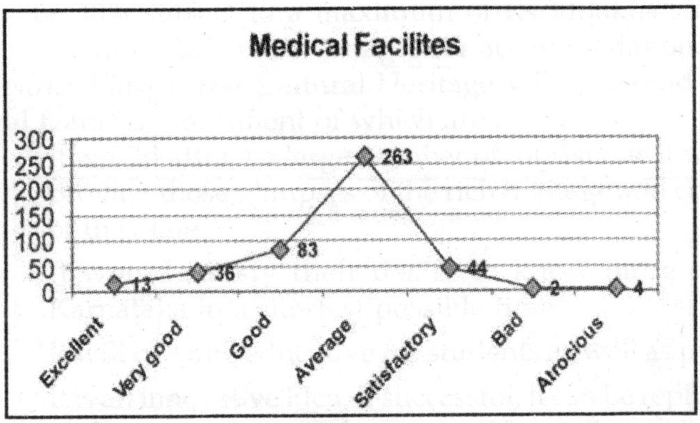

In response to the question of guide arrangement also tourists had different views. A majority of 75% stated that it was adequate. Though only a minority of 25% spoke of the need for enrichment and revision of guide, we cannot ignore the opinion of this minority. It is a fact that there is a shortage of well equipped guides. In order to raise to heights this highly competent industry and to increase the flow of foreign exchange, guides capable of dealing with foreign tourist traffic has to be made accessible Department of Tourism has to function efficiently in matters dealing with recruitment and registration of guides, training and protection of their rights (Table 76).

Table 76
Guide Arrangement At Tourist Spot

Facilities	*(N)Number*	*Percentage*	*(W)Weightage*	*(NxW)Rating*
Excellent	06	1	7	42
Very good	18	4	6	108
Good	74	17	5	370
Average	108	24	4	432
Satisfactory	237	53	3	711
Bad	02	01	2	04
Atrocious	—	—	1	00
Total	445	100		1667

Mean score = N x W / N = 1667 / 445 = 3.744.01

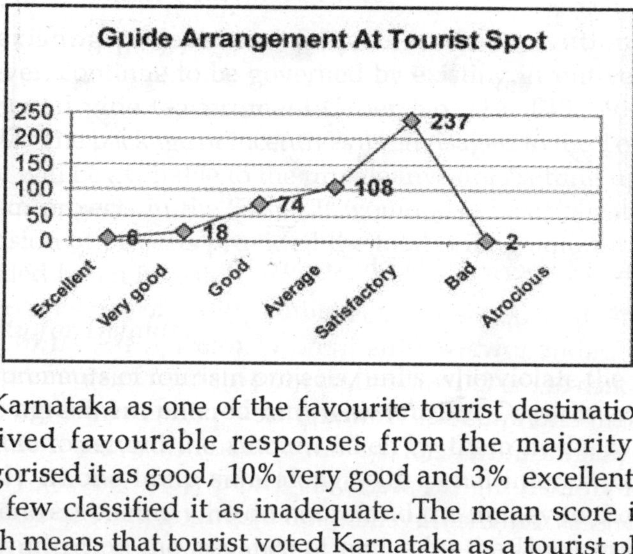

Karnataka as one of the favourite tourist destination also received favourable responses from the majority. 62% categorised it as good, 10% very good and 3% excellent. Only very few classified it as inadequate. The mean score is 4.84 which means that tourist voted Karnataka as a tourist place in more than average. Hence we infer that tourists are satisfied (Table 77).

Table 77
Karnataka As a Tourists Place

Facilities	*(N)Number*	*Percentage*	*(W)Weightage*	*(NxW)Rating*
Excellent	13	03	7	91
Very good	43	10	6	258
Good	276	62	5	1380
Average	93	21	4	372

Contd.

Facilities	(N)Number	Percentage	(W)Weightage	(NxW)Rating
Satisfactory	17	04	3	51
Bad	03	01	2	06
Atrocious	00	00	1	00
	445	100		2158

Mean score = N x W / N = 2158 /445 = 4.84

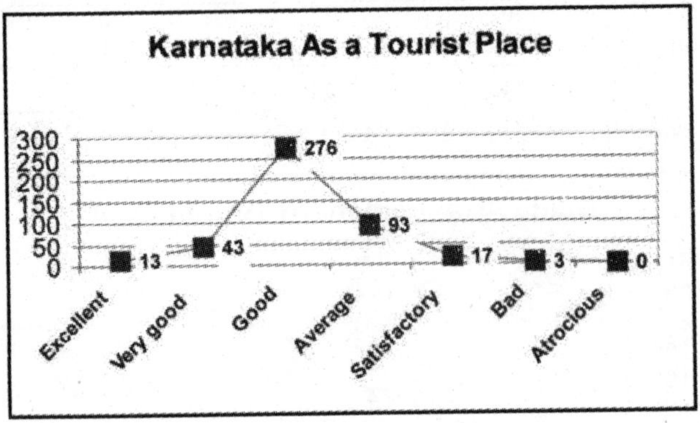

Personal Experience With Regard To

For the development of this industry and to attract more and more public towards this trend of touring, the attitude and approach of the tour operators towards their customers has be pleasant and amiable. From the view points of the tourists its clear that the attitude of the tour operators towards their clients in far from being appreciable. There were varying types of responses from the travellers some terming there behaviour as good 49% while some wants to the extremes and termed their attitude as bad and atrocious 4% and 5% respectively. 14% of travellers found their conduct quite satisfactory, 16% of the respondents opined that their performance was average. Only 13% and 3.5% of the respondents termed their behaviour as very good and excellent (Table 78).

Judgment of the tourists on the quality of food arranged also came under my scrutiny. 59% of the tourist replied that the food provided was good there was only a minor percentage of 6% who complained about food. 12% and 16% of the travellers found the food provided to be average and satisfactory in quality. Though most of them (66%) found the food facility as adequate, yet there was a substantial number of tourists (18%) who found it rather inadequate, it shows the sorry state of affairs prevalent in the consumer service (Table 79).

Table 78
First Meeting Experience With Travelling Agency

Experience	*(N)Number*	*Percentage*	*(W)Weightage*	*(NxW)Rating*
Excellent	14	3.50	7	98
Very good	60	13	6	360
Good	220	49	5	1100
Average	73	16	4	292
Satisfactory	60	14	3	180
Bad	16	04	2	32
Atrocious	02	0.50	1	02
	445	100		2064

Mean score = N x W / N = 2064 /445 = 4.16

Table 79
Quality of Food

Facilities	*(N)Number*	*Percentage*	*(W)Weightage*	*(NxW)Rating*
Excellent	04	1	7	28
Very good	26	6	6	156
Good	263	59	5	1315
Average	52	12	4	208
Satisfactory	69	16	3	207
Bad	31	06	2	62
Atrocious	00	00	1	00
	445	100		1976

Mean score = N x W / N = 1976 /445 = 4.44

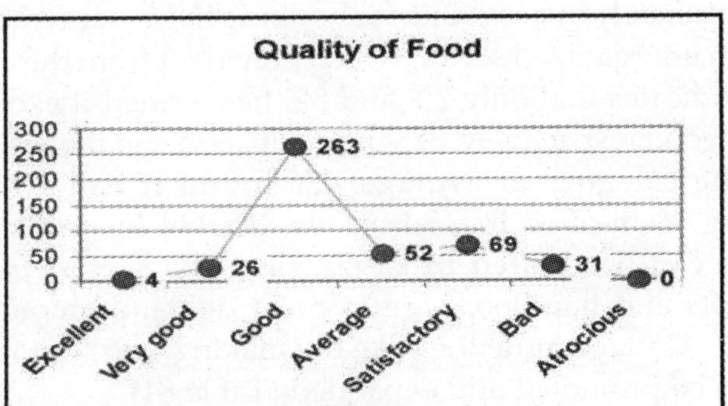

From the table its clear that the opinions of the traveller regarding the entertainment programme in more or less evenly distributed in the table from excellent to bad. Hence this segment of the tourism also require some urgent improvisation. 22%, 24% and 17% of the tourist traffic stated that the entertainment facility was just average satisfactory and good respectively only a minority of 5% mentioned that the entertainment was excellent and bad. Entertainment programmes has to be elaborated local fairs and festivals can be organized, more water bodies and amusement parks has tobe established. Local music and dance and local art and craft are also of considerable importance in increasing the tourist traffic (Table 80).

Table 80
Entertainment

Facilities	*(N)Number*	*Percentage*	*(W)Weightage*	*(NxW)Rating*
Excellent	23	05	7	161
Very good	119	27	6	714
Good	97	22	5	485
Average	106	24	4	424
Satisfactory	76	17	3	228
Bad	24	05	2	48
Atrocious	00	00	1	00
	445	100		2060

Mean score = N x W / N = 2060 /445 = 4.62

Shopping is one of the important past times of a visitors. In fact it is often the single most important activity of a visitor. But unfortunately in our country, shopping has so far remained largely an unorganized sector, which is evident from the above table it indicates that only 2% and 8% has termed it excellent and very good respectively. 37% found it good and the majority put in the category of average. 1% found it bad and the remaining 2% termed it as atrocious. Market for Indianised products can be created by organising this sector. Indian handicrafts and handloom are in great demand among the foreigners. Cottage industries like toy making, coir, terra cotta etc has to be promoted and expanded (Table 81).

Table 81
Shopping Facilities

Facilities	*(N)Number*	*Percentage*	*(W)Weightage*	*(NxW)Rating*
Exceilent	11	2	7	77
Very good	35	8	6	210
Good	166	37	5	830
Average	184	41	4	736
Satisfactory	39	09	3	117
Bad	06	01	2	12
Atrocious	04	02	1	04
	445	100		1986

Mean score = N x W / N = 1986 /445 = 4.46

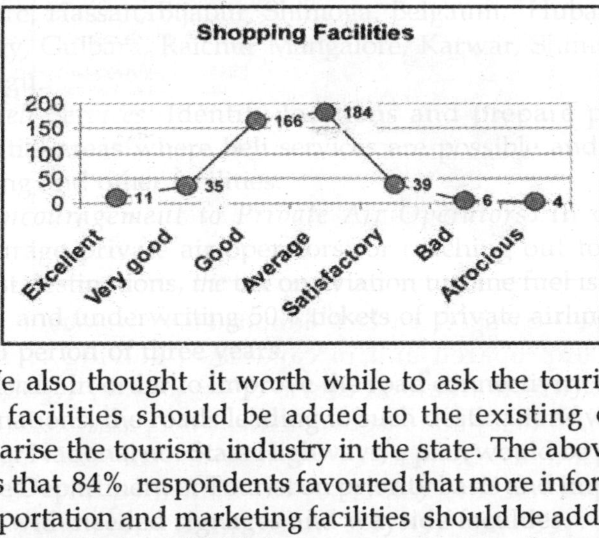

We also thought it worth while to ask the tourist what more facilities should be added to the existing ones to popularise the tourism industry in the state. The above table shows that 84% respondents favoured that more information, trans-portation and marketing facilities should be added, 65% mentioned hat the KSTDC does not properly perform the duty of travel agency, even though it is one of its objectives in their opinion KSTDC should also start working like a travel agency which will result in earning good profits. 89% recommended that historical places should be well maintained and more facilities should be created to attract more tourists another 66% of respondents made a plea for making large budget provisions for the development of hotel facilities. The fact remained that a lot of facilities need to be added to develop fully and realise the potentialities of the smokeless industry (Table 82).

Table 82
Tourist Feedback

Tourist Feedback	*Responses*	
	No.	*%*
Introduction, transport and marketing facilities should be added	373	84
Do you satisfy with the working of KSTDC as Travel Agency	289	65
Creation of new facilities and maintenance of historical places	397	89
Budget class hotels should be started	394	66

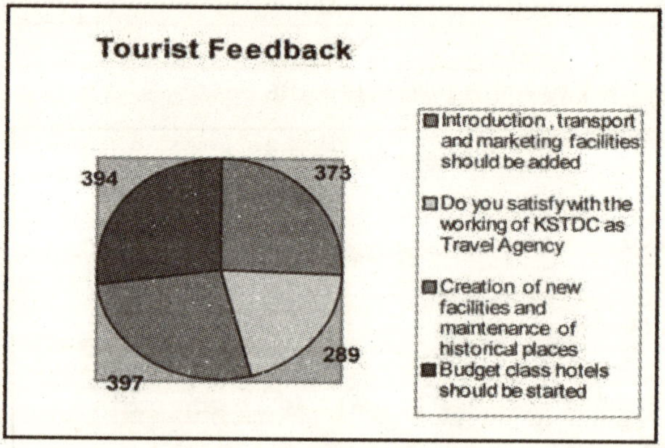

Of the 445 respondent 86% admitted that the tour operators proved unprepared and in capable of solving technical problems which arouse in course of the journey resulting in unnecessary delay and inconvenience to the passengers. It was important to assess whether the tourists had really enjoyed the trip or not, the response was almost equally divided between YES and NO 55% were content with the trip while 45% were discontent. Serious measures has to be taken to organize his sector and assure efficiency in its performance by all respect. Regarding the tour arrangements also 72% of the respondents expressed their dissatisfaction with an exception of a minority 28%. It could be seen from the table above that only 21% of the respondents retained any cherishable memory regarding the trip. A majority of 79% denied of having any sweet memories. When the researcher spoke to the travellers it was known that only 3% preferred to join a travel agency for their future tour, 69% were so dissatisfied that they disagreed (Table 83).

Table 83
Variables Worth to Note from Tourist Point of View

Variables	*Responses*		*Total*
	Yes	*No*	
Arrangement to solve problems	61(14)	384(86)	445(100)
Enjoyment of trip	243(55)	202(45)	445(100)
Satisfaction with tour arrangement	126(28)	319(72)	445(100)
Memorable experience	179(21)	266(79)	445(100)
Preference to join same operator	137(31)	308(69)	445(100)

Majority of the tourists choose the places to visit by word of guidance from friends and relatives and other miscellaneous sources (49% and 40% respectively). Tourist offices and travel agents contributed only to the extent of 21%, 9% of the respondents visited on their own judgment or previous experience advertisement and travel information bureaus to be almost ineffective for only 3% of the respondents were influenced by them (Table 84).

Table 84
Source Motivated to Join Tour

Source Motivated	*Number*	*%*
Own experience/judgment	38	9
Friends/relatives	218	49
Tourist information Bureaus	07	02
Advertisement/tourist branches	13	03
Any other	176	40

It was delightful to know that in spite of all the inconveniences that the tourists had to endure a majority of i.e. 74% wanted to revisit Karnataka, only 26% disagreed to the his question. This proves that Karnataka falls in the category of some of the interesting and eye capturing tourist destinations, hence if better facilities and more provisions are provide, the industry has high scope in this region (Table 85).

Table 85
Revisits to Particular Place of Karnataka

Revisit to Karnataka	*Number*	*%*
Yes	330	74
No	115	26

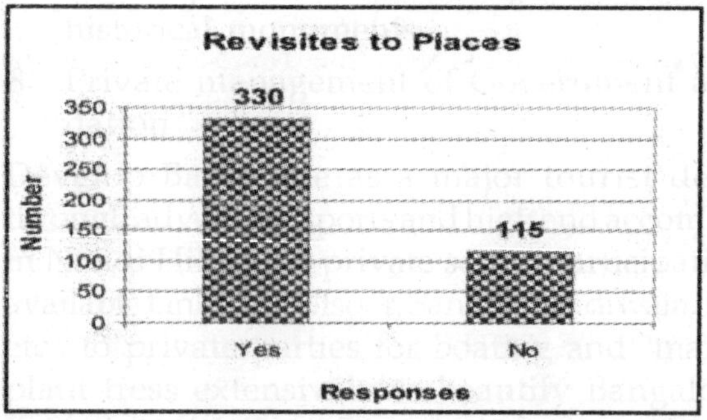

It is evident from the table that different classes of tourists reveals different motivations for their further visit to the state. 47% preferred created tourism of the state while 32% was inspired by the natural beauty, 49% of the respondents were motivated to visit religious and historically renowned places. There was another class of 40% who come to enjoy local food and hospitality (Table 86).

Table 86
Factors Motivated

Factors Motivated	*Number*	*%*
To see newly searched tourism of the state	211	47
To enjoy the natural beauty	142	32
To visit religious and historical monuments	217	49
To enjoy local food and hospitability	179	40

Choice of the respondents regarding various attractions were also assessed. 49% claimed that their trip was motivated by the desire to visit Auyurveda based health club. 39% voted for yoga and meditation camp. 26% of the respondents were interested to attend spiritual discourses. 18% voted for other miscellaneous activities (Table 87).

Table 87
Prefer to Visit

Prefer to Visit	*Number*	*%*
Yoga and meditation camp	173	39
Health club/Ayurveda based health club	219	49
Centre of spiritual discourse	114	26
Any other	79	18

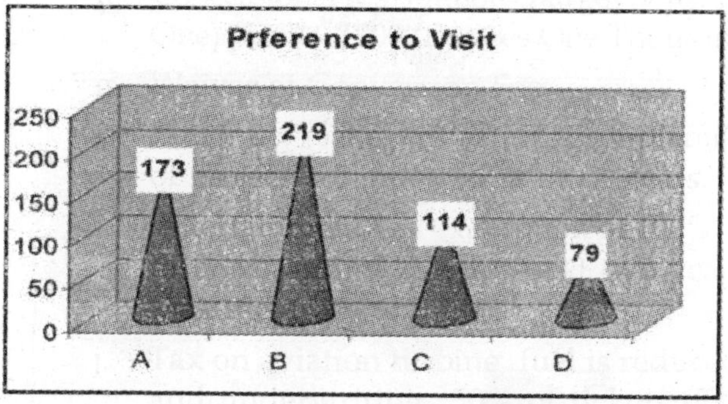

Judgment from the respondents were also invited on the various recreational activities attended. 40% stated that they enjoyed visiting wildlife sanctuaries. 55% of the traveller had liking for water sports. 32% voted for mountaineering clubs and 21% for adventure sports club (Table 88).

Table 88
Visited and Participated

Visited and Participated	*No.*	*%*
Wildlife sanctuaries	179	40
Mountaineering clubs	143	32
Water sports	246	55
Adventure sports club	93	21

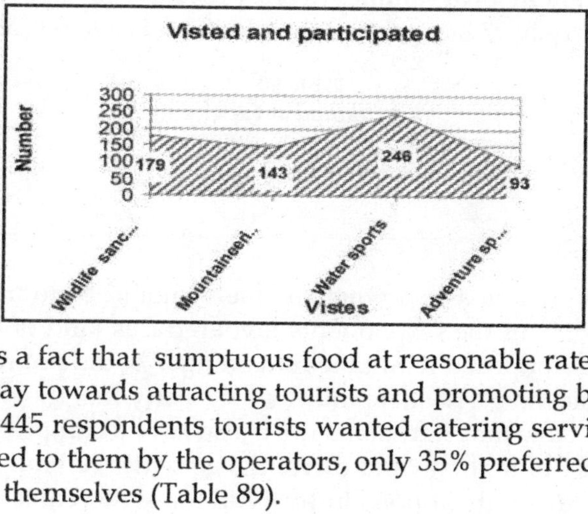

It is a fact that sumptuous food at reasonable rates goes a long way towards attracting tourists and promoting business. Of the 445 respondents tourists wanted catering service to be provided to them by the operators, only 35% preferred to deal with it themselves (Table 89).

Table 89
Catering Units

Response	*Number*	*%*
Yes	289	65
No	156	35

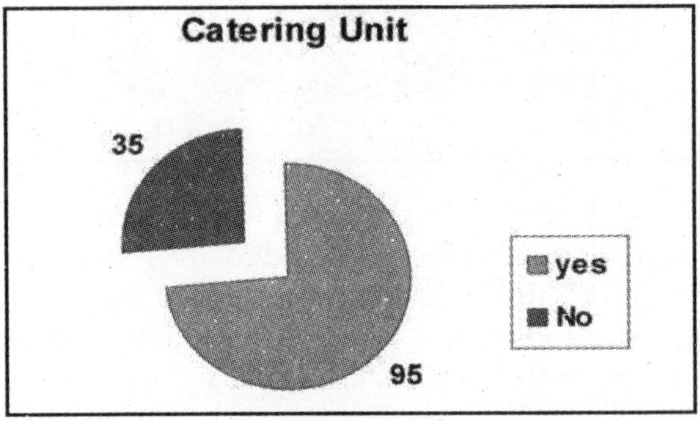

One of the major objectives of the tourists board has to be to provide entertainment for the tourists by way of cultural shows, dances, concerts, films, sports and games and other form of entertainment. Fairs and festivals of a locality has always enchanted and become source of publicity for the popularity of a region. Of the 445 respondents 75% claimed that they wanted entertainment programmes were provided to them by the operators only 25% expressed their indifference to it (Table 90).

Table 90
Entertainment Facility

Entertainment	*Number*	*%*
Yes	334	75
No	111	25

When it was asked whether there should be tourism act or not, 61% of the respondents favoured this kind of control while 32% opposed it and the remaining 7% did not respond to this question. The table indicates it clearly that the majority hold the view that Karnataka must also have a comprehensive tourist act to regulate and direct the activities of both public and private kinds of hotel industry in the state (Table 91).

Table 91
Response Regarding Tourism Act

Tourism Act	*Number*	*%*
Yes	342	61
No	179	32
N. A.	39	07
Total	560	100

In regard to the basic aims and objectives of the KSTDC 19% respondents replied that its primary function is to earn more and more profit, while 22% asserted that its task was to provide facilities to tourist at reasonable rates, 56% respondents emphasised that its policy ought to be multipronged, 3% said that they did know anything about it in an era of competitive and cooperative tourist in which a high level of services and other facilities are the need of the hour, both service and efficiency should be the motto of their pioneering body of tourism in the state. It has to cater the needs of domestic tourist in general and foreign tourist in particular to fulfill its basic objectives (Table 92).

Table 92
The Aims of KSTDC

Variable	*Number*	*%*
To earn profit	105	19
To provide facilities at reasonable rates	123	22
Both	314	56
Do not know	18	03
	560	100

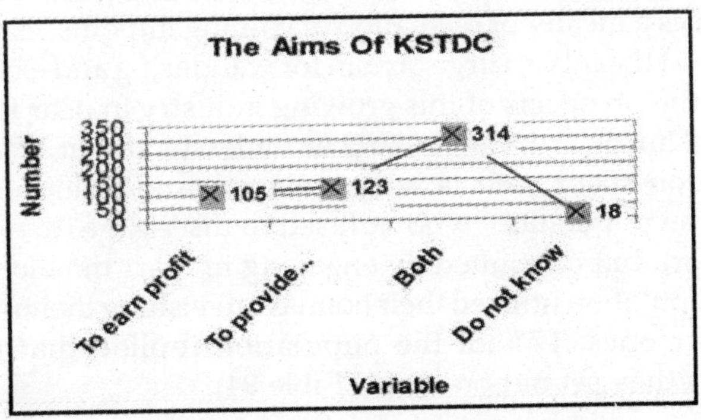

The respondents replied in the following way 23% respondents favored general administration, 71% of them suggested that specialists in tourist and hotel management should be appointed, 4% supported those who were experienced in this trade but may not hold any formal degree and 2% did not commit themselves to any formulation (Table 93).

Table 93
The Higher Administration of Board of Directors

Variables	*Number*	%
General administrators	128	23
Specialists in tourism and hotel management	397	71
Those who are experienced but do not have a formal degree	23	04
NR/NA	12	02
	560	100

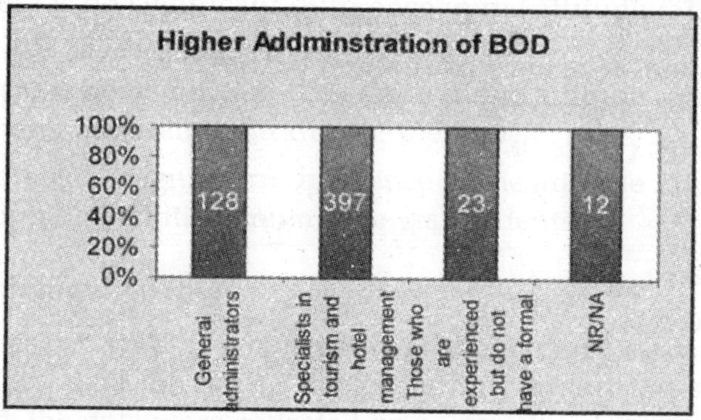

Though there are different ways of spending one's leisure, tourism as a means of recreation of gaining impetus, especially because of the inborn urge of man for wandering and exploring. Hence the prospects of this growing industry in near future is certain. During survey researcher understood that 37% of the population spent their holidays relaxing at house, there was 8% of the population who refused to disengage themselves from work but continued by engaging in part time jobs. 31% of the population utilized their holidays in visiting their relatives and dear ones. 17% of the population replied that during holidays they set out on tours (Table 94).

Table 94
Use of Holiday and Leaves

Use of Holidays	*Number*	%
Relaxation at home	210	37
Part time job	44	08
Visiting relatives	173	31
Arrange tours	97	17
Any other	36	07
	560	100

Section C
Hotel Owners/Managers

The number of years of establishment which in terms results in to experience of hotel owners plays very much positively significant roles in managing hotel business strategically. In the present study the observation with regards to establshment of the hotels reveals that majority of the respondents (25%), majority of respondents about 25% have their hotel establishment since last 25 years, whereas hotel owners having 11 to 15 years set-up or 16 to 25 years set-up comprises of 44% in total number of hotels. Only 18% respondents are having their hotel establishment set-up less than 5 years (Table 95).

Table 95
Year of Establishments

Age of Hotels	*Number*	%
Below 3 years	2	9
4 to 5 years	2	9
6 to 10 years	3	13
11 to 15 years	5	22
16 to 25 years	5	22
More than 25 years	6	25
Total	23	100

61% of the hotels were found to be under the control of appointed staff and a lower percentage(39%) was under the management of owner himself (Table 96).

Table 96
Management of Hotels

Management of Hotels	*Number*	*%*
By appointed staff	14	61
By owners staff	9	39
Total	23	100

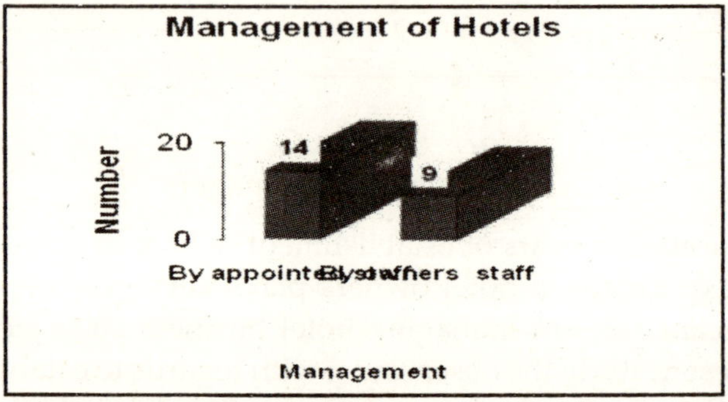

There has to be good co-ordination between the Karnataka State Tourism Development Corporation (KTDC), the travel agencies and the hotels for better functioning to bring, about tourism conscious dealings. Researcher observed that only 13% of the hotels arranged lodging facilities on a mass scale and for the tour operating agencies and only 9% had contact with such agencies for boarding 78% provided both (Table 97).

An evaluation was made on the facilities available. 61% of the hotel industry had AC room facilities. 100% had non AC facilities. Attached bathroom facilities were provided by 78% and 52% provided non attached room. Dormitory arrangement was found in 30% of the hotels (Table 98).

Table 97
Services to Tour Operating Agency

Services to Tour Operating Agency	*Number*	*%*
Lodging	3	13
Boarding	2	09
Both	18	78
Total	23	100

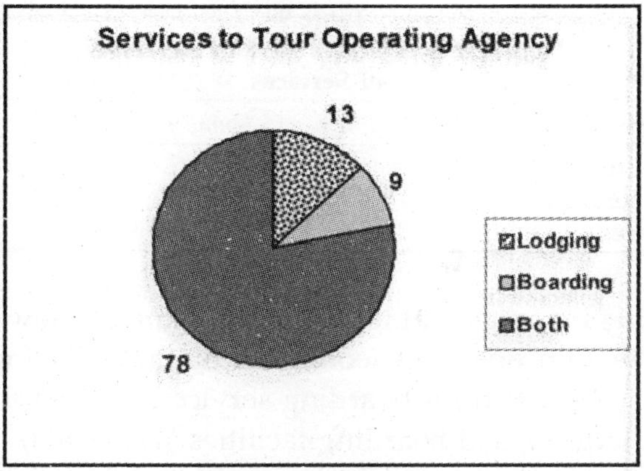

Table 98
Facilities at Hotels

Facilities at Hotels	*Number*	*%*
AC Rooms	14	61
Non AC Rooms	23	100
Attached	18	78
Non Attached	12	52
Dormitory	07	30

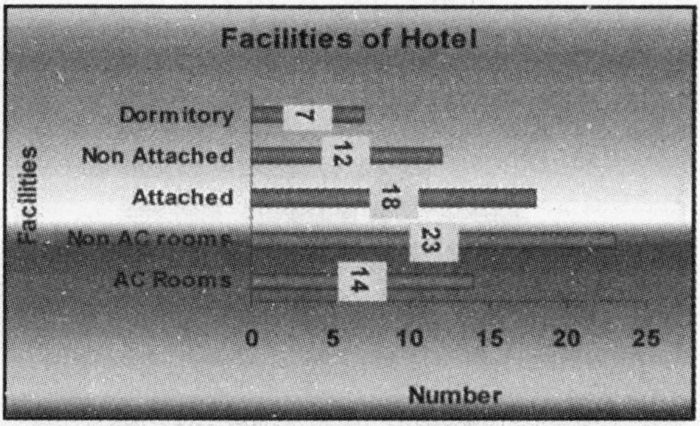

70% of the hotel owners maintained contact with the tour operator concerning lodging facility. Boarding arrangement contract existed between 78% of the tour operators and hotel owners (managers). Only 43% maintained an agreement on both (Table 99).

Table 99
Hotel Owners Travel Agency Agreement of Services

Agreement of Services	*Number*	%
Loading Services	16	70
Boarding Services	18	78
Both Services	10	43

During the questioning researcher came to know that only 13% of the tour operators contacted the hoteliers for lodging services. 17% asked for boarding services. 70% reached them for both lodging and boarding facilities (Table 100).

Table 100
Demand for Specific Hotel Services

Demand	*Number*	%
Only loading services	3	13
Only boarding services	4	17
Both services	16	70
Total	23	100

Among the 23 respondents i.e. 26% of the hoteliers stated that tour operators approached them for arranging lodging and boarding facilities but the majority 74% stated that no such contact existed (Table 101).

Table 101
Table Showing Arrangement of Hotels

Arrangement of Hotels	*Number*	%
Yes	06	26
No	17	74
Total	23	100

91% of the hoteliers did not provide any concessions to the tour operating agencies for mass scale booking on lodging and board. Only a minor percentage of 9% provided concessions (Table 102).

Table 102
Concession Offered

Concession Offered	*Number*	%
Yes	02	9
No	21	91
Total	23	100

The percentage of discount offered for mass reservation of lodging and boarding were also found to be scanty. 69% of the respondents provided only 5% discount. There was only a minimum of 7% of the hoteliers who provided a high discount of 15% and 17% respondents of the respondents did not go beyond 10% of discount (Table 103).

Table 103
Offer of Discount to Tourist

Offer of Discount	*Number*	%
5%	16	69
10%	4	17
15%	2	7
Any other	2	7
Total	23	100

Until and under the problems of tourism industry are taken note of the prospects of tourism, promotion will remain dim and low, it was revealed from the survey that there was very better co-ordination between the different segments of the industry like the hotel owners, tour operators, Karnataka Tourism Development operators etc. Only 17% of the respondents agreed on providing pamphlets with instructions for the stay. 23% of the hoteliers did not take note of any such arrangements (Table 104).

Table 104
Management Instructions to Tourist

Instructions	*Number*	%
Yes	4	17
No	19	83
Total	23	100

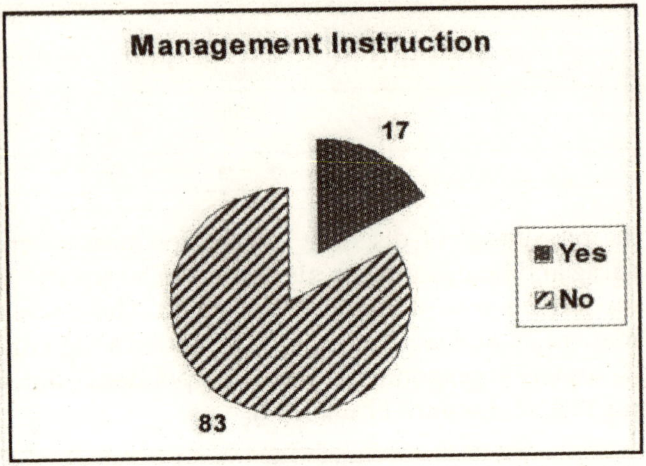

65% of the hoteliers experienced misbehaviour from the tourists. 35% were not disturbed by any such problems (Table 105).

Table 105
Misbehaviour of Tourist

Misbehaviour	*Number*	%
Yes	15	65
No	08	35
Total	23	100

Among the hoteliers 91% has complained about the misconduct of the tourists to the concerning tour operators. Only 9% tolerated or took it for granted (Table 106).

Table 106
Complaints About Tourist

Complaints About Tourist	*Number*	%
Yes	21	91
No	02	09
Total	23	100

Section D
Hypothesis Testing

Kolmogorov–Smirnov Test

This test is concerned with the degree of agreement between a set of observed values and the values specified by the null hypothesis. It is similar to the Chi-square test of goodness of fit. It is used when the researcher is interested in comparing a set of values as an ordinal scale.

Null Hypothesis (Ho)

Result: As the calculated "D" value exceeds the critical value of 0.6447 the Null Hypothesis Ho that there is no difference in the attitude rating for various concessions among the responses is rejected (Table 107).

Table 107
There is No Difference in the Attitude Rating for Various Concessions Among the Responses

Scale	*Observed Number*	*Observed Proportion*	*Observed Cumulative Proportion*	*Null Proportion*	*Null Cumulative Proportion*	*Absolute Difference Observed & Null*
1	0	0	0	0.142857143	0.142857143	-0.142857143
2	2	0.004494382	0.004494382	0.142857143	0.285714286	-0.281219904
3	77	0.173033708	0.17752809	0.142857143	0.428571429	-0.251043339
4	307	0.68988764	0.86741573	0.142857143	0.571428571	0.295987159
5	38	0.085393258	0.952808989	0.142857143	0.714285714	0.238523274
6	13	0.029213483	0.982022472	0.142857143	0.857142857	0.124879615
7	8	0.017977528	1	0.142857143	1	0
Total	445					
					MAX	0.295987159
	21.095				Critical Value	0.064470183

Result: As the calculated "D" value exceeds the critical value of 0.6447 the Null Hypothesis Ho that there is no difference in the attitude rating for Travel vehicle among the responses is rejected (Table 108).

Table 108
There is No Difference in the Attitude Rating for Travel Vehicle (Buses) Among the Responses

Scale	*Observed Number*	*Observed Proportion*	*Observed Cumulative Proportion*	*Null Proportion*	*Null Cumulative Proportion*	*Absolute Difference Observed & Null*
1	0	0	0	0.142857143	0.142857143	-0.142857143
2	16	0.035955056	0.035955056	0.142857143	0.285714286	-0.24975923
3	116	0.260674157	0.296629213	0.142857143	0.428571429	-0.131942215
4	273	0.613483146	0.91011236	0.142857143	0.571428571	0.338683788
5	26	0.058426966	0.968539326	0.142857143	0.714285714	0.254253612
6	14	0.031460674	1	0.142857143	0.857142857	0.142857143
7	0	0	1	0.142857143	1	0
Total	445					
					MAX	0.338683788
	21.095023				Critical Value	0.064470183

Result: As the calculated "D" value exceeds the critical value of 0.6447 the Null Hypothesis Ho that there is no difference in the attitude rating for punctuality aspect among the responses is rejected (Table 109).

Table 109
There is No Difference in the Attitude Rating for Punctuality Aspect Among the Responses

Scale	*Observed Number*	*Observed Proportion*	*Observed Cumulative Proportion*	*Null Proportion*	*Null Cumulative Proportion*	*Absolute Difference Observed & Null*
1	0	0	0	0.142857143	0.142857143	-0.142857143
2	21	0.047191011	0.047191011	0.142857143	0.285714286	-0.238523274
3	73	0.164044944	0.211235955	0.142857143	0.428571429	-0.217335474
4	317	0.712359551	0.923595506	0.142857143	0.571428571	0.352166934
5	22	0.049438202	0.973033708	0.142857143	0.714285714	0.258747994
6	12	0.026966292	1	0.142857143	0.857142857	0.142857143
7	0	0	1	0.142857143	1	0
Total	445					
					MAX	0.352166934
	21.095				Critical Value	0.064470183

Result: As the calculated "D" value exceeds the critical value of 0.6447 the Null Hypothesis Ho that there is no difference in the attitude rating for accommodation facilities among the responses is rejected (Table 110).

Table 110
There is No Difference in the Attitude Rating for Accommodation Facilities Among the Responses

Scale	*Observed Number*	*Observed Proportion*	*Observed Cumulative Proportion*	*Null Proportion*	*Null Cumulative Proportion*	*Absolute Difference Observed & Null*
1	0	0	0	0.142857143	0.142857143	-0.142857143
2	2	0.004494382	0.004494382	0.142857143	0.285714286	-0.281219904
3	23	0.051685393	0.056179775	0.142857143	0.428571429	-0.372391653
4	219	0.492134831	0.548314607	0.142857143	0.571428571	-0.023113965
5	183	0.411235955	0.959550562	0.142857143	0.714285714	0.245264848
6	16	0.035955056	0.995505618	0.142857143	0.857142857	0.138362761
7	2	0.004494382	1	0.142857143	1	0
Total	445					
					MAX	0.245264848
	21.1				Critical Value	0.064470183

Result: As the calculated "D" value exceeds the critical value of 0.6447 the Null Hypothesis Ho that there is no difference in the attitude rating for cleanliness and hygiene facilities among the responses is rejected (Table 111).

Table 111
There is No Difference in the Attitude Rating for Cleanliness and Hygiene Facilities Among the Responses

Scale	*Observed Number*	*Observed Proportion*	*Observed Cumulative Proportion*	*Null Proportion*	*Null Cumulative Proportion*	*Absolute Difference Observed & Null*
1	8	0.017977528	0.017977528	0.142857143	0.142857143	-0.124879615
2	73	0.164044944	0.182022472	0.142857143	0.285714286	-0.103691814
3	67	0.150561798	0.33258427	0.142857143	0.428571429	-0.095987159
4	25	0.056179775	0.388764045	0.142857143	0.571428571	-0.182664526
5	259	0.582022472	0.970786517	0.142857143	0.714285714	0.256500803
6	9	0.020224719	0.991011236	0.142857143	0.857142857	0.133868379
7	4	0.008988764	1	0.142857143	1	0
Total	445					
					MAX	0.256500803
	21.1				Critical Value	0.064470183

Result: As the calculated "D" value exceeds the critical value of 0.6447 the Null Hypothesis Ho that there is no difference in the attitude rating for first aid and medical facilities among the responses is rejected (Table 112).

Table 112
There is No Difference in the Attitude Rating for First Aid and Medical Facilities Among the Responses

Scale	Observed Number	Observed Proportion	Observed Cumulative Proportion	Null Proportion	Null Cumulative Proportion	Absolute Difference Observed & Null
1	4	0.008988764	0.008988764	0.142857143	0.142857143	-0.133868379
2	2	0.004494382	0.013483146	0.142857143	0.285714286	-0.27223114
3	44	0.098876404	0.112359551	0.142857143	0.428571429	-0.316211878
4	263	0.591011236	0.703370787	0.142857143	0.571428571	0.131942215
5	83	0.186516854	0.88988764	0.142857143	0.714285714	0.175601926
6	36	0.080898876	0.970786517	0.142857143	0.857142857	0.11364366
7	13	0.029213483	1	0.142857143	1	0
Total	445					
					MAX	0.175601926
	21.1				Critical Value	0.064470183

Result: As the calculated "D" value exceeds the critical value of 0.6447 the Null Hypothesis Ho that there is no difference in the attitude rating for guide arrangement at tourist spot among the responses is rejected (Table 113).

Table 113
There is No Difference in the Attitude Rating for Guide Arrangement at Tourist Spot Facilities Among the Responses

Scale	Observed Number	Observed Proportion	Observed Cumulative Proportion	Null Proportion	Null Cumulative Proportion	Absolute Difference Observed & Null
1	0	0	0	0.142857143	0.142857143	-0.142857143
2	2	0.004494382	0.004494382	0.142857143	0.285714286	-0.281219904
3	237	0.53258427	0.537078652	0.142857143	0.428571429	0.108507223
4	108	0.242696629	0.779775281	0.142857143	0.571428571	0.208346709
5	74	0.166292135	0.946067416	0.142857143	0.714285714	0.231781701
6	18	0.040449438	0.986516854	0.142857143	0.857142857	0.129373997
7	6	0.013483146	1	0.142857143	1	0
Total	445					
					MAX	0.231781701
	21.1				Critical Value	0.064470183

Result: As the calculated "D" value exceeds the critical value of 0.6447 the Null Hypothesis Ho that there is no difference in the attitude rating for first meeting experience with travelling agency among the responses is rejected (Table 114).

Table 114
There is No Difference in the Attitude Rating for First Meeting Experience with Travelling Agency Among the Responses

Scale	*Observed Number*	*Observed Proportion*	*Observed Cumulative Proportion*	*Null Proportion*	*Null Cumulative Proportion*	*Absolute Difference Observed & Null*
1	2	0.004494382	0.004494382	0.142857143	0.142857143	-0.13836276
2	16	0.035955056	0.040449438	0.142857143	0.285714286	-0.24526485
3	60	0.134831461	0.175280899	0.142857143	0.428571429	-0.25329053
4	73	0.164044944	0.339325843	0.142857143	0.571428571	-0.23210273
5	220	0.494382022	0.833707865	0.142857143	0.714285714	0.119422151
6	60	0.134831461	0.968539326	0.142857143	0.857142857	0.111396469
7	14	0.031460674	1	0.142857143	1	0
Total	445					
					MAX	0.119422151
	21.095				Critical Value	0.064470183

Result: As the calculated "D" value exceeds the critical value of 0.6447 the Null Hypothesis Ho that there is no difference in the attitude rating for Karanataka as a tourist place among the responses is rejected (Table 115).

Table 115
There is No Difference in the Attitude Rating for Karanataka As a Tourist Place Among the Responses

Scale	*Observed Number*	*Observed Proportion*	*Observed Cumulative Proportion*	*Null Proportion*	*Null Cumulative Proportion*	*Absolute Difference Observed & Null*
1	13	0.029213	0.029213483	0.142857	0.142857143	-0.11364366
2	43	0.096629	0.125842697	0.142857	0.285714286	-0.159871589
3	276	0.620225	0.746067416	0.142857	0.428571429	0.317495987
4	93	0.208989	0.95505618	0.142857	0.571428571	0.383627608
5	17	0.038202	0.993258427	0.142857	0.714285714	0.278972713
6	3	0.006742	1	0.142857	0.857142857	0.142857143
7	0	0	1	0.142857	1	0
Total	445					
					MAX	0.383627608
	21.09502				Critical Value	0.064470183

Result: As the calculated "D" value exceeds the critical value of 0.6447 the Null Hypothesis Ho that there is no difference in the attitude rating for Quality of food among the responses is rejected (Table 116).

Table 116
There is No Difference in the Attitude Rating for Quality of Food Among the Responses

Scale	*Observed Number*	*Observed Proportion*	*Observed Cumulative Proportion*	*Null Proportion*	*Null Cumulative Proportion*	*Absolute Difference Observed & Null*
1	0	0	0	0.142857143	0.142857143	-0.14285714
2	31	0.069662921	0.069662921	0.142857143	0.285714286	-0.21605136
3	69	0.15505618	0.224719101	0.142857143	0.428571429	-0.20385233
4	52	0.116853933	0.341573034	0.142857143	0.571428571	-0.22985554
5	263	0.591011236	0.93258427	0.142857143	0.714285714	0.218298555
6	26	0.058426966	0.991011236	0.142857143	0.857142857	0.133868379
7	4	0.008988764	1	0.142857143	1	0
Total	445					
					MAX	0.218298555
	21.095				Critical Value	0.064470183

Result: As the calculated "D" value exceeds the critical value of 0.6447 the Null Hypothesis Ho that there is no difference in the attitude rating for entertainment among the responses is rejected (Table 117).

Table 117
There is No Difference in the Attitude Rating for Entertainment Among the Response

Scale	*Observed Number*	*Observed Proportion*	*Observed Cumulative Proportion*	*Null Proportion*	*Null Cumulative Proportion*	*Absolute Difference Observed & Null*
1	0	0	0	0.142857143	0.142857143	-0.14285714
2	24	0.053932584	0.053932584	0.142857143	0.285714286	-0.2317817
3	76	0.170786517	0.224719101	0.142857143	0.428571429	-0.20385233
4	106	0.238202247	0.462921348	0.142857143	0.571428571	-0.10850722
5	97	0.217977528	0.680898876	0.142857143	0.714285714	-0.03338684
6	119	0.26741573	0.948314607	0.142857143	0.857142857	0.09117175
7	23	0.051685393	1	0.142857143	1	0
Total	445					
					MAX	0.09117175
	21.095				Critical Value	0.064470183

Result: As the calculated "D" value exceeds the critical value of 0.6447 the Null Hypothesis Ho that there is no difference in the attitude rating for shopping facilities among the responses is rejected (Table 118).

Table 118
There is No Difference in the Attitude Rating for Shopping Facilities Among the Responses

Scale	*Observed Number*	*Observed Proportion*	*Observed Cumulative Proportion*	*Null Proportion*	*Null Cumulative Proportion*	*Absolute Difference Observed & Null*
1	4	0.008988764	0.008988764	0.142857143	0.142857143	-0.13386838
2	6	0.013483146	0.02247191	0.142857143	0.285714286	-0.26324238
3	39	0.087640449	0.11011236	0.142857143	0.428571429	-0.31845907
4	184	0.413483146	0.523595506	0.142857143	0.571428571	-0.04783307
5	166	0.373033708	0.896629213	0.142857143	0.714285714	0.182343499
6	35	0.078651685	0.975280899	0.142857143	0.857142857	0.118138042
7	11	0.024719101	1	0.142857143	1	0
Total	445					
					MAX	0.182343499
	21.095				Critical Value	0.064470183

8

Strategic Management of Tourism

Strategy is generally viewed as a pattern of important decisions that (i) guides the organization in its relationships with its environment; (ii) affects the organization structure, and (iii) centrally affects the organization's performance (Hambrick, 1980; Howath & McMellion, 1979, Mintzbury, 1978). Thus, strategic management is an endeavour to deploy resources in such a manner as to create the future. Pertinent literature on strategic management argues that in a competitive environment, a focused strategy is required to align the organization with critical environment resources, to capitalise on the organization's distinct competencies, and to achieve a competitive edge (Schaffer, 1987; Andrew, 1972; Porter, 1980, 1985; Thompson, 1967; Newmen, 1967). Porter (1980) has identified three broad forms of strategy (i) lower cost, where production efficiency leads to value added to both consumer and producer e.g. matching market prices with greater profitability or being able to offer lower prices while maintaining average or above average profits; (ii) differentiation, where additional value is created for the consumer through adding value that allows a greater price to be commanded, e.g. branding, product features, or additional benefits and support and (iii) focus, relating to the breadth of markets cope, focus, referring to targeting specific niche markets or product ranges. Porter identifies that the essence of strategy formulation is coping with competition. However, three most prominent strategy forms relate to market concentration, market diversification (Olusoga, 1993; Ayal & Zif, 1979) or differentiation strategies (Verich & Calver, 1991).

The evolution process of strategic management research to the contemporary position has passed trough several stages with differing focus in each stage. From its emergence in the 1960's symbolizing a focus on budgetary control and forecasting, with allied issues reflecting improving the efficiency of administrative processes and organization structure; the 1970's represented a transitional stage where strategic stage where strategic management became more acknowledged notionally, the 1980's represented a further development stage in the process of globalization multi-disciplinary approaches leading to a greater degree of economic theory building; 1998's witnessed a maturation of the strategic management with focusing on organization's resources and capabilities (Kamra, 2001). The shifts in strategic management focus more on the need of strategic planning for future development.

Strategic Implications for Tourism Industry

The following points have strategic implications on tourism in India :

- Expansion of market awareness in new markets particularly in rural and lesser known tourism destinations.
- Increasing the availability of short-break packages targeted to regional markets.
- Developing and maintaining advocacy programmes that support industry.
- Creating a brand and product development programme with special forms destination and tourism resources.
- Developing entertainment and information sites around regional themes, resources and identities and also providing convenient packages to tourists that link with excursions.
- Monitoring the developments of new tourism and recreation products.

- Following an integrated approach to product development, marketing of tourism destinations and support ecology and environment.
- Evolving marketing strategies for tourists that can travel in the off season and less sensitive weather conditions.
- Improving database and MIS at regional level tourist destinations.
- Expanding regional networking in product development, marketing and advocacy in tourism promotion, development and sustainable environment.
- Encouraging tourism development programmes that include benefits for and utilization by local communities and supporting small business development opportunities to them.
- Promotion of environment conservation, protection, cultural and natural heritage conservation in tourism development programmes.
- Improving the efficiency of government organizations, built environment and physical infrastructure.
- Imparting education, training and skills for managing tourist destinations and extending in management of tourism services.
- Supporting programmes on the use and potential of electronic data base and linking service providers with regional offices, destinations and intermediaries.

Tourism has become a multiple activity focussed with integration of slopping and operation, entertainment and education and culture and meeting business centre development. The strategic tourism management demands positioning of tourism destinations and their effective marketing. As tourism industry grows, the competition is likely to grow intense. To face this competition and more tourists, tourism markets have to embrace all the marketing tools available. Their main challenge is to create a distinctive position in the mind of customers, a position which can differentiate the destination from the competitors. There has been a steady increase in the volume of international travel. The policy makers have recognized the value of tourism is the economics of their regions (Chacko, 2002). Interestingly, one of the most effective tools in tourism marketing is positioning. Importantly, strategic management of tourism involves managerial process of setting organization's goals and objectives analysis, planning and implementation of strategies. Moreover, environment and resource analysis, man power planning, corporate planning, business strategy formulation, target marketing, positioning and management of resource etc. are some of the crucial aspects of strategic management.

Environmental Analysis

Educational analysis of environment and resources is the first step in strategic marketing planning. The environment in which a tourism organization operates is complex and constantly changing. For analytical purposes, the environment can be divided into the following three components :

- The macro environment, which consists of those forces that create opportunities and pose threats to the destination to the tourism business units. These forces are factors that the tourism organization cannot control, and to which the tourism business units have to adopt. They include a wide variety of social, political, technological, economic and demographic factors.
- The competitive environment, which consists of all those suppliers of tourism offerings that compete for the same customers or target markets as particular tourism organizations and business of the destination.
- The market environment, which consists of the groups and other organizations that the regional tourism organization works with directly in order to accomplish its mission. In the tourism sphere, the main groups in the market environment are existing and potential tourists.

As indicated, the first major step in strategic marketing planning that a regional tourism organization should undertaker is a regional situation analysis. This can be divided into two elements :

- Careful analysis of both the present environment and the probable future environment so as to ascertain major threats and opportunities for the region at large, and also for the tourism business units in the region;
- The identification of the strengths and weaknesses of the regional tourism organizations, the region at large, and the tourism business units the region.

It is apparent from the Chart 6.1 that there is a large degree of consensus with regard to aspects that should be included in an environmental analysis. Kotler (1984), Jain (1985) and Abell and Hammond (1979) all agree that the analysis should incorporate external threats and opportunities and relate them to internal strengths and weaknesses Chart 1.

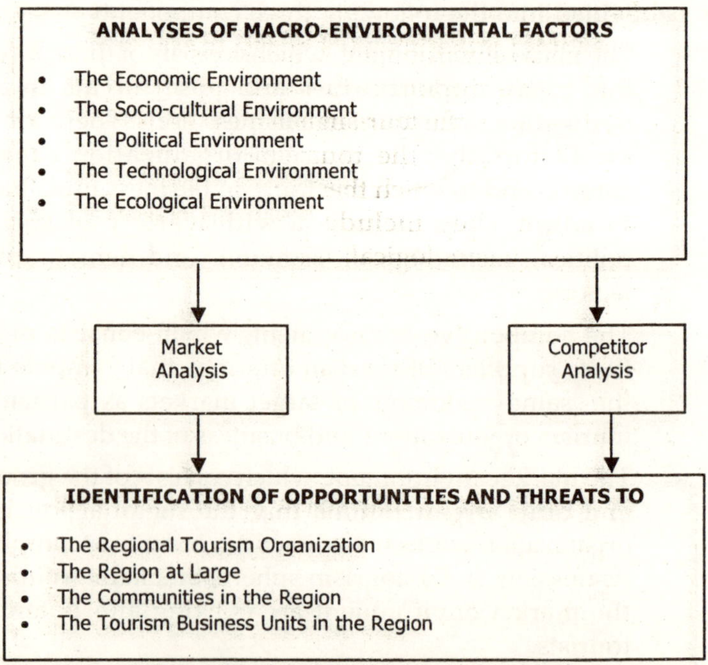

Chart 1: Regional Environmental Analysis

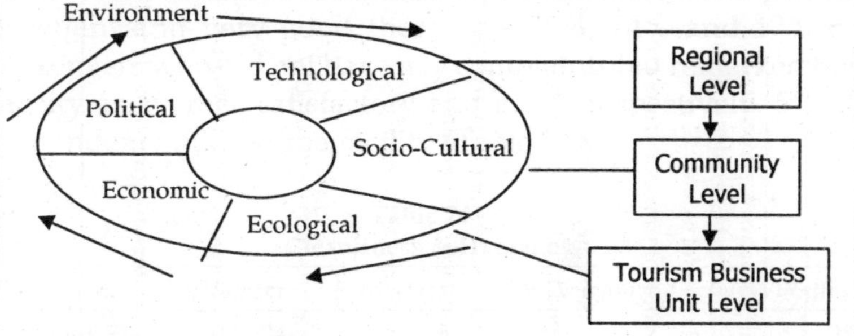

Source: After Jain(1985, p.252)

Chart 2: Constituents of the Regional Tourism Environment

The macro-environment poses both threats and opportunities to the regional tourism organization, the region at large, and the tourism businesses in the region. Elements of the macro-environment constantly are subject to change, and are largely outside the control of a regional tourism organization.

Five different types of environments can be distinguished: economic, socio-cultural, political, technological, and ecological. In addition, the regional tourism environment can be scanned at various levels· regional, community, and business unit. Perspectives on environmental scanning vary from level to levl in a region as indicated in Chart 2 and 3.

The process of tourism destination planning analysis comprises three principal aspects (Kamra, 2001):

- Market analysis and forecasts of infrastructure, facilities, services and amenities requirements to be used as input in the integrated analysis and synthesis.
- The integrated analysis and synthesis of physical (natural and built environment), socio-economic factors together with tourist attractions and activities, present policies and plans, and installation of general tourist carrying capacities at the national and regional levels.
- Analysis of the institutional elements.

The steady growth in numbers of tourists and tourist expenditure is a result of a realistic and pragmatic recognition of the country's lack of suitability for mass tourism and its

Chart 3
Regional Resources Analysis Sectors

Analysis Sectors	*Major Sector Components*	*Major Components Variables*
Accommodation	Hotels, motels, inns, friends and relatives, tourist homes, campgrounds and trailer parks	Length of stay, double occupancy, percentage of food and beverage utilization by residents versus visitors in accommodation form, etc.
Transportation	Automobiles, airplanes, trains, buses, and boats.	Origin/destination, mode of transportation, party size, etc.
Events and Attractions	Amusement and theme parks, museums and other cultural exhibitions, local festivities, fairs, events, and natural amenities.	Number of attendees, percentage of visitors versus residents, average expenditure, etc.
Outdoor Recreation and Parks	Parks and parklands, water bodies, outdoor recreational sports activities, and picnicing.	Percentage of visitors versus residents, party size, length of stay, and estimated expenditure.
Business and Conference	Conference centres, meeting rooms, communication networks, educational institutions.	Lodging form, length of stay, estimated expenditures.
Travel Services	Travel agencies, car rentals, travel information centres, and gas stations and other consulting and advisory services.	Percentages of revenue due to visitors, origin/destination, purpose of trip.
Retail Trade	Food services and general merchandise, automotive, and apparel and accessories outlets.	Percentage of sales to visitors, origin/destination, spending pattern.
Hospitality	Restaurants, fast-food services, bars and other beverage suppliers, and caterers.	Percentage of sales to visitors, lodging form, length of stay, spending patterns.

Source: After Vandermey (1984), Tourism Management, Vol. 5 (2).

potential to attract a small but growing number of tourists who mainly are interested in its natural environment. It is to be noted that present status of built environment and physical infrastructure as well as services are not upto the mark which affect the satisfaction of tourists. Environmental planning for sustainable and perspective development and tourism promotion.

Importantly, the market analysis helps in outlining the tourists markets that can be developed and also in setting its tourism goals and objectives. In the tourism development planning, market analysis provides the data base pertaining to tourists, their stay and visitation. Such information may be vital for planning the tourists attractions, activities, facilities, services, infrastructure and marketing destinations with positioning. Importantly, forecasting of accommodation, determination of transportation, tourist facility needs and infrastructure requirements etc. are important for integrated analysis and synthesis..

It is to be noted that market segmentation analysis is characterized by the following factors :

- Demographic or socio-economic background of tourists;
- Tourism products, attractions and facilities of the destination areas;
- Interest, life styles, attitudes, motivation etc. of tourist;
- Geographical features of destinations and tourist circuits along with the tourist infrastructure and service.

Significantly, carrying capacity analysis is a radical approach in tourism planning with the view of minimizing negative impacts of tourism on built environment, physical infrastructure, local ecology and environment. As regards planning at national and regional levels, the carrying capacities are usually determined for the planning area involving features of key attractions, development sites and even the tourist points etc. (Kamra, 2001). The carrying capacity analysis helps in understanding of the tourist arrivals, availability of existing services and infrastructure, needs of tourists and their behaviour towards nature and overall tourism development. It ultimately helps in minimizing the negative impacts of tourism on local environment and ecology. The major criteria for determining optimum capacity levels of environment encompasses: (i) physical; (ii) economic; (iii) socio-cultural and (v) infrastructure.

Man Power Planning

Human resources are very vital for organization's success. Importantly, organizations are becoming large and complex, with progressive industrialization and advent of new technologies. Over the years, governmental intervention in regulating organizational purpose and performance has increased. Social obligations, legal aspects and trade union pressures are actively shaping the environment. The environmental trends in terms of five principle environmental aspects viz. economic, demographic, socio-cultural, politico-legal and technological are important variables for shaping the present personnel environment. Today, there is a growing awareness of the importance of the human side of organizations as a vital factor in overall progresses (Dixit, 2001). Significantly, all managers have direct responsibilities for the human assets in an organization and are responsible for activities and decisions concerning personnel. Still most organizations have a separate personnel department whose main job is to coordinate all personnel activities. There is need for a close interaction between the personnel department which has the responsibility for the administration of personnel and line managers who have responsibility for optimizing the use of their resources viz. physical, financial and human. The personnel department is them required to maintain personnel information systems and comply with government's legal regulatory framework and union management agreements. Moreover, top management expects personnel specialists to devise ways and means for better utilization of human resources, in collaboration with line managers (Dixit, 2001).

Man Power Planning is a dynamic process as planning is amendable to modification, review and adjustments in accordance with the need of an organization and on the changing circumstances. The process of man power planning has the following steps: (a) deciding goals and objectives; (b) estimating future organizational structure and man power requirements; (c) auditing human resources; (d) planning job requirements and job descriptions; (e) developing a human resource plan. The basic objective of man power planning is to have the right people properly trained and motivated, available for the right jobs. Man Power Planning are : (i) determination of recruitment needs; (ii) anticipation of surplus to be corrected by natural shortage rather than redundancies or dismissal; (iii) indication of future training needs; (iv) provision of a basis for management development programme; (v) a factor in industrial relations and productivity bargaining; (vi) monitoring of labour costs; (vii) indication of staff facilities required and (viii) indication of critical or shortage areas where particular skills or experience will be missing.

Thus, it is clear that man power planning is a systematic approach to ensure that the right people are in the right job at the right time. This is especially important in tourism, which is a type of service activity, depending in large part for its success on human resources and the quality of personnel working in tourism. Man Power Planning in tourism should be approached systematically for all types and levels of tourism related personnel, including national, regional and community government tourism administration, accommodation and catering management and operations, tour and travel management and operations, and related tourist facility and service operations etc. (Gupta, 2002). Importantly, various types of education and training should be considered in a comprehensive education and training plan. This should include:

- On job training in the places of employment, such as hotels, restaurants, travel and tour offices, etc.;
- Short time courses on various aspects of tourism. These course may be started by Department of Tourism of various universities and academic institutions;

- Regular vocational and management programmes by academic and research institutions as well as departments of universities and colleges;
- Study tours of service providers and managers of travel, tour and tourism development and operations to different places for practical knowledge and insights;
- Corresponding courses for hotel catering, tour operations and tourism management by open universities and other academic institutions.

Goals and Strategy Formulation

Environment and resource analysis can be followed by regional goals formulation that can be achieved with tourism development. The goals and objectives of tourism development have already been detailed out in Tourism Policy And Action Plan. However, integrated approach is called for to achieve these goals and objectives.

In order to receive maximum benefits and minimizing negative impacts, Tourism development planning is essential. It is more true in case of natural and cultural heritage tourism. Tourism undoubtedly provides economic, social and cultural benefits to the residents of a number of holy places and other natural and cultrual heritage sites, but at the same time it creates various problems such as loss of potential economic and environmental benefits, environmental degradation, loss of cultural identity and damage to socio-cultural value system and distorting of our socio-cultural image. Therefore, tourism planning is important. Importantly, tourism policy should be integrated in the overall development policy , planning and strategy of the region or circuit. Planning and managing natural and heritage resources should be based on national or state tourism policy. The process of planning heritage attractions should include (Gupta, 2002) :

- determination of the development and conservation objectives;
- environmental/ecological analysis of flora and fauna, along with eco-systems to be preserved;

- carrying capacity analysis based on present and future use of resources and developing tourism destinations;
- projection of visitor demand by type of use be made with the carrying capacity analysis to arrive at optimum visitor use levels;
- determination of the type of visitor facilities needed and facility space requirements;
- formulation of action and financization of the selected plan for its effective implementation;
- tourism impact analsyis and
- implementation of plan and policies with the effective management of the resources and its visitor use.

The planning of architectural and historical sites is important for conservation and proper monitoring of visitor satisfaction levels and socio-cultural and environmental impacts of facilities development and visitor use. Arts and handicrafts and important attractions for tourists in all over India. Tourists are more interested in local arts, cultural traditions, traditions skills, techniques, crafts, performing arts, therefore, cluster development approach for promotion of local arts and crafts is needed for resources development as well as empowerment of artisans, artists and local poor dwellers.

Target Marketing and Regional Positioning

The tourism market can be approached as an aggregation of people, or one of the several segmentation approaches may be used. The tourism market segmentation bases are discussed in Chart 4.

There are four core attributes that are common to all market segments. These are value for money; variety of activities, friendliness of local people, and getting good services. However, consideration of other segments before preparing package tour and travel is necessary. These are mainly related to vacation attributes and are important for effective marketing of products and services.

Chart 4
Tourism Market Segmentation Bases

Geographic Variables	
Region	Circuits, destinations etc.
Market area	Urban, sub-urban, rural, cultural, historical etc.
Size of city or town	Town, city, metro, village, hamlet
Population density	Urban, sub-urban, rural.
Socio-economic and Demographic Variables	
Age	Children, youths, aged
Education	Primary, secondary, college/university.
Sex	Male, Female.
Income	Low, medium, high
Family size	Nuclear, joint, extended
Family life cycle	Young, married, without children, single
Occupation	Professional, executives, students, employees
Religion	Hindu, Muslim, Sikh, Christians, Jain, Buddhist
Psychographic Variables	
Social class	Upper class, middle class, lower class
Personality traits	Ambitious, authoritarian, impulsive
Lifestyle	Conservative, liberal
Behavioral Variables	
Benefits sought	Convenience, prestige, economy
Loyalty status	None, medium, strong, absolute.
Readiness stage	Unaware, aware, informed, interested, desirous
Attitude to regional tourism offering	Enthusiastic, positive, indifferent, negative, hostile.

Strategic Marketing Planning of Tourism encompasses Four Major Steps:

- Product differentiation which may be ensured through developing tour and travel packages and promotional measures to attract tourists;
- Market focus that may be ensured through giving priority and focus on customer's choice and satisfaction;
- Forecasting of tourists flow, required needs, anticipated results of tour packages and plans;
- Branding of tourism products and services for ensuring differentiation in natural and cultural heritage and other tourist destinations in the competitive business environment.

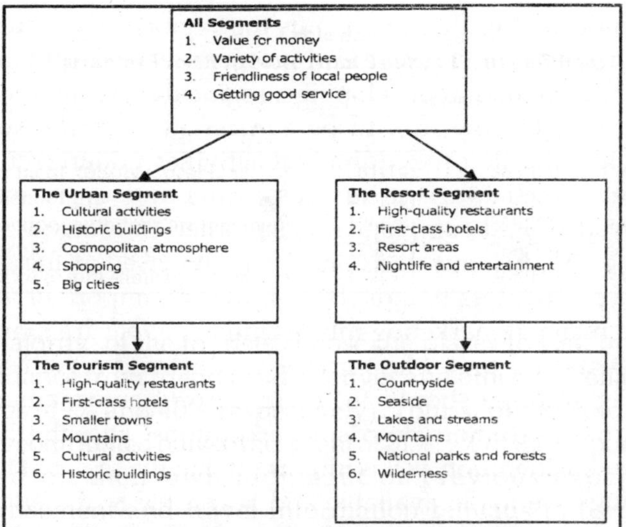

Source: After Canadian Government Office of Tourism (1984).

Chart 5: Attributes of Market Segmentation

Branding is necessary due to following reasons (Gupta, 2002):

- It identifies a particular product and distinguishes it from competitors;
- It is helpful for publicity and promotion provided it maintains level of quality;
- It provides the opportunity for service agencies in building their corporate image;
- It enhances image of the destination or reigon.

Marketing Mix

Once market segments have been identified and profiles drawn up, it is necessary to select which segment the well region will seek to attract and serve. The decisions on target markets can be made only after an analysis of sales potential, competition, costs and serviciability. Having selected target markets, a positioning strategy should be developed relative to other suppliers of similar tourism offerings serving the same target markets. This must be based on a thorough knowledge of the needs, wants and perceptions of the target market, along with the benefits offered by the destinations.

Importantly, the four P's in the regional marketing mix viz. products, price, place and promotion are important.. It is emphasized that in developing a regional marketing mix, it is important for the mix to be consistent with the region's capacity, and that the individual activities undertaken in the region by the tourism business units and every one else involved should complement each other. In tourism product strategy product mix decisions should be based on the analysis of the competitors brands. Price is also an important variable in the regional marketing mix. In India, people are more price conscious and prefer low priced product and services. Thus, pricing strategy should focus on current environment and potential customers/tourism perceptions. Distribution is a major consideration as it is important that the regional tourism offerings are made available and accessible to the envisaged target markets. Distribution decisions centre around what channels and institutions can and should be used to give the tourist the most effective access to regional tourism products. Importantly, promotion communicates the benefits of the regional tourism offerings to potential tourism and includes not only effective adventure but also sales promotion, public relations and personal selling.

Management Information System

UPSTDC has developed a detailed Management Information System. The MIS is based on the information received monthly from due hotels units spread across the state and APE's located in the six major cities outside the state. The data base has been computerized since 1988. Importantly, Department of Tourism has developed a MIS for policy formulation action plans. The Department, Directorate of Tourism, U.P.,prepares data base on the basis of information and data received from its various Regional Tourists offices located across the state. The Regional Tourists offices collects the information and data pertaining to tourist arrivals and stay at hotels, rest homes, dharmashalas etc. and other tourism related issues. The Department has also computerized accounting while UPSTDC has developed a detailed accounting system.

Promotional Tools: Marketing promotion is essentially the process of communication of with selected target markets. Most promotional activities requires an investment of time and money which may ensure better returns. Generally promotional activities include:

- Promotional print
- Public relations
- Advertising
- The internet and webs designing services
- Direct mailing
- Exhibition attendance
- Joint promotions through networking with other related organizations.

Importantly, marketing communication is vital for tourism promotion. The major elements of message are as follows:

- Kind of message
- Encoding the message
- Channel choice
- Advertising campaign
- Preparing and publishing attractive brochure
- Feedback and monitoring of advertising campaign.

Significantly, travel brochures are the most authentic and cost effective media of information dissemination. Publication of a brochure may include the following points:

- Quality paper, printing and cluster clear photography;
- Relevant content and attractive design;
- Special features of destination along with essential details of services, infrastructure, amenities etc.;
- Arranging natural and attractive coloured photographs;
- Essential details of package tour, events, cultural and natural heritage etc.;
- Relevant details of excursions and their importance along with essential details of available services and infrastructure;

- Brief and relevant information content.

Promotional measures may focus on sales promotion techniques and promotional programmes. These may include:

- Incentives to workers, employees and visitors;
- Bonus to staff members;
- Contests and competition for visitors;
- Free distribution of gifts, souvenir usually barring the name of service provides and destination;
- Trade exhibition, travel mart, cultural fairs and festivals;
- Publication of literature;
- Preparation of publicity materials and audio-visual materials;
- Effective advertising;
- Organizing seminars, workshops and symposiums;
- Wider coverage of destinations in media.

Public relations activities are important for the promotion of tourism resources. Effective public relations can influence a vast range of different groups of people, encouraging them to buy the product. Public relations activities may include (Buggs, 1997):

- Lobbying publications and opinion formers to improve services;
- Convincing opinion formers in local community to support activities and encouraging others to do so;
- Initializing positive media coverage of activities through selected media by issuing press release or invitations to members of the media to expenses facilities first hand;
- Developing contacts with local, national and specialist media and developing a reputation as a spokesperson in the field.

Thus, public relations is essentially about developing and maintaining awareness of the product. Being the low cost and effective that can help in informing the public and generation sales. Importantly, in the dynamic business environment, modern promotional and sales techniques such as internet, websites, e-mail etc. should be adopted for tourism development and promotion.

Thus, the above analysis suggests that proper management of tourism resources may ensure maximum returns of investment and reduce the negative impacts. Moreover, proper man power planning, strategic planning and management of tourist destination may lead to increased demand of tourism and benefits to the local community. Sustainable development of tourism needs the effective participation of both the public sector and private sector as well as community at large.

References

Ansoff, H. Igor (1968), Corporation Strategy, Mcgrew Hill, New York.

Briggs, S. (1997), Successful Tourism Marketing, Kogan Page Ltd., London.

Brots and Ziegler (1984), Integrated Tourism and Recreation Planning for the 1980's, Heidemij Consultancy.

Chacko, H.E. (2002), Positioning Tourism Destinations, Marketing Mastermind, Sept.

Dixit, M. (2001), Dimensions of Indian Tourism, Bharat Book Centre, Lucknow.

Gunn, C.A. (1988), Tourism Planning, Tylor and Frances, New York.

Gupta, S.K. (2002), Tourism and Heritage Resources in Garhwal Himalaya, Kaveri Pub., Delhi.

Hambrick, D. (1983), High Project Strategies in Mature Industrial, The Academy of Management Journal, 26.

Health, E. & Wall, G. (1992), Marketing Tourism Destinations, Johnvilly & Sons, New York.

Hofer, C.W. and Schendil, D.E. (1978), Strategy Formation: Analytical Concepts, West Pub. Comp. St. Paul, Minnesota.

Kamra, K.K. (2001), Managing Tourist Destinations, Kanishka Pub. Delhi.

Kevitt, T. (1975), Marketing Myopia, Harvard Business Review, Sept.-Oct.

Mathieson, A, & Wall, G. (1982), Tourism : Economic, Physical And Social Impacts, Longman, London.

Meddik, S. (1985), Paying Guests, Confederation of British Industry, July.

Mill, R.C. & Morision, A.M. (1985), The Tourism Systems: An Introductory Text, PHI, New Jersey.

Mintzberg, H. (1978), Patterns in Strategy Formation, *Management Science*, 24.

Murphy, P. (1985), Tourism: A Community Approach, Methuen, London.

Nigam, Devesh (2002), Tourism Environment and Development of Garhwal Himalaya, Mittal Pub. Delhi.

Porter, M. (1987), From Competitive Advantage to Corporate Strategy, *Harvard Business Review*, May-June.

Porter, M.E. (1980), Corporate Strategy, Free Press, New York.

Schwaninger, M. (1987), A Practical Approach to Strategy Development, *Long Range Planning*, Vol. 20.

9

Concluding Observations and Policy Recommendations

Tourism with multi-dimensional activity has evolved one of the largest and lucrative industries of the new millennium. Despite varied and rich cultural heritage, India's share in world tourism has been reported to be dismal. Protected areas play an important role in evolving challenge of maintaining a sustainable world. Not only they provide shelter for biological diversity, but they play an equally significant role in the changing economic and social structure of local communities and nations. The protected areas are increasingly becoming a source of tourist revenue and alternative tourism forms. However, eco-tourism requires a multi-disciplinary approach, careful planning and strict guidelines and regulations that will guarantee sustainable operation and conservation of nature. The present development and proposals of eco-tourism promotion across the country no doubt will lead promotion and conservation of nature, however, it is difficult to meet the eco-tourism parameters. Therefore, acceptable change planning process demand to evolve the sound mechanism for assessing recreational carrying capacity of eco-tourism destinations and minimizing the negative environmental impacts of visitors on local built up environment, eco-system and biological diversity. The recent developments in the hill stations and other eco-tourism destinations for the promotion of tourism activities and also to facilitate tourist have led distortions of cultural value system and adverse impact on built up environment and eco-system. This has caused natural hazards and environmental consequences.

WTO has estimated that there will be 1.6 billion international tourists by the year 2020 and Asia will emerge as the second region to be the most visited in the world. India being rich in cultural and natural heritage is likely to experience its share in global tourism. India, however, faces two major challenges in the globalized world i.e. exploitation of tourism potential and designing strategies for tapping such potential. Therefore, 'Tourism 2020 Vision' document has identified the following priorities:

- Strategic marketing
- Product differentiation and quality improvement
- Sustainable tourism development
- Private-Public partnership
- Improving brand image and positioning
- Strategic planning and management of resources
- Development of new destinations
- Use of electronic and internet services for facilitation and data base preparation

It has been estimated that India's travel and tourism potentials can provide its economy substantial resources in the coming years. It is expected that tourism has potential to provide 7 million new jobs, provided that potential of tourism resources is effectively exploited. The potential of tourism in India can be viewed against the global scenarios. Globally tourism has touched $ 476 billion tourism receipts with the 10.6 per cent of the global workforce, 10.2 per cent contribution to GDP, generating tax revenues of $ 655 billion and gross out put of $ 3.4 trillion. However, India's share in global tourism is dismal. It is to be noted that tourism in India during last 50 years has shown tremendous progress. From a beginning of 17000 international tourists in 1950 contributing Rs. 7.7 crore to the economy the present arrival of 2.64 million tourists contributing about $ 3.5 billion in foreign exchange earnings and the number of domestic tourists has swelled to a massive 200 million is really a substantial progress. Thus, India has to evolve the strategies of tourism development to make a respectable position in the global tourism industry. India has the potential of becoming a major player in the world tourism league, endowed as it is with unrivalled resources ranging from its millennia old heritage, Kaleidoscopic landscape, a wide variety of delectable cuisine and a rich mosaic of culture an people's traditions. Tourism industry being the labour intensive has potential to solve the problem of unemployment and reducing poverty. Moreover, tourism is most effective instrument for natural integration, harmony and thus leading towards social transformation and upliftment of rural poor. It has already proved that the return on investment in tourism from the point of view of employment generation is much higher to agriculture and manufacturing sector. The tourism policy and action plan has also pointed out that multi-dimensional efforts are needed to exploit the tourism potential and managing tourism resources. Tourism has many advantages over other industries. Some of the beneficial aspects of tourism are:

- Tourism initiates harmonic growth in nation incomes. The demands of the foreign tourist denote a direct export of goods and services.
- Tourism is much more pervasive in its economic impacts as it promotes purchasing power and stimulates every sector of economy.
- Tourism is highly labour intensive with high rate of employment potential.
- Tourism promotes other industries and help to correct regional imbalance.
- Proper and planned tourism encourages and ensures the protection of vulnerable cultural and natural heritages.
- Tourism contributes significantly in GDP.
- Tourism contributes human resources.

- Tourism promotes micro-enterprises and self-employment.
- Tourism investment has better returns.
- Tourism ensures sustainable development of natural resources.
- Tourism promotes social harmony, cohesion and national integration.
- Tourism is a multi-dimensional activity and it covers a large number of economic activities.
- Tourism helps development of backward regions because they are not area specific.
- Tourism also helps promotion of handicrafts, crafts, traditional culture, and preservation of heritage.

Constraints in Tourism Development

Tourism industry is facing challenges, constrains and difficulties that may be categorised in the following manner:

Physical Environment

- Quality water
- Quality of air
- Quality of climate and weather
- Geographical situation

Human and Built Environment

- Negative image of people
- Negative image of service providers
- Negative image of businessmen, artisan and artists.
- Unethical business behaviour
- Negative image of poor quality products
- Negative image of polluting factors
- Unplanned and mushrooming of buildings
- Mushrooming of business activities
- Beggars and touts

- Unattractive image of destinations
- Poor maintenance of historical sites; monuments and heritage
- Traffic congestion
- Environmental degradation and ecological threat
- Theft, cheating and poor security to tourists
- Unhygienic food stuff and drinks at destinations
- Poor health and medical facilities

Tourism Infrastructure

- Poor provision of all weather facilities
- Poor reasonable and inadequate accommodation facilities
- Inadequacy of budget hotels for middle class
- Poor quality of services
- Non-availability of public transport
- Lack of information about excursions
- Lack of basic amenities to tourists
- Lack of marketing approach
- Poor road conditions
- Poor quality of communication
- Poor facilities of transport - low paid taxi, tourist buses and inter-city trains
- Lack of publicity and brand positioning of destinations
- Poor segmentation and marketing strategies
- Capacity deficiencies in accommodation and catering sector
- Less entertainment in accommodation sector
- Poor exposure of local arts, traditions, crafts and performing arts
- Poor linkages by national and international air services
- Poor and erratic power supply
- Poor and less investment in tourism sector

Management of Tourism Resources

- Poor tourism planning
- Ineffective implementation of plan & policies
- Less conduct of studies on carrying capacities and tourism impacts
- Poor human resource planning
- Poor brand positioning
- Poor and ineffective public relations
- Lack of corporate planning
- Poor management of parks, sanctuaries and other eco-sites
- Lack of data base and information system
- Lack of marketing segmentation, goal setting and marketing communication
- Lack of marketing approach
- Untrained, unskilled and low educated service providers-tour and travel operators, travel guides, accommodation and catering managers
- Poor advertising of tourism resources

Public and Private Sector

- Less number of tourist circuit house, rest houses, tourist bunglows, dak bunglow, forest rest houses etc.
- High tariff rates in tourist bunglows and government hotels
- Lack of marketing approach in government hotels and tourist bunglows
- Poor quality of services in government run hotels and catering centres
- Less number of tour and travel packages for tourists from regional tourist offices
- Lack of complete, authentic and detailed information regarding tourist destinations and excursions at regional tourist offices

- Commission agents charge high rate and try to influence tourist desire to choose accommodation. This trends is encouraged by private hotels
- Hawkers, rickshapullers, taxi drivers etc. harass foreign tourists.

Main Thrust Areas of Tourism Development

There are a few major thrust areas that can be taken into consideration for tourism development in India :

- Eco-friendly sustainable development according to natural settings
- Creating awareness and people's participation in decision making process for developing tourism products and services, maintenance of heritage tourism sites and exposure cultural deposits
- Improving the quality of services through capacity building to human resources and service providers
- Developing tourist friendly culture and strict enforcement of laws. Tourist police may be introduced to provide assistance to tourists and conservation of heritage sites, flora and fauna
- Improving basic amenities at newer tourist destinations and wayside to major tourist destination
- Brand positioning of tourism resources and though evolvement of local community based organizations
- Information dissemination through published materials, developing websites, and MIS
- Developing new tourist destinations, such as water parks, wild life park and sanctuaries, resorts, cottages heritage and cultural sites etc.
- Developing beach tourism for recreation purpose at major destinations in southern states
- Developing wildlife tourism in protected areas and promotion of natural heritage, resources, environment protection and flora and fauna

- Adventure tourism promotion for developing sports, trekking, and establishing cottages, rest houses in remote and isolation areas in the dense forest for stay of tourists under struck monitoring and regulation
- Promotion of rural tourism in natural settings for development of crafts, arts, traditional performing arts, floriculture, crops fields, rivers, folk lore, dances, theatre, folk songs, ritual performance, fairs and festivals etc. as well as to attract tourists
- Promotion of ethnic tourism for upliftment of socio-economic conditions of the tribal people, and conservation of cultural deposits
- Pilgrimage tourism development for promotion of domestic tourism since India has rich and varied religious tourism resources
- Developing marketing plan and promotional campaign for attracting domestic tourists and international tourists from abroad.

Travel Circuits for Intensive Development

The following travel circuits are needed for intensive development:

- Kullu - Manali - Leh
- Gwalior - Shivpuri - Orcha - Khajuraho
- Bagdogra - Sikkim - Darjeeling - Kalimpong
- Bhubaneshwar - Puri - Konark
- Hyderabad - Nagarjunsagar - Tirupati
- Madras - Mamallapuram - Pondicherry
- Rishikesh - Narendra Nagar - Gangotri - Badrinath
- Indore - Ujjain - Mahewar - Omkareshwar - Mandu
- Jalasalmer - Jodhpur - Bikaner - Barmer
- Bangalore - Mysore - Hassan
- Raigad Fort - Sirvardhan - Harihareshwar - Sivdhuberg
- Varanasi (Sarnath) - Kashinagar - Kapilvastu -Srawasti

- Patna - Bodhgaya - Nalanda - Ratnagiri - Vaishali
- Bhubaneshwar - Ratnagiri - Sun Temple
- Kochi - Madurai - Rameshwaram
- Hirkund - Sambhalpur
- Ahmadabad - Patna - Mount Abu
- Ahmadabad - Rajkot - Dwarka - Somnath
- Guwahati - Kaziranga - Shillong - Tawang
- Nainital - Almora - Pindari Glacier - Valley of Flowers-Massoorie - Dehradoon - Corbett Park
- Lucknow - Naimish - Ayodhaya - Varanasi - Vindhyachal
- Kanpur - Jhansi - Orchcha - Khajuraho - Ajanata - Ellora
- Delhi - Pinjaur - Shimla - Kullu - Manali - Leh
- Delhi - Chandigarh - Jammu - Vaishno Dham - Sri Nagar

Development of tourist circuits will ensure the following benefits to society, economy and visitors at large:

- Socio-economic benefit to community by improving quality of life
- Employment generation through investment and economic enterprises at wayside for extending facilities and amenities
- Preservation of national heritage and environment through extending support in exposure of performing arts, crafts and cultural traditions
- Touristic awareness for visiting domestic tourism destinations that will lead to nation building through national integration
- Encouraging international tourism and optimization of forex through offering wider choice of destinations with facilities and comfort
- Diversification of tourism product by developing image of cultural and natural heritage and thereby responding to the changing consumer needs

- Increase in India's viability and stake in global tourism through developing alternative and sustainable tourism resources.

Policy Recommendations

Role of Tourism Industry

- Protecting the biosphere and minimizing the environmental impact of tourism on built and physical infrastructure
- Sustainable use of resources and compensating the environment damage and degradation
- Reducing and disposing of wastes by recycling, re-using and reducing waste disposal such as plastic bags, polythene packaging and other hazardous wastes
- Adopting energy efficiency devices by tapping potential of bio-energy
- Undertaking projects for green marketing and promoting plantation in the fragile area
- Motivating environmental damage by replacing or compensating for local adverse impacts of tourism
- Providing authentic and complete information to tourists through offering them package tours, public relations and creating visit for friendly environment
- Conducting regular environmental audits, carrying capacities analysis and tourism impacts assessment to evolve action plan
- Conducting programmes for promotion of performing arts, crafts and traditions - fairs, festivals and exhibitions etc. to attract tourists as well as empowerment of local community

Government Role

- Government should undertake area and sector specific research into built environment, carrying capacities, tourism impacts and managerial aspects

- Government should development standards and regulatory framework for environmental and cultural impact assessments, monitoring and proposed tourism development in new areas
- Government should evolve environmental adding system for tourism industry along with corporate planning and strategic management of resources
- Government should design and implement educational and awareness programmes to sensitive people for sustainable tourism development
- Government should regulate and control tourism in environmental fragile area and culturally sensitive zones
- Government should create tourism advisory boards at regional level, involving all stakeholders
- Government should enhance investment on basic tourism infrastructure, human resource development and tourism services in newly emerged tourist destinations
- Government should take initiative to create tourist police, special trains and basic services leading towards major tourist destinations.

Role of NGO's

- NGO's should be strengthened, encouraged and assisted for taking active role in sustainable tourism development.
- NGO's should take active part in development of eco-tourism and empowerment of local communities and also providing training to service provides.
- NGO's should take active interest in tourism education and making local community sensitive towards sustainable development of tourism.
- NGO's should promote the use of local residents to assist in sustainable tourism research and data collection.
- NGO's should involve in developing tourism literature, public relations, brand positioning and strategic marketing of tourism resources.

- NGO's should be given opportunities in creation of physical infrastructure, services and maintenance of heritage resources since they provide cost effective services.
- NGO's should be assisted for organizing tours and travels event management, exposure visits as well as organizing fairs, festivals and performing arts.
- NGO's should be encouraged to identify and communicate to government agencies those issues related to sustainable tourism solution to these problems.

Eco-Tourism Development

- There is a need for healthy and regular interaction between tour promoters and managers. Strengthening the overall management in protected areas must always precede steps towards tourism development.
- Government needs to strengthen the staff support and infrastructure development for tourism in protected areas and provide funds for tourism promotion programmes and staff training.
- Government needs to create a legal mechanism to facilitate the use of revenue generated through wild life tourism for development of protected areas and its management.
- Local people's cooperatives, associations and NGO's need to be encouraged, promoted and strengthened to manage middle and low income group accommodation, catering, guide services, sale of artifacts and handicrafts and in organizing cultural programmes for visitors.
- The decisions for promoting tourism in protected areas should be taken after assessing the potential and possible ecological impacts of tourism in the area. The managers, representatives, ecologists. NGO's and tourism promoters should be involved in the decision making process.
- Considering the socio-economic and ecological impacts of wild life tourism, landuse, tourist facilities, complexes and other infrastructure outside the protected area should be strictly regulated and monitored.

- Conducting of eco-development works in the surrounding villages like soil conservation, solar energy, plantations on barren lands, development of pastures, horticulture, sericulture, bee-keeping, development of handicrafts and artifacts, fisheries, animal husbandry, child and women health care etc. as per the needs of local people should be ensured by government.
- Water bodies needs to our attention for their development to convert into abode of migratory birds and also for promotion of bird sanctuaries.
- The tourists should be told how to love, respect and care of animals even as they watch them in their habitats.
- The forests forts and heritage palaces (havelis) are needed to develop for accommodation of tourists and day visitors. There is strong need to restore these forests forts as each structure is a potential battlement from where poachers can be encountered.

Bibliography

Adhikari, P.S., Tourism and its Impact on Himalayan Environment, *Himalaya Man and Nature,* Vol. 14 No. 1, Himalaya Seva Sangh, New Delhi, 1990.

Adhikari, P.S., Tourism Industry of Dehradun Districts : A Geographical Analysis, Unpublished Ph.D. Thesis, Garhwal University, Srinagar (Garhwal), U.P. India, 1985.

Ashuorth, G.J., Recreation and Tourism Man and Environment, Bell and Hyman Publisher, London, 1985.

Bagri, S.C., Mountain Tourism in The Himalaya; Some Observation On Trekking in Garhwal Himalaya, *Journal of Tourism,* Vol. 1 No. 1, 1988.

Bagri, S.C., Mountain Tourism, Problem of Resources Use and Environmental Conservation - Case of Kashmir and Garhwal, *Journal of Tourism and Hotel Management,* Vol. (iii), 1988.

Bansal, S.P. (Ed.), Tourism in the New Millenium, Abhishek Pub. Delhi, 2002.

Basu, A.R. and Gautam, P.M., Natural Heritage of India - Essays On Environment Management, H.K. Publishers and Distributors, Delhi, 1989.

Batta, R.N., Tourism And The Environment : A Quest for Sustainability, Indus Pub. Com. Delhi, 2000.

Bedi, R., Corbett National Park. Clarion Books, Delhi, 1985.

Bejbarua, M.P., Frontiers Of New Tourism, Gyal Pub. Delhi, 2002.

Berkmaller, K.L., Mukherjee. S.K. and Mishra, B., Environmental Impact of Tourism to Hemkund Lake and Valley of Flowers. Wildlife Institute of India, Dehradun, Unpublished, 1987.

Berton, Lt-Col. R.W., Wildlife Reserves in India : Uttar Pradesh. *Journal of the Bombay Natural History Society,* 1950.

Bhandari, R.K. and Gupta, C., Problems of Landslides in the Himalaya and Future Directions. In J.S. Singh (ed.), Environmental Regeneration in the Himalaya. Central Himalayan Environment Associations, Nainital, 1985.

Bhanumathi, R., The Enchanting Valley, World Wildlife Fund (W.W.F.) *India Quarterly,* New Delhi, Vol. 4, No. 1, 1993.

Bharadwaj, S.M., Hindu Places of Pilgrimage in India. Thomson, New Delhi, 1993.

Bisth, D.S., Guide to Garhwal and Kumaun Hills, Dehradun, Tirshul Publication, 1992.

Bisht, Harshvati, Tourism in Garhwal Himalaya With Special Reference to Mountaineering and Trekking in Uttarkashi and Chamoli Districts, Indus Publishing Company, New Delhi,1994.

Bond, Ruskin, Beautiful Garhwal Heaven in Himalayas, EBD Educational Pvt, Ltd, Dehradun, 1988.

Boo, E., "Planning for Eco-tourism", *Parks,* Vol. 2, No.3, November, 1991.

Brandon, K., and M. Wells, "Planning for People and Parks : Design Dilemmas". *World Development,* Vol. 20, No. 4, April, 1992.

Burkast & Medlik, S., Tourism Past & Present, Heineman, London, 1974.

Butler, R.W., "The Concept of Carrying Capacity for Tourism Destinations: Dead or Merely Buried? Progress, *Tourism and Hospitality Research,* Vol. 2, 1996.

Butler, R.W., "The Concept of The Tourist Area Cycle of Evolution : Implications for Management of Resources", *Canadian Geographer,* Vol. 24, 1980.

Butler, R.W., Tourism, Heritage and Sustainable Development, in J.G. Nelson and S. Woodley (Eds.), Heritage Conservation and Sustainable Development, 1990.

Ceballos-Lascurain, H., "Tourism, Eco-tourism, and Protected Areas". *Parks,* Vol. 2, No. 3 November, 1991.

Ceballos-Lascurain, H., "Tourism, Ecotourism, and Protected Areas", in J.A. Kusler, *Ecotourism and Resource Conservation,* Vol. 1, 1991.

Ceballos-Lascurain, H., Tourism, Ecotourism, and Protected Areas, IUCN, Gland, Switzerland, 1996.

Chadha, S.K. (Ed.), Himalayas : Ecology and Environments, Mittal Publications, New Delhi, 1980.

Chadha, S.K., Himalayan Ecology, Ashish Publishing Company, New Delhi, 1989.

Chakraborty, P., Adventure Tourism in the Himalaya, *Yojana,* Vol. 40, No. 8, 1996.

Chatopadhyay, K., Economic Impact of Tourism Development : An Indian Experience, Kanishka Publisher, New Delhi, 1995.

Christofer, J.H., The Business Of Tourism, Longman, New York, 1998.

Clarke, M.D., Ecological Impact On The Nanda Devi Area. *The American Alpine Journal,* 1979.

Cohen, E., The Impact of Tourism on the Physical Environment, *Annals of Tourism Research,* Vol. 5, No. 2, 1977.

Conlin, M.V., and Baum, T., Island Tourism : Management Principles and Practice, Wiley, 1995.

Cooper, C. and Wanhill, S.R., Tourism Development : Environmental and Community Issues, Wiley, 1997.

Dang, H., A Natural Sanctuary In The Himalaya : Nanda Devi and the Rishiganga Basin. *Journal of the Bombay Natural History Society,* 1961.

Datar, B.N., Himalayan Pilgrimage, Publication Division, Ministry of Broadcasting, New Delhi, 1961.

Dixit, Manoj, Dimensions of Indian Tourism, BBC, Lucknow, 2001.

Doswell, R., Tourism: Understanding its Development and Management, Butterworth Heinemann, 1995.

Dutta, D.M., Step To Reduce The Conflict Between Tourism Industry and Environment in India, in Tourism in 21st Century, Edited by Prof. G.S. Batra, Anmol Publications Pvt. Ltd., New Delhi, 1996.

Eagles, P., B. Higgins, "Ecotourism Market and Industry Structure," Ecotourism : A Guide for Planners and Managers, Vol. 2, The Ecotourism Society, North Bennington, Vermont, 1998.

Edington, J.M. and M.A. Edington, Ecology, Recreation and Tourism, Cambridge University Press, New York, 1986.

Farrel, B.H., D. Runyan, Ecology and Tourism, *Annals of Tourism Research,* Vol. 18, 1991.

Farrel, B. (Ed.), Tourism And The Physical Environment Pergamon, 1987.

Forsyth, T., Sustainable Tourism : Moving from Theory to Practice, Tourism Concern/Worldwide Fund for Nature, 1996.

Getz, D. and Page, S., Business of Rural Tourism, International Thomson Business Press, 1997.

Getz, D., Festivals, Special Events and Tourism, Van Nostrand Reinhold, 1990.

Glasson, J. Godfrey, K. and Goodey, B., Towards Visitor Management, Anthony Rowe, 1995.

Goldfrey, K. & Clark, J., Tourism Development, Handbook, Classel, London, 2000.

Gopal, Rajesh, Fundamentals of Wildlife Management, Justice Home Allahabad, 1993.

Gupta, S.K., Tourism and Heritage Resources in Garhwal Himalaya, Kaveri Books, Delhi, 2002.

Gupta, S.P., etal., Cultural Tourism In India, D.K. Printwell, Delhi, 2003.

Gupta, S.K., Tourism In Garhwal Himalaya : Strategy For Sustainable Development, Bhardwaj, D.S., Kandari, O.P., (Eds), Domestic Tourism in India, Indus Publishing Company, New Delhi, 1988.

Gurber, G.R., Impact of Tourism on Mountain Environment in S.C. Singh (Ed.) Impact of Tourism on Mountain Environment, Research India Publishers, Meerut, 1989.

Harja, P.K., A contribution To The Botany of Nanda Devi National Park in Uttar Pradesh, India. Botanical Survey of India, Howrah, 1938.

Heath, E. and Wall, G., Marketing Tourism Destinations, John Villy & Sons, New York, 2000.

Hummell, John., Nature Tourism in Govind Pashu Vihar (U.P.): Case for Ecotourism, in Shalini Singh (Ed) Profiles of India Tourism, A.P.H. Publishing Corporation, New Delhi, 1996.

Hunter, C. and Green, H., Tourism and the Environment : A Sustainable Relationship, Routledge, 1995.

Inskeep, E., Environmental Impact in Tourism Planning on Integrated and Sustainable Approach, Van Nostrand Reinhold, New York, 1991.

Inskeep, E., Socio-economic Impact in Tourism Planning, An Integrated and Sustainable Development Approach, Reinhold, New York, 1991.

Inskeep, E., Tourism Planning : An Integrated and Sustainable Development, Van Nostrand Reinhold, 1991.

Iyer, H.R.S., Towards an Eco-environment Friendly Society, *Kurukshetra,* Vol. XLV. No. 55, 1997.

Jenkin, C.L., Environmental Constractions in Tourism Development, in the Approach to Tourism Management, Edited by Dr. N. Mathur et. al., Print House, Jodhpur, 1992.

Joshi, S.C., Joshi, D.R. and Dari, D.D., Singh, T.V., Corbett National Park, in Singh, T.V. (Ed.) Tourism Wildlife Parks and Conservation, Metropolitan Book Company, New Delhi, 1982.

Joshi, S.C., Joshi, D.R. and Dari, D.D., Wildlife of Garhwal Himalaya: A Study of Recreation Resource for Tourism Promotion. Unpublished Ph.D. Dissertation, Institute of Himalayan Studies, Garhwal University, Srinagar, Garhwal, 1985.

Kamlesh Kumar and Nityanand,, The Holy Himalaya : A Geographical Interpretation of Garhwal, Daya Publishing House, Delhi, 1989.

Kamra, Krishan, K., Economics Of Tourism, Kanishka Publishers, Distributors, New Delhi, 2000.

Kamra, Krishan, K., Tourism : Theory, Planning and Practice, Indus Publications, New Delhi, 1997.

Kandari, O.P. and Singh, T.V., Govind Pashu Vihar : Exploring Natural Environment. Johsard, Vol. 7 & 8, 1983-84.

Kandari, O.P., A Note On The National Parks and Wildlife Sanctuaries of Garhwal Himalaya. *Journal of Himalayan Studies and Development,* 9 & 10 , 1985-86.

Kandari, O.P., Wildlife of Garhwal Himalaya : A Recreational Resource for Tourism Promotion. Doctoral Dissertation Submitted to University of Garhwal, Srinagar Garhwal, (Unpublished), 1984.

Kandari. O.P. and Singh, T.V., Corbett National Park. In Singh T.V. (Ed.) Tourism Wildlife Parks and Conservation, Metropolitan, New Delhi, 1982.

Kangas, P., M. Shave, P. Shave, "Economics of an Ecotourism Operation in Belize," *Environmental Management,* Vol. 19, No. 5, 1995.

Kaur, J. and Singh, D.P. (Eds), Studies in Tourism Wildlife, Parks and Conservation, New Delhi, Metropolitan Book Company, 1982.

Kaur, J. and Singh, D.P. (Eds.), Paradox of Mountain Tourism : Case Reference from the Himalaya, *Industry and Environment,* Vol. IX, No. 1, Paris, U.N.E.P., 1986.

Kaur, J., "Evaluating Recreation Resources : Case of Garhwal Himalaya", Johsard, Vol. 4, 1980.

Kaur, J., "On Protecting Nature Monumetns : Case of Nanda Devi", *Tourism Recreation Research,* Vol. V. No. 1, 1980.

Kaur, J., "Pilgrims' Progress to Badrinath", In Singh, T.V. et al. (Eds), Tourism Wildlife, Parks Conservation, Metropolitan, New Delhi, 1982.

Kaur, J., "The Valley of Flowers : Himalayas Youngest Park in Making", In Singh, T.V. and Kaur. J., (Eds.) Himalayas Mountains and Men, Print House, Lucknow, India, 1982.

Kaur, J., "Thrills of Trekking", *Tourism Recreation Research,* Vol. V. No. 2., 1980.

Kaur, J., Bibliographical Source for Himalayan Pilgrimages and Tourism Studies in Uttarakhand, *Tourism Recreation Research,* Vol. IV, No. 1, 1979.

Kaur, J., Himalayan Pilgrimage and the New Tourism, Himalayan Books, New Delhi, 1985.

Kaur, J., The Valley of Flowers : An Exploratory Survey of the Bhyundar Valley along the Alaknanda for Recreation Planning of High Altitude Flora, Seminar on Mountain Ecology & Hill Area Development, Institute of Himalayan Studies & Regional Development, Garhwal University, Srinagar (Garhwal), March 6-8, 1978.

Kayastha, S.L., Impact of Tourism in the Himalayan Region, Proceedings. International Geographical Union. (I.G.U.), Symposium on Environmental Problems, Plama de Mallorca, Spain, 19983.

Khachchar, L.K., The Nanda Devi Sanctuary, Journal of the *Bombay Natural History Society,* Vol. 75, No. 3, 1978.

Khanna, D.P.S., Uttarakhand - The Cradle of Human Race, Seminar on Mountain Ecology and Hill Area Development, Institute of Himalayan Studies and Regional Development, Garhwal University, Srinagar, March 6-8, paper No. 24, 1978.

Kharakwal, S.C., Physico-Cultural Environment and Development in U.P. Himalaya, Nutan Publications, Kotdwar Garhwal, 1993.

Kohil, M.S., Mountaineering in India, Vikas Pub. House, New Delhi, 1989.

Lakshminarasaiah, M., Tourism and the Environment, *Kurukshetra,* Vol. XLV. No. 4 and 5, 1997.

Lindberg et al. (Ed.), Eco-Tourism : A guide for planners and Managers, Vol. 1 & 2, Natraj Pub. Dehradun, 1999.

Lindberg, K., D.E. Hawkins, Ecotourism : A Guide for Planners and Manager, Volume 1, The Ecotourism Society, North Bennington, Vermont,1993.

Lindberg, K., S.F. McCool, G.H., Stankey, Rethinking Carrying Capacity, *Annals of Tourism Research,* Vol. 24, No. 2, 1997.

Marison, J.L., Environmental Auditing: Capabilities and Management Utility of Recreation Impact Monitoring Programmes, *Environmental Management,* Vol. 19, No. 5, 1995.

Mathew, T., Rajaji Crisis Ahead : Recipe for Disaster, W.W.F. *India Quarterly,* Vol. 4, No. 1, 1993.

Mathieson, A., and Wall, G., Tourism : Economic, Physical and Social Impacts, Longman, New York, 1982.

McKercher, R.D., The Business of Nature-based Tourism, Hospitality Press, Melbourne, Australiea, 1998.

Mill, R.C., & Morison, A.M., The Tourism System, PHI, New Jersey, 1985.

Mill R.C., Tourism : The International Business Prentic Hall, 1990.

Naithani, S.P., Uttrakhand Ke Tirth and Mandi (in Hindi), Pavetri Prakashan, Srinagar Garhwal, 1994.

Negi, J.M.S., Himalayan Heritage : A Socio-Economic, Cultural and Tourism Analysis, Gitanjali Publishing House, New Delhi, 1995.

Negi, P.S., Uttarakhand Himalaya Mein Van Vinash Karan Aur Upai, Tehri Garhwal, U.P., 1984.

Negi, S.S., Garhwal: The Land and People, Indus Publishing Company, New Delhi, 1994.

Negi, S.S., Handbook of National Parks, Sanctuaries and Biosphere Reserves in India, Indus Publishing Company New Delhi, 1995.

Negi, S.S., Himalayan Rivers, Lakes and Glaeters, Indus Publishing Company, New Delhi, 1991.

Nigam, D., Tourism Environment and Development of Garhwal Himalya, Mittal Pub. Delhi, 2002.

O'Reilly, A.M., Tourism Carrying Capacity, Tourism Management, Vol. 7, No. 4, 1986.

Rodgers, W.A. and Panwar, H.S., Planning a Wildlife Protected Area Network in India. 2 vols. Project, FAO, Dehradun, 2000.

Sah, Anup., The Nanda Devi Sanctuary, *Cheetal Wildlife Society of India,* Vol. 18, No. 1 and 2 Sept.-Dec., 1976.

Saharia, V.B., Wildlife in India, Natraj Publishers, Dehradun, 1982.

Seshadri, B., India's Wildlife And Wildlife Reserves. Sterling Publishers, New Delhi,1986.

Sharma, M.M., The Valley of Flowers, New Delhi, Vision Books, 1985.

Siddiqui, S., Eco-Friendly Tourism in U.P. Himalayas, B.R. Pub. Delhi, 2000.

Singh, T., Tourism Environmental Sustainability in Kullu Valley Report, Prepared for CIDA - SICI Project on Sustainable Development of Mountain Environments in India and Canada, Department of Geography, University of Delhi, 1995.

Singh, T.V. and Kaur, J.(Ed), Studies in Himalayan Ecology and Development Strategies, Himalayan Books, New Delhi., 1989.

Singh, T.V. and Kaur, J., The Valley of Flowers in Garhwal Himalaya: An Ecological Preview. Studies in Himalayan Ecology (Revised edition) Metropolitan, New Delhi, 1989.

Singh, T.V. and Kaur, J., Tourism in the Himalaya : Some Experiences in Tourist Ecology, in T.V. Singh and J. Kaur (Eds.) Studies in Himalayan Ecology and Development Strategies, English Book Store, New Delhi, 1980.

Singh, T.V. and Shalini Singh, Tourism and Himalayas Tribes : Searching for Sustainable Development Option for the Bhotias of Bhyunder Valley. In Pearce, Douglas, G. and Richard W. Butler (Eds) : Complementary Issue in Tourism Development Analysis and Application, Riotledge, London, 1998.

Singh, T.V., "Tourism Takes A Leap Into The Himalaya Planners Predicament" in Hawkins, D.E., et al. (Eds) 1980, Tourism Planning and Development Issues, Washington, George Washington, Goerge Washington University, 1980.

Smith, K., Environmental Hazards : Assessing Risks And Reducing Disasters, Routledge Pub. London, 1992.

Smythe, F.S., The Valley of Flowers, Natraj Publishers, Dehradun, 1988.

Tyagi, N., "Hill Resorts of Uttar Pradesh Himalayas : A Geographical Study", New Delhi, Indus Publishing Company, 1991.

Wahab, S., Tourism Management, Tourism International Press, London, 1975.

Wahab, S., Crampon, L.J. and Rothfield, L.M., Tourism Marketing, Tourism International Press, London, 1976.

Walle, A., "Tourism And Traditional People : Torging Equitable strategies", *Journal of Travel Research,* Winter, 1993.

Williams, P., "Tourism Technology and Environment", *Journal of Travel Research,* Vol. 29, No. 2, 1990.

Yale, P., The Business of Tour Operations, Longman, 1995.

Questionnaires

Questionnaire for Tour & Travel Operating Agency

1. Name of the tour and travel agency : -
   Address :
   Head Office :
   Year of Establish :
2. Location of office : -
   i) Near bus station
   ii) City
   iii) Railway station
   iv) Airport
   v) Others
3. Do you conduct following types of tours: -
   vi) State tours
   vii) All India tours
   viii) International tour
4. What type of transportation media do you use : -
   i) By video coach bus
   ii) By train
   iii) By air
5. What is the duration of tour?
   i) One day
   ii) One week
   iii) Fortnight
   iv) Month
6. Do you conduct package tours Yes / No

7. On an average what is the number of state tour do you conduct in a year
   - i) More than 1 and up to 5 tours.
   - ii) More than 6 and up to 10 tours
   - iii) More than 11 and up to 15 tours
   - iv) More than 16 and up to 20 tours
   - v) Any other (Please specify the number)
8. On an average what is the number of All India tour do you conduct in a year
   - i) More than 1 and up to 5 tours
   - ii) More than 6 and up to 10 tours
   - iii) More than 11 and up to 15 tours
   - iv) More than 16 and up to 20 tours
   - v) Any other (Please specify the number)
9. On an average what is the number of International tour do You conduct in a year?
   - i) More than 1 and up to 5 tours.
   - ii) More than 6 and up to 10 tours
   - iii) More than 11 and up to 15 tours
   - iv) More than 16 and up to 20 tours
   - v) Any other (Please specify the number)
10. How much cost to you the following types of tours (for example 50 passengers = 1 bus) (in Rupees)

    One day : Rs.8000 to 10000, Rs.10001 to 12000 , Rs. 12001 to 14000, Any other

    One Week : Rs. 40000 to 45000, Rs. 45000 to 50000, Rs.50001 to 55000, 55001 to 60000 , Any other

    Fortnight : Rs.70000 to 75000, Rs.75000 to 80000, Rs. 80001 to 85000, Rs. 85000 to to 90000, Any other

    Month : 250000 to 260000, 260001 to 270000 , 270001 to 280000 , 280001 to 290000 , 290001 to 300000, any other
11. How much do you charge from the customers for the following type, of tours. (in Rs.)

    One day : Rs. 250, 275, 300, 325, 350 Any other

    One Week : 1000, 1250, 1500, 1750, 2000 Any other

    Fortnight : 2000, 2500, 3000, 3500, 4000 Any other

    Month : 8000, 10000, 12000, 14000, 16000 Any other

12. On an average how much do you earn from your tour business
    - (a) 10% to 15%
    - (b) 16% to 20%
    - (c) 21% to 25%
    - (d) 26% to 30%
    - (e) Any other
13. Do you pay following taxes ?
    Sales tax, Commercial tax, Municipal tax, Others
14. Do you pay following facilities for your passengers at you tour and travel office.
    - i) Computers for office administration
    - ii) Waiting room
    - iii) T.V.
    - iv) Refreshment stall
    - v) Sulabh Toilet
    - vi) Porters
    - vii) PCO / STD
    - viii) Baggage insurance
    - ix) Health requirement
    - x) Documentary requirement
    - xi) Ticket arrangements for theator and music fetival
    - xii) Foreign currency exchnge
15. a) Do you have your own bus for tours Yes / No
    b) If yes how you have purchased the bus
       - i) By own funds
       - ii) By loan from financial
       - iii) By leave basis
    c) If no, Do you take buses on rental basis Yes / No
16. Do you give any kind of gifts to your tourist when they returned from tour and go back to their home? Yes / No
17. Do you observe punctuality in departing buses for tour Yes/No
18. Do your offer cash discount to your tourist Yes / No
19. Do you offer credit facility to your tourist Yes / No
20. Do you charge penal interest form tourist if payment is delayed Yes/No

21. What is an average expenditure on advertisement annually
    i) Rs. 5000
    ii) Rs. 10000
    iii) Rs. 15000
    iv) Rs. 20000
22. Do you observe punctuality in providing to tourist.
    i) Accommodation
    ii) Tea and Snacks
    iii) Lunch
    iv) Dinner
23. Do you observe punctuality while taking tourists on various tourist spots Yes/No
24. Do you make arrangement of guide on tourist spots? Yes/No
25. Do you arrange cultural programmes in the evening during tour Yes/No
26. Have you experienced any kind of suddenly arrised problem with regards :
    i) Accommodation
    ii) Food arrangement
27. Do you make any substitute arrangement on the spot when such problems arises ? Yes /No
28. Do you get harassed by passengers during tour Yes/No
29. Do you get any kind o trouble by Road Transport Office during tour Yes/No
30. Do you face any problem due to frequent modification/ Amendments of Road Transport Office rules and regulations? Yes/No
31. What is the number of total staff members in your tour and travel unit
    i) 10 ii) 15
    iii) 20 iv) 25
    v) any other
32. What is an average monthly expenditure on staff payments
    i) 5000 ii) 10000
    iii) 15000 iv) 20000
    v) Any other

33. Do you have permanent staff? Yes / No

34. What is the frequency of staff turnover

    i) Low ii) Medium

    iii) High

35. Do you find inadequacy of experienced staff? Yes / No

36. How do you recruit staff?

    i) Internal source ii) External sources

37. Do you recruit staff?

    i) Trained ii) Untrained iii) Both

38. Do you give training to untrained staff Yes / No

39. Do you offer to your staff following motivation

    i) Monetary ii) Non-Monetary

    iii) Both iv) No

40. Do you have any authorized ticket reservation agency ? Yes / No

41. Does ticket reservation agency book reservations for their passengers at your tour and travel agency on commission basis Yes / No

42. What is the rate of commission for ticket reservation agency for seat / ticket / tourist

    i) 5% ii) 7%

    iii) 9% iv) 10%

    v) Any other

43. What is on an average percentage of tickets reserved by ticket reservation agency ?

    10%, 20% 30% 40% 50% 60% 70% 80% 90% 100%

44. How much you invested to start a tour agency (in Rs.)

    i) 30000 to 35000 ii) 36000 to 40000

    iii) 41000 to 45000 iv) 46000 to 50000

    v) Any other (please specify)

45. Which media do you prefer ?

    News Paper, Magazines, Modern media (Cable Media), Professionals journals, Others

46. Did you face following problems at promotional stage

    i) Procurement of loan

    ii) Location

47. Did you face following problems at functional stage
    a) Water scarcity
    b) Purchasing for catering untis
    c) Accommodatio
    d) Medical
    e) Expansion of tourist activities
    f) Gernation of new tourist sites
    g) Providign bais cammenties
    h) Promotion of tourist activites in the off seacon
48. Did you face any factual problem
    a) Unhelath climate
    b) High state entry tax
    c) Harrashments from tourist and government officials
    d) Land sliding at hill station
    e) Raod transport officer problems
    f) Technicla problems
49. Do you conduct all tour by
    a) By bus only
    b) By train only
    c) By both
    d) By air

Questionnaire for Tourist

1. Name :
2. Address : Age :
3. Sex : Male/Female
4. Marital Status : Married/Unmarried
5. Member in the family :
6. Education :
   Non-matric
   Matric
   Intermediate
   Graduate
   Post-Graduate
   Others
7. Nature of job :
   Employed – Govt. organisation
   Employed – Private organisation
   Self employed – Businessman
   Others
8. Annual Income
9. What is total number of holidays and leaves for you in a year :
10. How do you make use of these holidays & leaves
    i) Relaxation at home
    ii) Part time job
    iii) Visiting relatives
    iv) Arrange tours
    v) Any others
11. How do you arrange/go on tours
    i) By own arrangement
    ii) By approaching travel agency

12. Do you get LTA facilities Yes / No
13. How many days tour do you prefer?

    One day, One week, Fortnight, One month,

    More than one month
14. What type of tour do you prefer

    State tour, All India tour International tour
15. What type of journey do you prefer?

    By Bus/By Train/By Air
16. How much proportion of your annual income to you spent on tour :

    10%, 15%, 20%, 25%, 30%
17. Have you traveled with Travel Agency? Yes/No
18. If yes, on an average how many times you have traveled with travel agency?

    One time, Two time, Three time, Four times, Five times

    Any other more than five times
19. Mention first meeting experience with travel agency while fixing tour :

    Excellent, Very Good, Good, Average, Satisfactory, Bad, Atrocious
20. Mention your experience when you are on tour with regard to : :

    i) Travel vehicle (Buses)

    ii) Punctuality aspect

    iii) Accommodation facilities

    iv) Quality of food

    v) Cleanliness & Hygiene

    vi) Entertainment

    vii) First aid and medical facilities

    viii) Shopping facilities

    ix) Various concessions
21. Do you face any health problem due to :

    a) Change in water Yes/No

    b) Change in food Yes/No

    c) Change in climate Yes/No

    d) Daily travel Yes/No

    e) Air pollution Yes/No

    f) Water pollution Yes/No

22. Did you face any unreasonable help up of tour vehicle due to:
    i) Technical problem
    ii) Road Transport Officer Problem
    iii) Other state entry problem
23. Did travel agency take immediate action to solve the unreasonable held up problem of tour vehicle : Yes/No
24. Did you encounter (find) any problem during tour due to the
    i) Lack of professional knowledge of tour operators
    ii) Encashment problem of traveller's cheques
    iii) Non-availability of language study materials
    iv) Unreasonable charges for traditional handicrafts.
    v) High pollution
    vi) Lack of tourist guides
25. Did you enjoy the tour Yes/No
26. Are you satisfied with the tour arrangement Yes/No
27. Did you feel that you tour was really a memorable experience in your life. Yes/No
28. Would you prefer to join with some tour operator for your next tour Yes/No
29. Which source motivated to visit the tourist spot :
    i) Own experience/judgement
    ii) Friends/relative
    iii) Tourist office/travel agents
    iv) Advertisement/tourist broucher
30. a) Would you like to come to Karnataka again Yes/No
    b) If Yes, Why
        i] To see created tourism of the state
        ii] To enjoy the naturl beauty
        iii] To visit religious and historical monuments
        iv] To enjoy local food and hospitality
31. As a tourist do you prefer to visit
    i) Yoga and meditation camp
    ii) Health club/Ayurved based health club
    iii) Centre of spiritual discourse
    iv) Any other

32. During your tour in Karnataka did you visit or participates in :
    - i) Wildlife sanctuaries
    - ii) Mountainering clubs
    - iii) Water sports
    - iv) Adventure sports club
33. How do you rate Karnataka on the whole as a tourist place :
    Excellent, Very Good, Good, Average, Satisfactory, Bad, Unsafe.
34. Do you prefer travel agencies having their own catering units
    Yes/No
35. Do you prefer travel agencies conducting cultural programmes during tour period. Yes/No
36. What more facilities should be added to the existing ones to popularize the tourism industry in the state :
    - i) Information, transport and marketing facilities should be added
    - ii) As KSTDC is not developed in its working as travel agency
    - iii) Creation of new facilities and maintenance of historical places
    - iv) Budget class hotels should be started.
37. Whether there should be tourism act or not Yes/No
38. What kind of personnel would be needed for the higher echelons of administration ?
    - i) Generl administrators
    - ii) Specialists in tourism and hotel management
    - iii) Those who are experienced but not have a formal degree
    - iv) NA/NR
39. What should be the basic aim of objectives of the KSTDC
    - i) To earn profit
    - ii) To provide facilities at reasonable rates
    - iii) Both
    - iv) Do not know

Questionnaire for Hotel Owners/Management

1. Name of the Hotel :
   Grade
   Address
   Year of Establish
2. Managed by :
   Mangers
   Owners (Self)
3. Do you provide following service o tour operating agency on mass scale
   a) Loading b) Boarding c) Both
4. Loading facilities
   a) A/c rooms b) Non A/c rooms
   (c) Attached d) Non attached
   (e) Dormitory
5. Do you have any contract / agreement to provide following services to tour operating agencies.
   a) Loading b) Boarding c) Both
6. Do the tour operating agencies ask for
   a) Only loading services
   b) Only boarding services
   c) Both services
7. Does the tour operating agencies approach you for loading and boarding services of your hotel Yes/No
8. Do you grant concession to tour operating agencies when they ask for lodging and boarding services on mass scale. Yes/No
9. How much concession / discount do you offer
   a) 5% b) 10%
   c) 15% d) Any other

10. Does you hotel provide pamphlets with the do's and do not's that will guide the tourist during their stay Yes/No
11. Have you observed/experienced any tourist misbehavior/misconduct in your hotel. Yes/No
12. Have you complained about misbehavior/misconducts of tourist to tour operator or agency. Yes/No